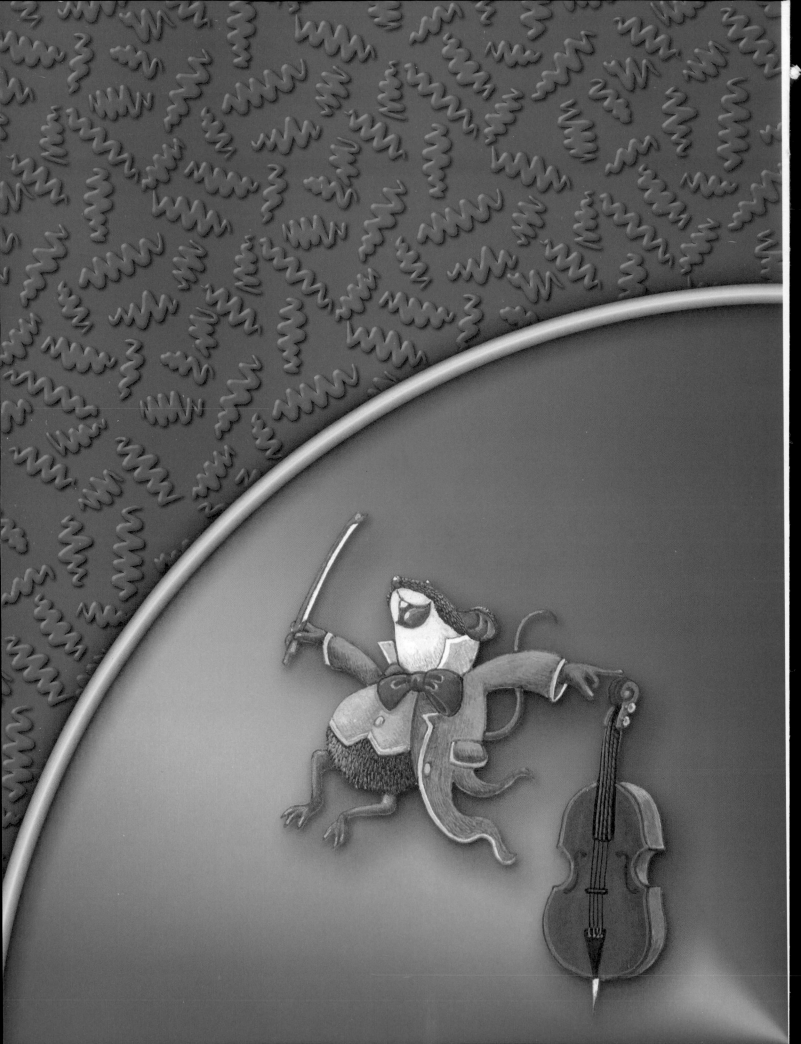

SPOTLIGHT on MUSIC™

Authors

Judy Bond

René Boyer

Margaret Campbelle-Holman

Emily Crocker

Marilyn C. Davidson

Robert de Frece

Virginia Ebinger

Mary Goetze

Betsy M. Henderson

John Jacobson

Michael Jothen

Chris Judah-Lauder

Carol King

Vincent P. Lawrence

Ellen McCullough-Brabson

Janet McMillion

Nancy L. T. Miller

Ivy Rawlins

Susan Snyder

Gilberto D. Soto

Kodály Contributing Consultant

Sr. Lorna Zemke

HAL•LEONARD®

Macmillan McGraw-Hill

ACKNOWLEDGMENTS

Creative Direction and Delivery: The Quarasan Group, Inc.

From the Top-On National Radio! student features are adapted from the nationally distributed public radio program, *From the Top.* CEOs/ Executive Producers: Jennifer Hurley-Wales and Gerald Slavet. Authors: Ann Gregg and Joanne Robinson. © 2001, 2002, 2003 From the Top, Inc.

The Broadway Junior® logo and MTI® logo are trademarks of Music Theatre International. All rights reserved.

Grateful acknowledgment is given to the following authors, composers and publishers. Every effort has been made to trace the ownership of all copyrighted material and to secure the necessary permissions to reprint these selections. In the case of some selections for which acknowledgment is not given, extensive research has failed to locate the copyright holders.

Songs and Speech Pieces

Addams Family Theme, The, Music and Lyrics by Vic Mizzy. Copyright © 1964, Renewed 1992 by Unison Music Company. Administered by Next Decade Entertainment, Inc. International Copyright Secured. All Rights Reserved.

Ballad of the Bedbugs and the Beetles, traditional. Reprinted in Ready-to-Use Activities for Before and After School Programs, by Verna Stassevitch, Patricia Stemmler, Rita Shotwell, and Marian Wirth. The Center for Applied Research in Education, Copyright © 1998. Music by Carol King. All Rights Reserved. Used by Permission.

Bohm (Spring Has Come!), Words by Chu Shik Ham. Music by Sou Chul Chang. Copyright © by SEH KWANG PUBLISHING CO. International Copyright Secured. All Rights Reserved.

Boo!, Words and Music by Cheryl Lavender. Copyright © 2002 by HAL LEONARD CORPORATION. International Copyright Secured. All Rights Reserved.

Butterfly, Come Play with Me, from the Come Children Sing Institute SONG LIBRARY. Words and Music by Mary Ellen Pinzino. Copyright © 2003 by Mary Ellen Pinzino. International Copyright Secured. All Rights Reserved.

Chag Asif (Harvest Time), Original Words and Music by Sarah Levy-Tanai. English Words by Laura Koulish. Original Words and Music Copyright © by Levy-Tanai & Rappaport Moshe, Israel. English Words Copyright © Laura Koulish. International Copyright Secured. All Rights Reserved. Reprinted by Permission of ACUM, Ltd.

City Life, Words and Music by John Jacobson and Alan Billingsley. Copyright © 2000 by HAL LEONARD CORPORATION. International Copyright Secured. All Rights Reserved.

Colors of the Wind, from Walt Disney's POCAHONTAS. Music by Alan Menken. Lyrics by Stephen Schwartz. © 1995 Wonderland Music Company, Inc. and Walt Disney Music Company. All Rights Reserved. Used by Permission.

Consider Yourself, from the Columbia Pictures - Romulus Film OLIVER! Words and Music by Lionel Bart. © Copyright 1960 (Renewed) Lakeview Music Co. Ltd., London, England. TRO - Hollis Music, Inc., New York, controls all publication rights for the U.S.A. and Canada. International Copyright Secured. All Rights Reserved Including Public Performance For Profit. Used by Permission.

Digga Digga Dog, from Walt Disney Pictures' 102 DALMATIANS. Words and Music by Pamela Phillips Oland, Mark Brymer, George Clinton, Jr., Garry M. Shider and David L. Spradley. © 2000 Walt Disney Music Company, Bridgeport Music, Inc. and Southfield Music, Inc. All Rights Reserved. Used by Permission. Contains sampling of "Atomic Dog" by George Clinton.

Ding Dong Diggy Diggy Dong, Words and Music by Carl Orff. Copyright © 1958 by Schott & Co. c/o European American Music. International Copyright Secured. All Rights Reserved.

Eight Days of Hanukkah, The, Words and Music by George David Weiss. Copyright © 1987 by ABILENE MUSIC, INC. c/o THE SONGWRITERS GUILD OF AMERICA. All Rights Reserved.

El arroyo que murmura. from *90 Songs Of The Americas.* Compiled and Arranged by Ruth DeCesare. © 1993 EMI MILLS MUSIC, INC. Worldwide Print Rights on behalf of EMI MILLS MUSIC, INC. Administered by WARNER BROS. PUBLICATIONS U.S. INC. All Rights Reserved. Used by Permission.

El atole (The Atole), Mexican Folk Song. Adapted by José-Luis Orozco. Copyright © 1987 by José-Luis Orozco/Arcoiris Records, Inc. International Copyright Secured. All Rights Reserved.

Evergreen, Everblue, Words and Music by Raffi Cavourkian. Copyright © by Homeland Publishing, a div. of Troubadour Music, Inc. International Copyright Secured. All Rights Reserved.

Flip, Flop and Fly, Words and Music by Charles Calhoun and Lou Willie Turner. Copyright © 1955 by Unichappell Music Inc. Copyright Renewed. International Copyright Secured. All Rights Reserved.

Frosty, the Snowman, Words and Music by Steve Nelson and Jack Rollins. Copyright © 1950 by Chappell & Co. Copyright Renewed. International Copyright Secured. All Rights Reserved.

Frosty Weather, from *Singing Games and Play Parties, Vol. I.* Traditional Singing Game. Adapted by Jill Trinka. Copyright © 1996 by JILL TRINKA. International Copyright Secured. All Rights Reserved.

Gong xi fa cai (Chinese New Year Song), Words and Music by Chooi-Theng Lew. English Words by John Higgins. Copyright © 2001 by MUSIC EXPRESS LLC. International Copyright Secured. All Rights Reserved.

Greatest Show on Earth, The, from the Paramount Motion Picture THE GREATEST SHOW ON EARTH. Words by Ned Washington. Music by Victor Young. Copyright © 1952 (Renewed 1981) by Famous Music Corporation. International Copyright Secured. All Rights Reserved.

Happy Wanderer, The, Words by Antonia Ridge. Music by Friedrich W. Moller. Copyright © 1954 and 1982 by Bosworth & Co., Ltd., London for all countries. All Rights for the United States of America and Canada assigned to Sam Fox Publishing Company, Inc., Santa Barbara, California. International Copyright Secured. All Rights Reserved.

I Walk in Beauty, Words and Music by Arliene Nofchissey. Copyright © Laminite Publishers. International Copyright Secured. All Rights Reserved.

I'm a Believer, Words and Music by Neil Diamond. © 1966 (Renewed), 1978 STONEBRIDGE MUSIC and FORAY MUSIC. All Rights Reserved. International Copyright Secured. Used by Permission.

Interjections, from MTI's Broadway Junior Broadway for Kids SCHOOL-HOUSE ROCK LIVE! Junior. Music and Lyrics by Lynn Ahrens. Copyright © Music and Lyrics 1995 and TM American Broadcasting Companies, Inc. The above copyright notice may be subject to change to conform to new or different requirements upon written notification from American Broadcasting Companies, Inc. All Rights Reserved. Used by Permission.

Interplanet Janet, from MTI's Broadway Junior Broadway for Kids SCHOOLHOUSE ROCK LIVE! Junior. Music and Lyrics by Lynn Ahrens. Copyright © Music and Lyrics 1995 and TM American Broadcasting Companies, Inc. The above copyright notice may be subject to change to conform to new or different requirements upon written notification from American Broadcasting Companies, Inc. All Rights Reserved. Used by Permission.

It's Time to Get Ready for Christmas, Words and Music by Emily Crocker and John Higgins. Copyright © 1992 by Jenson Publications. International Copyright Secured. All Rights Reserved.

Jamaica Farewell, Words and Music by Irving Burgie. Copyright © 1955; Renewed 1983 Cherry Lane Music Publishing Company, Inc. (ASCAP), Lord Burgess Music Publishing Company (ASCAP) and Dimensional Music Of 1091 (ASCAP). Worldwide Rights for Lord Burgess Music Publishing Company and Dimensional Music Of 1091 Administered by Cherry Lane Music Publishing Company, Inc. International Copyright Secured. All Rights Reserved.

Jasmine Flower, Chinese Folk Song collected and transcribed by Kathy Sorensen. © 1991 Kathy B. Sorensen. All Rights Reserved.

continued on page 409

A

ii

CONTRIBUTORS

Consultants

Brian Burnett,
Movement

Stephen Gabriel,
Technology

Magali Iglesias,
English Language Learners

Roberta Newcomer,
Special Learners/Assessment

Frank Rodríguez,
English Language Learners

Jacque Schrader,
Movement

Kathy B. Sorensen,
International Phonetic
Alphabet

Patti Windes-Bridges,
Listening Maps

Linda Worsley,
Listening/Singable
English Translations

Sr. Lorna Zemke,
Kodály Contributing
Consultant

Recordings

Executive Producer: John Higgins

Senior Music Editor/Producer: Emily Crocker

Senior Recording Producer: Mark Brymer

Recording Producers: Steve Millikan, Andy Waterman

Associate Recording Producers: Alan Billingsley, Darrell Bledsoe, Stacy Carson, Rosanna Eckert, John Egan, Chad Evans, Darlene Koldenhoven, Chris Koszuta, Don Markese, Matthew McGregor, Steve Potts, Edwin Schupman, Michael Spresser, Frank Stegall, David Vartanian, Mike Wilson, Ted Wilson

Project/Mastering Engineer: Mark Aspinall; Post-Production Engineer: Don Sternecker

Selected recordings by Buryl Red, Executive Producer; Michael Rafter, Senior Recording Producer; Bryan Louiselle and Buddy Skipper, Recording Producers; Lori Casteel and Mick Rossi, Associate Recording Producers; Jonathan Duckett, Supervising Engineer

Contributing Writers

Allison Abucewicz, Sharon Berndt, Rhona Brink, Ann Burbridge, Debbie Helm Daniel, Katherine Domingo, Kari Gilbertson, Janet Graham, Hilree Hamilton, Linda Harley, Judy Henneberger, Carol Huffman, Bernie Hynson, Jr., Sheila A. Kerley, Elizabeth Kipperman, Ellen Mendelsohn, Cristi Cary Miller, Leigh Ann Mock, Patricia O'Rourke, Barbara Resch, Soojin Kim Ritterling, Isabel Romero, Carl B. Schmidt, Debra Shearer, Ellen Mundy Shuler, Rebecca Treadway, Carol Wheeler, Sheila Woodward

Multicultural Consultants

William Anderson, Chet-Yeng Loong, Edwin Schupman, Kathy B. Sorensen, Gilberto D. Soto, Judith Cook Tucker, Dennis Waring

In the Spotlight Consultant

Willa Dunleavy

Multicultural Advisors

Brad Ahawanrathe Bonaparte (Mohawk), Emmanuel Akakpo (Ewe), Earlene Albano (Hawaiian), Luana Au (Maori), Bryan Ayakawa (Japanese), Ruby Beeston (Mandarin), Latif Bolat (Turkish), Estella Christensen (Spanish), Oussama Davis (Arabic), Mia Delguardo (Minahasa), Nolutho Ndengane Diko (Xhosa), Angela Fields (Hopi, Chemehuevi), Gary Fields (Lakota, Cree), Gilad Harel (Hebrew), Josephine Hetarihon (Bahasa Indonesian, Minahasa, and Maluko dialect), Judy Hirt-Manheimer (Hebrew), Rose Jakub (Navajo), Elizabeth Jarema (Fijian), Rita Jensen (Swedish), Malou Jewett (Visayan), Alejandro Jimenez (Hispanic), Chris Jones (Hungarian), Wendy Jyang Shamo (Mandarin), Amir Kalay (Hebrew), Michael Katsan (Greek), Silvi Madarajan (Tamil), Georgia Magpie (Comanche), Nona Mardi (Malay), Aida Mattingly (Tagalog), Mike Kanathohare McDonald (Mohawk), Vasana de Mel (Sinhala), Marion Miller (Czech), Etsuko Miskin (Japanese), Mogens Mogenson (Danish), Kenny Tahawisoren Perkins (Mohawk), Pradeep Nayyar (Punjabi, Hindi), Renu Nayyar (Punjabi), Mfanego Ngwenya (Zulu), Wil Numkena (Hopi), Samuel Owuru (Akan), Nina Padukone (Konkani), Hung Yong Park (Korean), James Parker (Finnish), Jose Pereira (Konkani), Berrit Price (Norwegian), John Rainer (Taos Pueblo, Creek), Lillian Rainer (Taos Pueblo, Creek, Apache), Arnold Richardson (Haliwa-Saponi), Ken Runnacles (German), Trudy Shenk (German), Ron Singer (Navajo), Ernest Siva (Cahuilla, Serrano [Maringa']), Bonnie Slade (Swedish), Cristina Sorrentino (Portuguese), Diane Thram (Xhosa), Elena Todorov (Bulgarian), Zlatina Todorov (Russian), Tom Toronto (Lao, Thai), Rebecca Wilberg (French, Italian), Sheila Woodward (Zulu), Keith Yackeyonny (Comanche)

Contents

Spotlight on Music Reading..........241

In the Spotlight

Shine the spotlight on music!
Shine the light from above!
Shine the spotlight on music
because music's what we love!

Step into the Spotlight

Spotlight CD
Track 1 **Verse**

Words and Music by John Jacobson,
Emily Crocker, and John Higgins

Bb   Cm/Bb

1. Lis - ten to the world a - round you, There is
2. In a world of sound and col - or, in a

F/A   Bb   F/A   Gm7

mus - ic ev - 'ry - where.___ Just step out - side___ your
rhy - thm all its own,___ It's the heart - beat of___ A -

Dm7   Db9   Bb6/C   C9   F   Eb/F   F

door - way, and you can hear mus - ic in the air!___
mer - i - ca, the land we proud - ly call our home!_

Gm   D/F#

From the cit - y to the farm and field,___ to the
From the cit - y to the farm and field,___ there's a

A

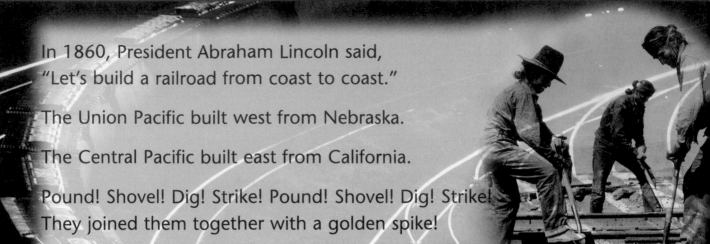

In 1860, President Abraham Lincoln said,
"Let's build a railroad from coast to coast."

The Union Pacific built west from Nebraska.

The Central Pacific built east from California.

Pound! Shovel! Dig! Strike! Pound! Shovel! Dig! Strike!
They joined them together with a golden spike!

I've Been Working on the Railroad

Spotlight CD
Track 4

Traditional American

I've been work-ing on the rail - road, all the live-long day. I've been work-ing on the rail - road just to pass the time a - way. Can't you hear the whist-le blow - ing. Rise up so ear - ly in the morn.

Changing the world doesn't always take a chorus.
Sometimes it only takes one small voice.

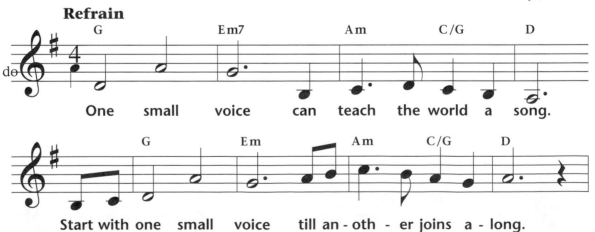

One Small Voice

Spotlight CD
Track 7

Words and Music by Jeff Moss

Refrain

One small voice can teach the world a song.

Start with one small voice till an-oth-er joins a-long.

Then you'll feel the mu - sic grow-ing full and sure and strong.

One small voice can teach the world a song.

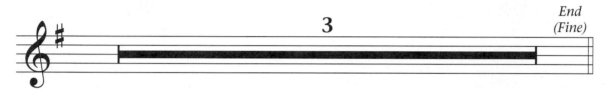

3

*End
(Fine)*

Verse

Ev - 'ry song the world sings, each was once un-known.

Some-bod-y felt a song in-side and was-n't a-fraid to sing a-lone.

If you feel the mu - sic and you sing it clear and true,

*Go back to the beginning and sing to the End.
(Da Capo al Fine)*

then the world can sing with you.

Shine the spotlight on America!
Let us sing the songs.
Let us tell the stories.
Let us dance the dances and play the tunes.
Shine the spotlight on America
and let us shine! Shine! Shine!

Patriotic Medley

You're a Grand Old Flag, This Land Is Your Land, America

Spotlight CD
Track 10

Words by George M. Cohan,
Woody Guthrie, and Katharine Lee Bates.

You're a Grand Old Flag, you're a high flyin' flag.

And forever in peace may you wave.

You're the emblem of the land I love,

The home of the free and the brave.

Ev'ry heart beats true for the red, white, and blue,

Where there's never a boast or brag.

But should auld acquaintance be forgot,

Keep your eye on the grand old flag.

This land is your land, this land is my land

From California to the New York Island.

From the redwood forest to the Gulf Stream waters,

This land was made for you and me.

As I was walking that ribbon of highway,

I saw above me that endless skyway.

I saw below me that golden valley.

This land was made for you and me.

America! America! God shed His grace on thee.

And crown thy good with brotherhood,

From sea to shining sea! *(Repeat last two lines)*

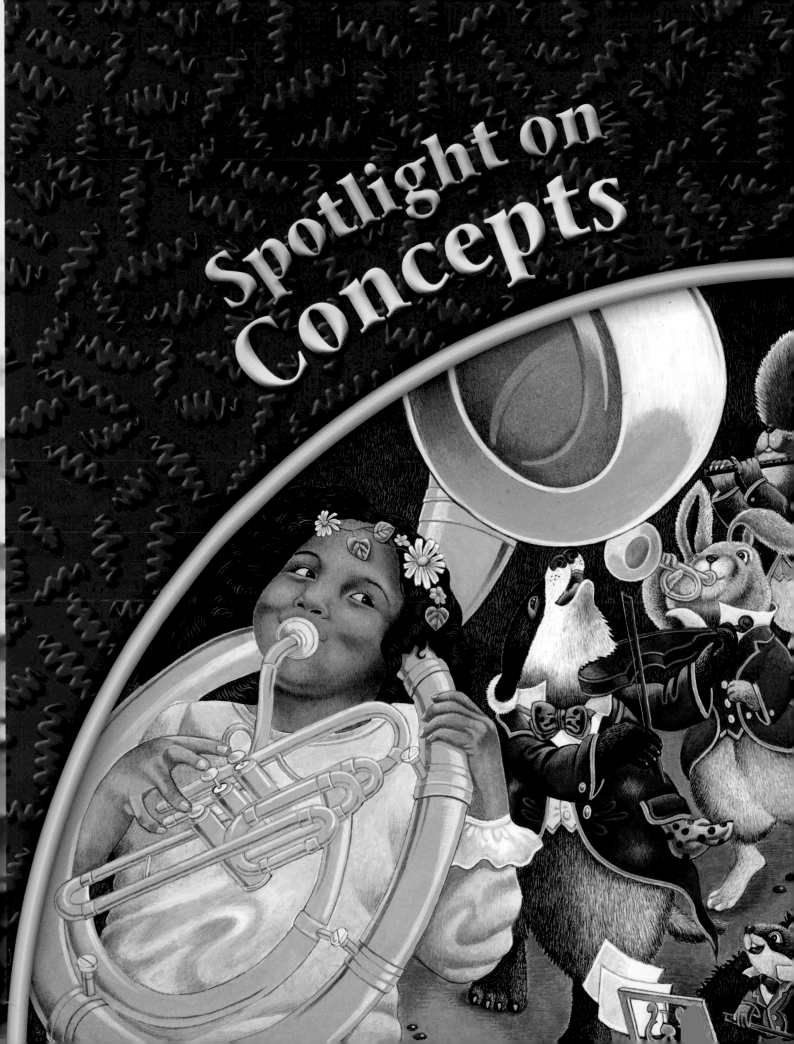

Spotlight on
Concepts

Spotlight on Concepts

Spotlight on Concepts

Music for the Fun of It!

Music makes sharing and playing more fun. Music can bring fun to many things you do. Look at the picture. How are these children sharing through music?

Coming Attractions

Listen to music for a king's party.

Explore the sounds your voice can make.

Play rhythms and create your own music!

There are many games you can play with music. Here is a musical way to play Simon Says. **Sing** as you move to the words.

CD 01:01

Words and Music by Elliot Chiprut

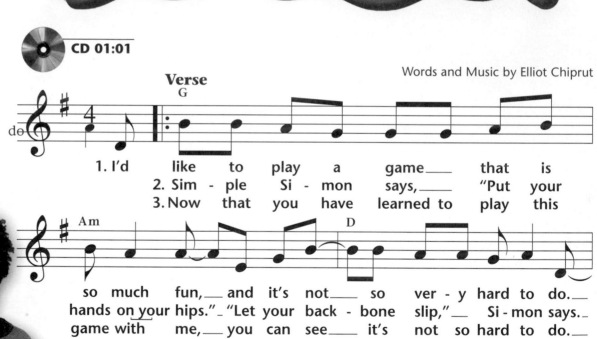

Verse
G

1. I'd   like   to   play   a   game____   that   is
2. Sim - ple   Si - mon   says,____   "Put   your
3. Now   that   you   have   learned to   play   this

Am   D

so   much   fun,__ and   it's   not___   so   ver - y   hard   to   do.__
hands on your hips." _ "Let your   back - bone   slip," ___   Si - mon   says._
game with   me,__ you   can   see____   it's   not so   hard   to   do.__

Follow the Rhythm

CONCEPT
RHYTHM
SKILLS
SING,
MOVE
LINKS
READING,
LANGUAGE ARTS

Children all over the world have fun with singing games. Learn this new singing game. Then have more fun when you teach the game to a friend.

Sing the counting song "Billy."

Move to the first words of the song "Billy." Point out these words in this song.

Look at the pictures and learn how to move to the words. **Move** to the song as you sing it again.

cross	down	when

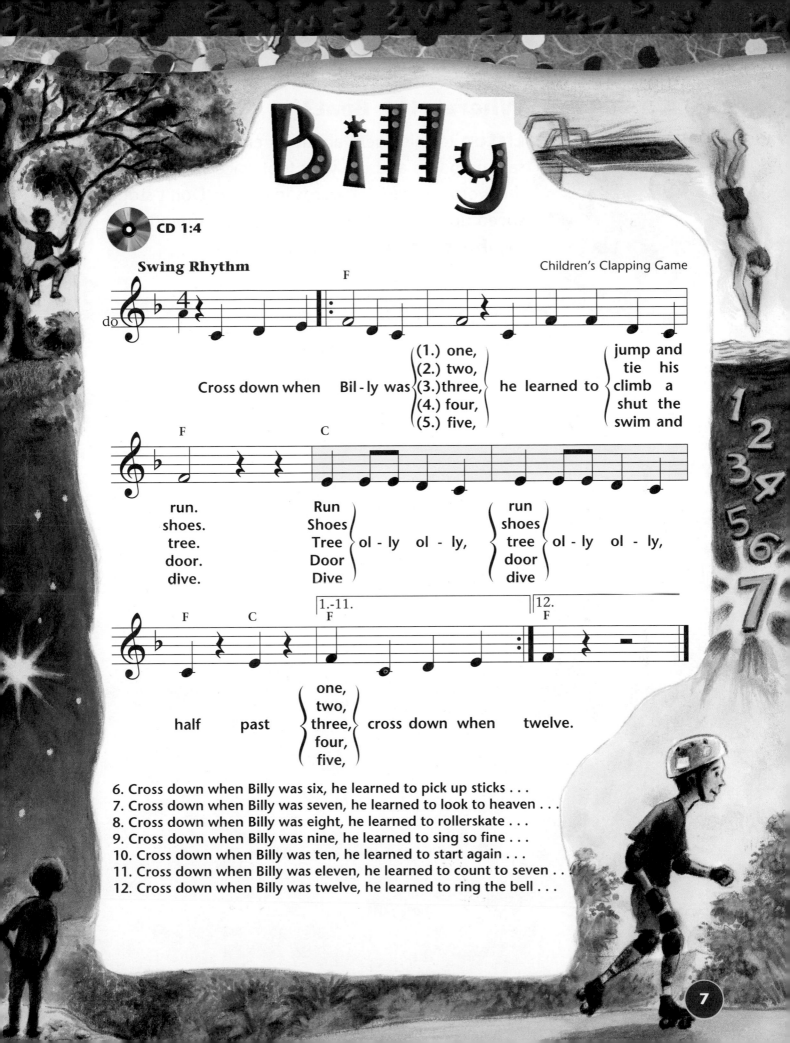

Billy

CD 1:4

Swing Rhythm Children's Clapping Game

6. Cross down when Billy was six, he learned to pick up sticks . . .
7. Cross down when Billy was seven, he learned to look to heaven . . .
8. Cross down when Billy was eight, he learned to rollerskate . . .
9. Cross down when Billy was nine, he learned to sing so fine . . .
10. Cross down when Billy was ten, he learned to start again . . .
11. Cross down when Billy was eleven, he learned to count to seven . . .
12. Cross down when Billy was twelve, he learned to ring the bell . . .

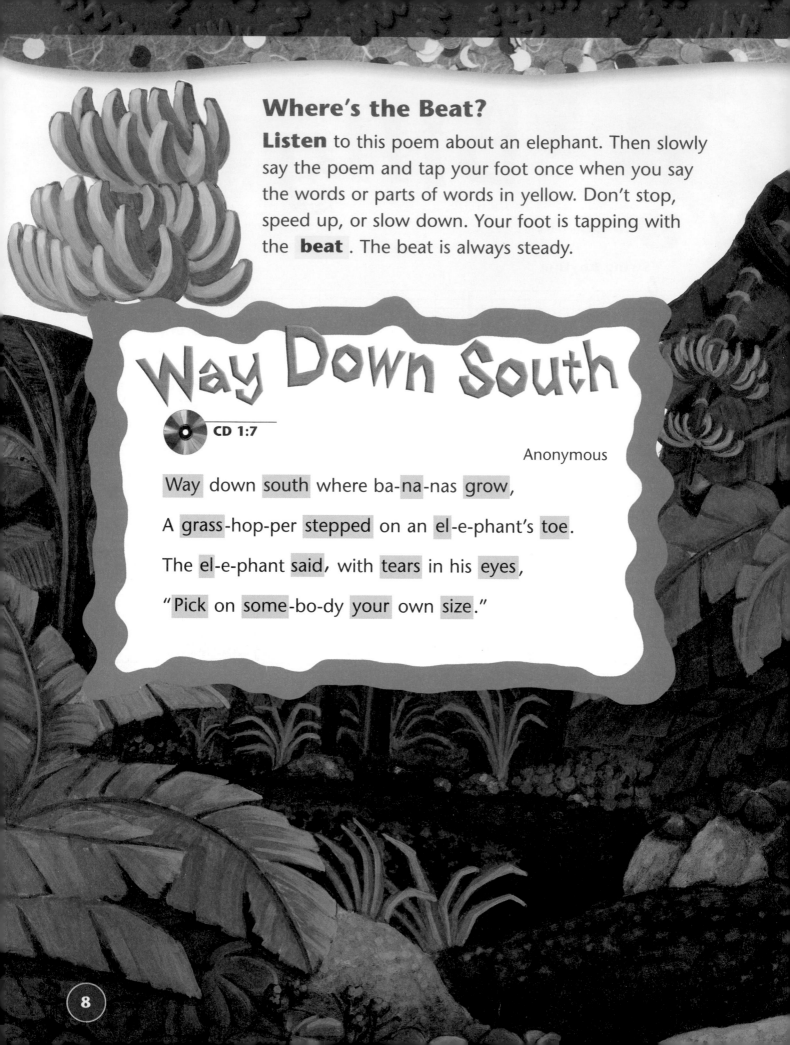

Where's the Beat?

Listen to this poem about an elephant. Then slowly say the poem and tap your foot once when you say the words or parts of words in yellow. Don't stop, speed up, or slow down. Your foot is tapping with the **beat**. The beat is always steady.

Way Down South

CD 1:7

Anonymous

Way down south where ba-na-nas grow,

A grass-hop-per stepped on an el-e-phant's toe.

The el-e-phant said, with tears in his eyes,

"Pick on some-bo-dy your own size."

Listen for some words with long sounds and some words with short sounds. The long and short sounds you hear are called the **rhythm** of the words. Say the poem and clap the rhythm of the words.

| Way | down | south | where ba- | na- | nas | grow, |

| A | grass- | hop- per | stepped | on | an | el- e- | phant's | toe. |

| The | el- e- | phant | said, | with | tears | in | his | eyes, |

| "Pick | on | some- | bo- dy | your | own | size." |

THINK! How do beat and rhythm of the words differ?

The Shape of Melody

CONCEPT
MELODY
SKILLS
LISTEN, SING
LINKS
HISTORY, CULTURE

"Chan mali chan" is a popular song from Singapore. It tells the story of a baby goat walking to town. He talks with people he meets along the way. The words do not mean anything at all—they are just fun to sing! **Sing** the song.

MAP

UNITED STATES

SINGAPORE

CD 1:10

Singaporean Folk Song

Refrain

Malay: **Chan ma - li chan, chan ma - li chan,**
Pronunciation: chan ma li chan chan ma li chan

Chan ma - li chan Ke - ti - pung____ pa - yung.
chan ma li chan kə ti pɔng pa yəng

Chan ma - li chan, oi! oi! Chan ma - li chan, oi! oi!
chan ma li chan oi oi chan ma li chan oi oi

(3rd time)
Fine

Chan ma - li chan Ke - ti - pung.____ pa - yung.
chan ma li chan kə ti pɔng pa yɔng

Sing "Chan mali chan" again. On what words does the tune go upward? On what words does the tune go downward? On what words does the tune repeat the same notes?

chan mali chan

oi oi

Verse 4

1. Di - ma - na di - a   a - nak kam - bing sa - ya
   di ma na di a   a nak kam bing sa ya
2. Di - ma - na di - a   a - nak kam - bing sa - ya
   di ma na di a   a nak kam bing sa ya

A - nak kam - bing sa - ya   per - gi   ke Ko - ta Bha - ru;
a nak kam bing sa ya   pe gi   ke ko ta ba ɾu
A - nak kam - bing sa - ya   ma - kan   te - pi pe - ri - gi;
a nak kam bing sa ya   ma kan   ta pi pe ɾi gi

Di - ma - na di - a   chin - ta   ha - ti   sa - ya
di ma na di a   chin ta   ha ti   sa ya
Di - ma - na di - a   chin - ta   ha - ti   sa - ya
di ma na di a   chin ta   ha ti   sa ya

D.C. al Fine

chin ta ha - ti sa - ya   yang pa - kai ba - ju   bi - ru.
chin ta ha ti sa ya   yang pa kai ba ju bi ru
chin ta ha - ti sa - ya   yang ti - dak a - da gi - gi.
chin ta ha ti sa ya   yang ti dak a da gi gi

Trace the Tune

"A String of Pearls" is a dance tune that was popular in the 1930s. Many people still enjoy the melody and listen to this music today. A **melody** is a string of connected pitches moving upward, downward, or repeating the same pitches. **Pitch** is the highness or lowness of a sound. Every melody has a shape.

Listen to "A String of Pearls." Trace the shape of the melody by pointing to each pearl on the string.

 LISTENING CD 1:14

A String of Pearls by Glenn Miller

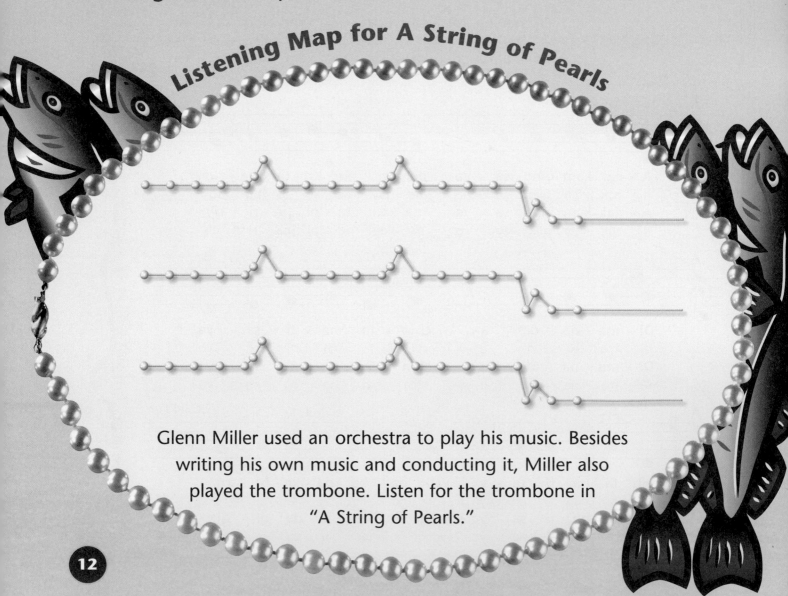

Listening Map for A String of Pearls

Glenn Miller used an orchestra to play his music. Besides writing his own music and conducting it, Miller also played the trombone. Listen for the trombone in "A String of Pearls."

"I's the B'y" is a fun song from the island of Newfoundland. It is about a fisherman's busy job catching fish. Look at the melody. Some of the pitches go upward, some go downward, and some repeat. **Sing** this song. Listen to the words *I's the b'y that*. Does the melody go upward, downward, or stay the same?

MIDI

For another activity with "I's the B'y," see *Spotlight on MIDI*.

MAP

UNITED STATES   NEWFOUNDLAND

I's the B'y

CD 1:15

Newfoundland Folk Song

Verse

1. I's the b'y that builds the boat, And I's the b'y that sails her!
2. Sods and rinds to cov-er your flake,___ Cakes and tea for sup-per,
3. I don't want your mag-got-y fish,___ That's no good for win-ter,

I's the b'y that catch-es the fish, And brings them home to Liz - er.
Cod-fish in the spring o' the year,___ Fried in mag-got-y but - ter.
I could buy as good___ as that___ Down in Bon - a - vis - ta.

Refrain

Hip your part-ner, Sal - ly Tib - bo, Hip your part-ner, Sal - ly Brown!

Fo-go, Twil-lin-gate, Mor-ton's Har-bour, All a - round the cir - cle.

Rhythm Around the House

CONCEPT
RHYTHM
SKILLS
SING, READ, LISTEN
LINKS
READING, VISUAL ARTS

Did you know that you can use things around your house to make music? Years ago people used things they found around the house as instruments. They found that even spoons could make music! Name some things in your classroom that you could use.

Listen to "Great Big House," a song from Louisiana. Listen for the sound of the spoons. **Sing** the song.

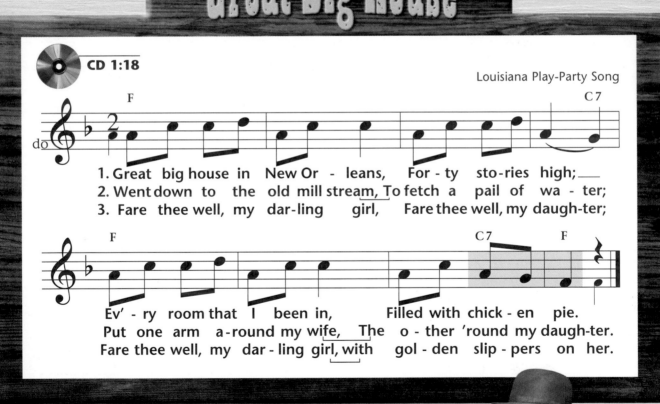

CD 1:18

Louisiana Play-Party Song

1. Great big house in New Or - leans, For - ty sto - ries high;
2. Went down to the old mill stream, To fetch a pail of wa - ter;
3. Fare thee well, my dar - ling girl, Fare thee well, my daugh - ter;

Ev' - ry room that I been in, Filled with chick - en pie.
Put one arm a - round my wife, The o - ther 'round my daugh - ter.
Fare thee well, my dar - ling girl, with gol - den slip - pers on her.

The "drummer" in this group of musicians is playing pie tins and a washboard, as well as a kazoo.

The rhythm of "Great Big House" uses one sound, two sounds, and even no sounds to the beat.

one sound	two sounds	no sounds
♩	♫	𝄽
quarter note	**eighth notes**	**quarter rest**
the word *pie*	the word *chicken*	no words

Clap this rhythm as you say *pie* for each quarter note (♩) and *chicken* for each pair of eighth notes (♫).

Play the rhythm on a rhythm instrument while saying *chicken* and *pie*. Repeat the rhythm on rhythm instruments while you sing "Great Big House."

Look at the music below. Find the **bar lines**. How many are there? The space between the bar lines is called a **measure**. Next, find the **meter signature**. The top number shows how many beats are in each measure. How many beats are in these measures?

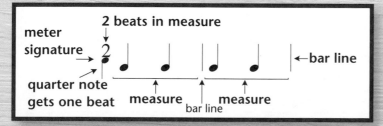

Rhythm All Around

This Creole folk song is also from Louisiana. **Listen** to "Sweet Potatoes." You will hear a washboard used as percussion.

Sweet Potatoes

CD 1:21

Louisiana Creole Folk Song

1. Soon as we all cook sweet po - ta - toes,
2. Soon as sup - per's gone, Mam - ma calls us,
3. Soon's we touch our heads to the pil - low,
4. Soon's the roost - er crow in the morn - ing,

sweet po - ta - toes, sweet po - ta - toes.
Mam - ma calls us, Mam - ma calls us.
to the pil - low, to the pil - low.
in the morn - ing, in the morn - ing.

Soon as we all cook sweet po - ta - toes,
Soon as sup - per's gone, Mam - ma calls us,
Soon's we touch our heads to the pil - low,
Soon's the roost - er crow in the morn - ing,

Eat 'em while they're hot.
Get a - long to bed.
Go to sleep right smart!
Got - ta wash our face.

The rhythm of "Sweet Potatoes" uses quarter notes, eighth notes, and quarter rests. Look at the song. How many quarter rests are there?

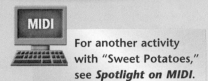

For another activity with "Sweet Potatoes," see *Spotlight on MIDI*.

 **THINK!** **How many beats are in each measure of "Sweet Potatoes"?**

You can play these pitches on instruments. The pitches go with "Sweet Potatoes."

Play the pitches as you sing the song.

Move with Melody

CONCEPT
MELODY
SKILLS
LISTEN, SING, PLAY
LINKS
READING

Imagine that you are walking along. A song that you like pops into your head. You start to sing quietly to yourself. Then you begin to sing more loudly. Your steps start to match the beat of the song. How do you feel?

Listen to "The Happy Wanderer." How does the singer feel about hiking in the mountains?

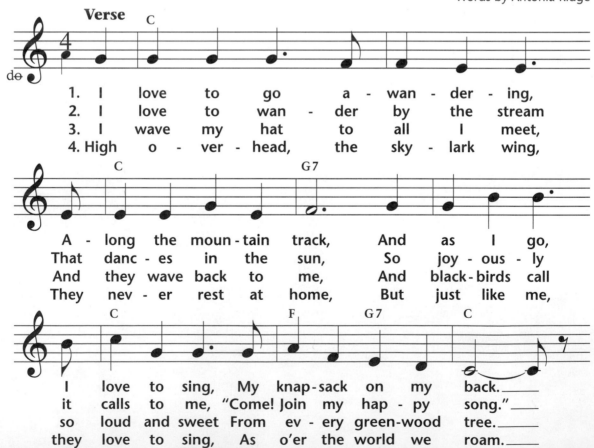

CD 1:24

Music by Friedrich W. Möller
Words by Antonia Ridge

Verse

1. I love to go a - wan - der - ing,
2. I love to wan - der by the stream
3. I wave my hat to all I meet,
4. High o - ver - head, the sky - lark wing,

A - long the moun - tain track, And as I go,
That danc - es in the sun, So joy - ous - ly
And they wave back to me, And black - birds call
They nev - er rest at home, But just like me,

I love to sing, My knap - sack on my back.___
it calls to me, "Come! Join my hap - py song."___
so loud and sweet From ev - ery green - wood tree.___
they love to sing, As o'er the world we roam.___

The last three words of "The Happy Wanderer" use three pitches. Trace the melodic shape of *on my back*.

The three pitches you sing for *on my back* are called *mi*, *re*, and *do*. **Sing** "The Happy Wanderer." Sing the pitch syllables *mi, re,* and *do* instead of the words *on my back*.

Sing the song again, and use the hand signs shown in the pictures for *mi, re,* and *do*.

mi

re

do

Refrain

G7   C   G7

Val - der - ri,   Val - de - ra,   Val - de - ri,

C   G7

Val - de - ra ha ha ha ha ha, Val - de - ri,

C   F   G7   C

Val - der - ra,   My knap - sack on my back.____

Show Me the Notes

Pitches are written on a **staff** that has five lines and four spaces. The lines and spaces of the staff are numbered from bottom to top.

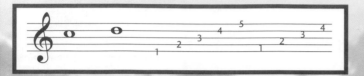

In which space is the first note?
Which line goes through the second note?

This staff shows the pitches *mi*, *re*, and *do* that you sang on the words *chicken pie* in "Great Big House" on p. 14.

mi   re   do

In which space is *mi*? On which line is *re*? In which space is *do*?

Listen to "The Happy Wanderer" again. **Sing** the pitch syllables of the playalong as you listen.
Play the notes on a pitched instrument.

Playalong

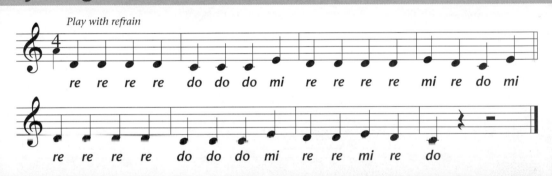

Play with refrain

re re re re do do do mi re re re re mi re do mi

re re re re do do do mi re re mi re do

Different Sounds, Same Voice

CONCEPT
VOCAL TONE COLOR

SKILLS
SING, COMPARE, PERFORM

LINKS
READING, CULTURE

Your voice can make different sounds. You can use your voice to speak, whisper, shout, and sing.

This song is a counting song, like "Billy" on page 6. It is about counting apples, and it comes from Hungary. **Listen** to this song. Are the performers using their speaking, whispering, or singing voices?

Perform this song with your singing voice.

MAP

UNITED STATES — HUNGARY

Egy üveg alma

One Jar of Apples

🔘 **CD 1:27**

Hungarian Folk Song
English Words by Mary Goetze

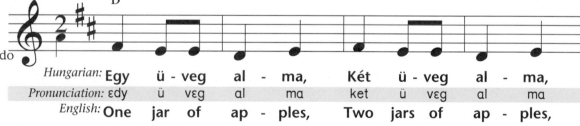

Hungarian: Egy ü - veg al - ma, Két ü - veg al - ma,
Pronunciation: ɛdy ü vɛg al ma ket ü vɛg al ma
English: One jar of ap - ples, Two jars of ap - ples,

Há - rom ü - veg al - ma, Négy ü - veg al - ma,
ha rom ü vɛg al ma nɛdy ü vɛg al ma
Three jars of ap - ples, Four jars of ap - ples,

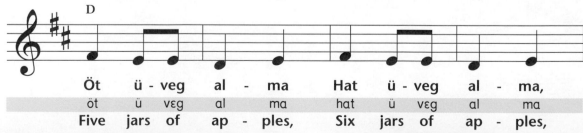

Öt ü - veg al - ma Hat ü - veg al - ma,
öt ü vɛg al ma hat ü vɛg al ma
Five jars of ap - ples, Six jars of ap - ples,

This chart shows the numbers one to ten in English and in Hungarian.

Pair up with a friend.

One speaks the numbers in Hungarian and the other whispers the same numbers in English.

Listen to the song again to hear all the numbers sung in Hungarian.

	1	2	3	4	5
English	one	two	three	four	five
Hungarian	egy	két	három	négy	öt

	6	7	8	9	10
English	six	seven	eight	nine	ten
Hungarian	hat	hét	nyolc	kilenc	tíz

D

Hét ü - veg al - ma, Nyolc ü - veg al - ma,
het ü veg al ma nyolts ü veg al ma
Sev-en jars of ap - ples, Eight jars of ap - ples,

D

Ki - lenc ü - veg al - ma, Tíz ü - veg al - ma,
ki lɛnts ü vɛg al ma tiz ü vɛg al ma
Nine__ jars of ap - ples, Ten jars of ap - ples,

F♯m

Tíz, tíz, tisz - ta víz, Ha nem tisz - ta, vidd visz - sza
tiz tiz tis ta viz ha nɛm tis ta vid vis sa
Ten, ten, wa - ter's clean, Dir - ty wa - ter, take it back,

A7   D

Ott a sza - már meg - isz - sza.
ot a sa mar mɛg is sa
Let the don - key drink it up.

Choose a Voice

Silently read this poem from Hungary.

Apple Tree

Apple tree, apple tree,
Will your apple fall on me?
I won't cry and I won't shout
If your apple knocks me out.

—*Katalin Forrai*

Perform "Apple Tree" using the rhythm shown below. How does this change the way you speak the poem?

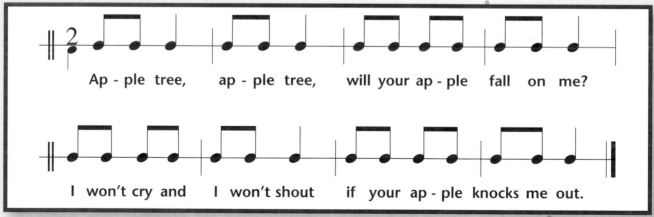

Ap - ple tree,   ap - ple tree,   will your ap - ple   fall   on   me?

I   won't cry and   I   won't shout   if   your ap - ple   knocks me   out.

Think about the words for which you might use your speaking, whispering, or singing voice. You could whisper *apple tree* the second time you say it. Then it would sound like an echo. Practice how you would like to perform this poem for the class with a partner.

Gathering Apples

Lajos Karcsay (1860–1932) was born in Hungary. Growing up, he wanted very much to be a painter. When Karcsay was 18 years old he moved to Germany to study at an art school. He lived in Germany, but he showed his paintings in Hungary.

The Color of Music

CONCEPT
TONE COLOR
SKILLS
LISTEN, ANALYZE, DESCRIBE
LINKS
READING, HISTORY

Many things have their own special sound. Think about your school. You know the sound of footsteps in the hall, the crunching of paper, and the ring of the school bell. Instruments and voices have their own special sounds too. This sound is called **tone color**.

Follow the map as you listen to "Hornpipe" from *Water Music Suite* by George Frideric Handel.

Meet the Musician

George Frideric Handel (1685–1759) lived most of his life in England. He was a composer and conductor who wrote a large number of songs for voice and other instruments. In 1717, Handel wrote this music for a party that King George I of England was hosting on several boats on the River Thames. The king liked the music so much that the musicians played it over and over as the party boats floated up and down the river. For this reason, this set of pieces is called *Water Music*.

LISTENING CD 1:31

Hornpipe (excerpt) from *Water Music Suite*
by George Frideric Handel

Each barge on the next page has a different group of instruments on it. You can tell when the music gets to each new barge by the instrumental tone color. When all of the instruments play together, you'll see the Italian word *tutti* on the barge.

Listen to the instruments as you look at the listening map. Why do you think Handel put certain instruments together?

Log on to **music.mmhschool.com** to learn more about Handel.

Listening Map for Hornpipe from *Water Music Suite*

START

tutti

Tone Color

"When I First Came to This Land" tells a story that includes many characters.

Tone color is a good way to tell the characters in this story apart.

Sing the song and learn the story.

When I First Came to This Land

CD 1:32

Words and Music by
Oscar Brand

Verse

1.-5. When I first came to this land, I was not a wealth-y man.

Then I built my-self a shack.
Then I bought my-self a cow.
Then I bought my-self a horse. } I did what I could.____
Then I got my-self a wife.
Then I got my-self a son.

Repeat these four measures for additional lines in verses 2-5

I { called my shack Break-my-back.
    called my cow No-milk-now,
    called my horse Lame-of-course, } I
    called my wife Joy-of-my-life.
    told my son My work's done. }

Refrain

Still the land was sweet and good, I did what I could.____

28

This playalong gives each character tone color. Every character will have its own instrumental sound.

Playalong

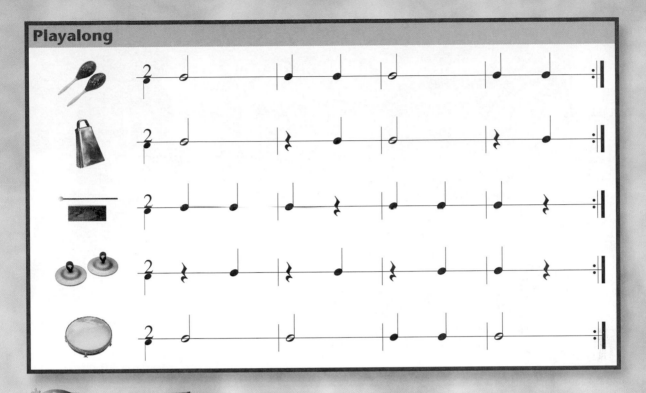

THINK! What instruments would you use for the characters in the song "When I First Came to This Land"? Why?

CONCEPT
RHYTHM

SKILLS
LISTEN, MOVE, IDENTIFY

LINKS
SOCIAL STUDIES, CULTURE

Learn About Carnaval

Carnaval in the Andes Mountains is a time for celebration. People wear fancy, colorful clothes. They play lots of music. Name some times or events when you celebrate with music.

Listen to "Guadalquivir," which is often heard at Carnaval time.

LISTENING CD 2:1

Guadalquivir Andean Dance Song

People from different cultures live in the Andes today. They share their culture through the music they play. Some of the rhythms and melodies in the music have been created by people from Spain.

Quechua men playing flute at village festival

Quechua woman playing siku (panpipes)

quena

siku

charango

In "Guadalquivir," you heard different sounds made by different kinds of instruments. These instruments can be put in three different groups: string, wind, and percussion.

String Instruments
String instruments have strings that are plucked, strummed, or bowed.

violin	banjo	guitar

Wind Instruments
A wind instrument makes sound when someone blows through it.

clarinet	recorder	siku

Percussion Instruments
Percussion instruments make sound when you hit them or shake them.

snare drum	tambourine	bombo

Clapping Rhythms

Listen to this song from Peru. Do you hear the *bombo,* a drum from Peru? Now sing "De aquel cerro."

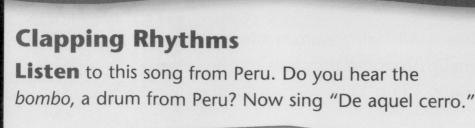

MAP

UNITED STATES

PERU

De aquel cerro

On the Darkened Hillside

CD 2:3

Peruvian Folk Song
Collected by R. and M. D'Harcourt

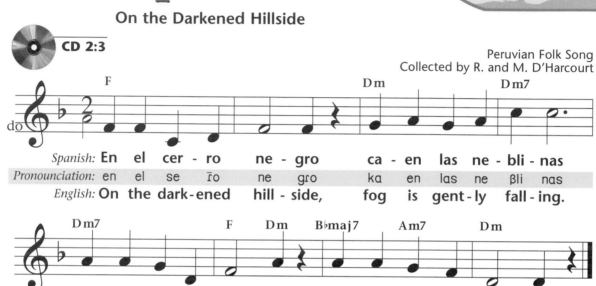

F   Dm   Dm7

do

Spanish: **En el cer - ro   ne - gro   ca - en las ne - bli - nas**
Pronunciation: en el se ɾo   ne gɾo   ka en las ne βli nas
English: **On the dark-ened   hill - side,   fog is gent-ly fall - ing.**

Dm7   F   Dm   B♭maj7   Am7   Dm

De tus lin-dos   o - jos,   a - guas cris - ta - li - nas.
ðe tus lin dos o xos   a gwas kɾis ta li nas
From your eyes so love - ly,   crys - tal tears are flow - ing.

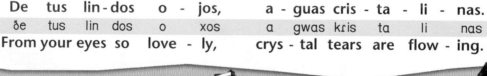

Bombo and siku players

Music from the Andes has special rhythms. Here are two rhythms you heard in "Guadalquivir" and "De aquel cerro."

Musicians from Ecuador

THINK! What makes music from the Andes Mountains different from "Billy," "Great Big House," and "The Happy Wanderer"?

Art Gallery

quenas

Carnaval
Haydee Mendizabal has studied art in South America and in the United States. People from all over the world have seen her works of art.

CONCEPT
RHYTHM
SKILLS
SING, ANALYZE,
COMPOSE
LINKS
CULTURE,
DANCE

All songs have rhythm. One of the rhythms you know is ♫ You heard this rhythm in "Egy üveg alma," "Simon Says," and "The Happy Wanderer." Name some other songs you know that have this rhythm. This is a fun song from South Africa. How many ♫s are in this song?

Hey, Motswala

MAP

UNITED
STATES

SOUTH AFRICA

CD 2:8

South African Folk Song

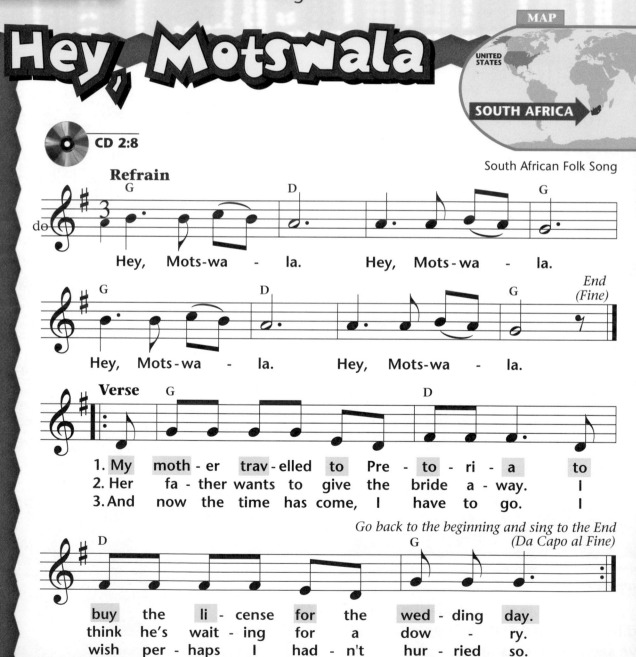

Refrain

Hey, Mots-wa - la.   Hey, Mots-wa - la.

Hey, Mots-wa - la.   Hey, Mots-wa - la.

End (Fine)

Verse

1. My moth - er trav - elled to Pre - to - ri - a to
2. Her fa - ther wants to give the bride a - way. I
3. And now the time has come, I have to go. I

Go back to the beginning and sing to the End (Da Capo al Fine)

buy the li - cense for the wed - ding day.
think he's wait - ing for a dow - ry.
wish per - haps I had - n't hur - ried so.

You can sing "Hey, Motswala." Look at the pictures and learn how to move to "Hey, Motswala"!

Sing the song. **Move** to the words.

My	mother	travelled	to

 **LISTENING** CD 2:11

Pata Pata by Miriam Makeba and Jerry Ragovoy

 Meet the Musician

Miriam Makeba (b. 1932) was born in South Africa. She is a well-known singer all over the world. In the United States she has performed for the President, starred on Broadway, and recorded many albums. She lived in the United States for many years. She returned to South Africa in 1980.

Create Some Rhythm

You have learned a lot about rhythm. You have learned that a beat can have one sound, two sounds, and no sounds. **Clap** these rhythms.

1.

2.

3.

4.

Shaka Zulu Day in Durban, South Africa

Zulu woman in South Africa

Use what you know about rhythms to make your own music. **Create** a rhythm piece that has eight beats in all.

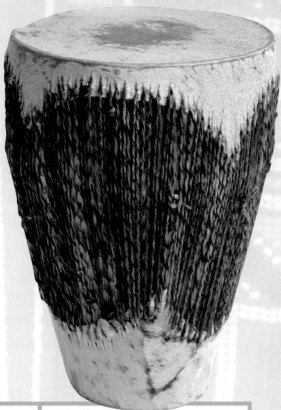

East African cowhide drum

1 Use ♩, ♫, and 𝄽

2 Choose your own order for the beats of your rhythm.

3 Write your rhythm on paper.

4 Use the meter signature ² for your rhythm pattern.

5 Be sure each measure has two beats.

Share your music with the class.

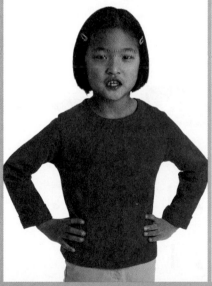

Clap your rhythm piece.

Speak your rhythm piece. Use the word *pie* for the quarter notes and *chicken* for the eighth notes.

Play your rhythm piece on a rhythm instrument.

Spotlight Your Success!

REVIEW

1 What do you call a group of pitches that moves higher, lower, or stays the same?

    a. pitch   **b.** melody   **c.** rhythm   **d.** beat

2 If the meter signature of a song is ⅜, how many beats are in the measure?

    a. 3   **b.** 8   **c.** 4   **d.** 2

3 This staff shows the pitches *mi, re,* and *do.* How does this melody move?

    a. higher   **b.** lower   **c.** stays the same

READ AND LISTEN

 CD 2:12

1 **Read** these rhythms. Then **listen**. Which do you hear?

    a.   **b.**

    c.

2 **Listen** to this melody. With your index finger, trace the shape of the melody in the air. How did the melody move?

    a. upward   **b.** downward   **c.** stayed the same

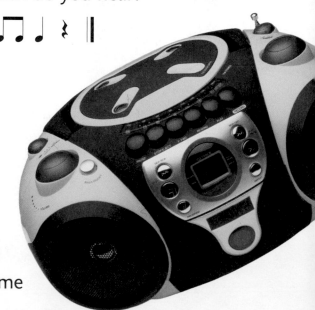

3 **Read** these melodies with *do*, *re*, and *mi*. **Listen** to the melody. Which melody do you hear?

a.

b.

c.

THINK!

1 How do beat and rhythm of the words differ?

2 The shape of a melody moves upward. How would the pitches of the melody appear on a musical staff?

3 **Write** about the tone color of an instrument you like.

CREATE AND PERFORM

Create your own melody.

1 Use ² for your meter signature.

2 Use ♩, ♫, and 𝄽 to create your rhythm pattern.

3 Use *mi*, *re*, and *do* for your pitches.

4 **Write** your melody on a piece of paper.

5 Quietly practice what you wrote.

Perform your own melody.

Meet the Musician
ON NATIONAL RADIO!

Names: Ariana and Rexton Park
Ages: 10 and 11
Instrument: Piano
Hometown: Lexington, Massachusetts

Before Ariana and Rexton Park started playing piano, they used to bicker all the time. "We would quarrel for no reason at all," says eleven-year-old Rexton. "The more we play piano, the less we seem to fight." Ten-year-old Ariana agrees. "The piano has changed us!" she says.

Ariana and Rexton are now so close, they sometimes find themselves saying the same thing at the same time. "Our imaginations are alike," explains Rexton. The two enjoy spending time together, especially when they are playing piano duets.

 LISTENING CD 2:13–15 **RECORDED INTERVIEW**

The Funny Road by David Dvorin

Listen to Ariana and Rexton's performance and interview on the national program **From the Top**.

Spotlight on the Guitar

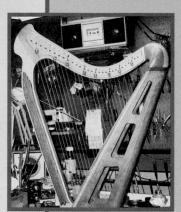

When Jimmy Kane started his part-time job in college, he never realized it would become his full-time career.

Mr. Kane only played guitar and piano before he began working in a family-owned music store. At first, he sold music and instruments. But customers also brought broken instruments for repair, and Mr. Kane's duties changed.

By watching others do repairs, Mr. Kane learned much more about instruments. Today he fixes many types of instruments. He can even play a little on all of them.

Mr. Kane is sure you can learn by experience. He says, "You need a teacher who knows the instrument and to practice *every* day."

Did You Know?

Guitar players produce sound by plucking the six strings.

The guitar's soundboard, the flat surface next to the strings, makes the vibrations of the strings sound louder and clearer.

The guitar is widely used in popular music, but many classical pieces were written for it.

 LISTENING CD 2:16–17

Jesu, Joy of Man's Desiring
by Johann Sebastian Bach

Concierto de Aranjuez, First Movement (excerpt)
by Joaquin Rodrigo

Listen to two pieces. Although not originally for guitar, Bach's music has been adapted for it. Rodrigo's concerto uses melodies that give it a Gypsy sound.

The World Around You

The sounds of music are all around you. You hear music in nature. You hear music in the sounds of the city. You can hear music in the sounds of voices. All you have to do is listen!

Coming Attractions

Sing a fun song quickly, slowly, loudly, and softly.

Learn about Native American traditions.

Create movement to imitate a clock.

As you listen to this song, make a list of the everyday sounds that it mentions. **Sing** "Music of the World A-Turnin'."

Music of the World A-Turnin'

 CD 2:19

Words and Music by
Estelle Levitt and Don Thomas

(sing refrain before each verse)

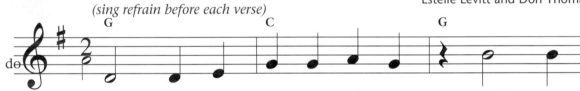

Refrain	I	hear	the	mu - sic	of	the	world	a -
Verse 1.	I	hear	the	mu - sic	of	the	world	a -
Verse 2.	I	hear	the	sym - pho - ny	of	traf-fic in	the	
(Verse 3.)	wind	writes	a	spe - cial song	for	each and ev' - ry		

turn-in'.	Can't you	hear the sweet sounds___	of	the
turn-in'.	There are	some___ folks laughin',	There are	
cit - y.	There are	horns___ a - blow-in',	There are	
day.___	It's got the	rain___ a - danc-in',	And the	

world   a - turn-in'?_____   Stop,   look and
some folks cry - in',_____   Kids   play - in'
heels a - click-in',_____   Ash   cans a -
thun-der a - clap-pin',_____   Don't   just ig -

lis - ten; you can   hear___things a - grow-in'._____
in the street sound   sweet-er than a cho - ir._____
rat-tlin' as the   sun be - gins to ri - se,_____
nore it: there's a   con - cert all a - round you._____

You___ can have mu - sic   wher - ev - er you go.
(1.-3.) All you got - ta do___   is lis - ten to hear.   3. The

LESSON 1

CONCEPT
FORM
SKILLS
LISTEN, SING,
DESCRIBE
LINKS
CULTURES,
READING

Focus on Form

Before you put a toy together, write a story, or have a party, you need a plan. Before a song or piece of music is created, there is a plan. In music, this plan is called **form**. The form for "El florón" has one section. This section is given the letter A.

El florón

The Flower

CD 2:22

Mexican Game Song
English Version by MMH

		D	G	D

Spanish: El flo - rón es - tá en las ma - nos, Y en las
Pronounciation: el flo ɾon es ta en las ma nos yen las
English: In my hand is a love - ly flow - er, Pret - ty

D	A 7	D	G

ma - nos es - tá el flo - rón. A - di - vi - nen quién lo
ma nos es ta el flo ɾon a ði βi neng kyen lo
flow - er I hold in my hand. Now, I won - der who will

D		A 7	D

tie - ne, O se que - da de plan - tón.
tye ne o se ke ða ðe plan ton
have it, Or will it stay in my hand?

46

When a song has two sections that are the same, the form is AA. When the two sections of a song are different, the form is AB. **Listen** to "Nigun Atik." How many different sections do you hear?

 **LISTENING** CD 2:26

Nigun Atik Israeli Folk Dance

The music for this folk dance has two different sections that take turns like this: ABABA. The dance to "Nigun Atik" also has different movements for the A and B sections to match the music.

The Form Is Set

All music has form. **Listen** to "Sun Don't Set in the Mornin'." How many sections do you hear? Are any of them the same? Which of these describes the form?

AAA   ABA   ABB

CD 2:27

Virginia Folk Song

A

D   Bm

do

Sun don't set in the morn-in',   Sun don't set in the morn-in', Lord,

D   A   D

Sun don't set in the morn-in',   Light shines round the world.

B

D

Sing on,_____ sing-in' sis-ter, Sing on,_____ sing-in' sis-ter

THINK!

Think about the songs and dances you know. Which have A and B sections?

Sing on,____ sing-in' sis-ter, Light shines round the world.

A

Sun don't set in the morn-in', Sun don't set in the morn-in', Lord,

Sun don't set in the morn-in', Light shines round the world.

Rhythm for a Reason

CONCEPT
RHYTHM
SKILLS
LISTEN, READ, SING
LINKS
READING, DANCE

There are many ways to honor people for how they help others. They can receive a medal or a statue. Some people are honored by having buildings named after them. What are some other ways people are honored? You will hear a story that the Iroquois people tell to honor a special animal.

Listen to this ancient Iroquois story honoring the rabbit.

 LISTENING CD 3:1

Tehahontanekenhnêha' (Rabbit Dance Story)

Iroquois Story
In this story, the rabbit is remembered for the many ways it helps the Iroquois people.

cornhusk doll

Iroquois dancer

Listen to this song that tells the story "Tehahontanekenhnêha'."

 LISTENING CD 3:2

Tehahontanekenhnêha' (Rabbit Dance Song)

Iroquois Song

Singers from the Iroquois Nation perform this song. It is another way the Iroquois people remember the rabbit for the many ways it helps them.

How many instruments do you hear in this song? Listen to the tone color of the instruments. Name the instruments.

THINK! **How do the instruments help the singers tell the story?**

Listen to the song again and **read** the music below. The top line is the music for the rattle. The middle line is the music for the drum. Both the rattle and the drum play eighth notes. **Tap** your foot to the quarter notes in the bottom line.

tree bark rattle

water drum

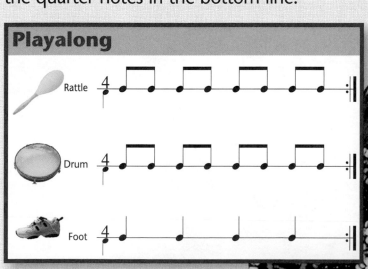

Playalong

Rattle

Drum

Foot

beadwork

I Have Reason to Dance

The Iroquois people often dance. They dance for many reasons. They dance to celebrate, to tell a story, or to remember events. The Rabbit Dance is a traditional Iroquois dance.

RECORDED INTERVIEW CD 3:3

Jerry Thundercloud McDonald

Listen to Jerrry Thundercloud McDonald talk about traditional music and dance.

Iroquois dancer

Meet the Musician

Jerry Thundercloud McDonald (b. 1962) is a singer, storyteller, dancer, and actor. He created a group called Peacemakers Drum. Peacemakers Drum is a group of Mohawk Native Americans who perform traditional dances like the Rabbit Dance.

turtle carving

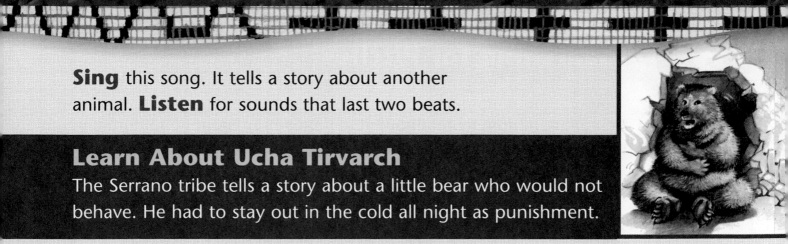

Sing this song. It tells a story about another animal. **Listen** for sounds that last two beats.

Learn About Ucha Tirvarch

The Serrano tribe tells a story about a little bear who would not behave. He had to stay out in the cold all night as punishment.

Ucha Tirvarch

Little Bear Song

CD 3:4

Serrano (Maringá) Indian Lullaby
As Sung by Ernest Siva

Searching for Pitches

CONCEPT
MELODY
SKILLS
SING, ANALYZE,
DESCRIBE
LINKS
READING,
CULTURES

Children from all over the world play games. "El florón" is a game that Mexican children play with a small flower. **Listen** to the song and then play the game.

1 Hold your hands behind your back and listen to the song with your eyes closed.

2 At the end of the song, close your hands and open your eyes. The person who was "it" will ask one person at a time to guess who has the flower.

3 Whoever guesses right will be "it" when the game begins again.

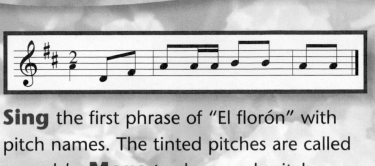

Sing the first phrase of "El florón" with pitch names. The tinted pitches are called *so* and *la*. **Move** to show each pitch as you sing "El florón."

do   re   mi   so   la

do   re   mi

so   la

Baa *So La*

Identify *so* and *la* in this song.

Shepherd, Shepherd

CD 3:8

Swing Rhythm

African American Spiritual

Shep - herd, shep - herd, where'd you lose your sheep?
Shep - herd, shep - herd, where'd your leave your lambs?

Shep - herd, shep - herd, where'd you lose your sheep?
Shep - herd, shep - herd, where'd you leave your lambs?

Shep - herd, shep - herd, where'd you lose your sheep? }
Shep - herd, shep - herd, where'd you leave your lambs? } O, the

sheep all gone a - stray. _____ The

sheep all gone _ a - stray. _____

Play these rhythms on rhythm instruments while you listen to "Shepherd, Shepherd."

Time and a Half Note

CONCEPT
RHYTHM
SKILLS
SING, ANALYZE, DESCRIBE
LINKS
READING, CULTURES

In Nigeria, Africa, some people fish in long boats. The people in the boats have to row for the boats to move. To help everyone row together, the people might sing a song like "Eh Soom Boo Kawaya."

Look at the notes in "Eh Soom Boo Kawaya," a song from Nigeria. Notes show how many beats there are to a sound. A quarter note (♩) shows one beat to a sound. A **half note** shows two beats to a sound. Find the half notes (♩). **Listen** to the song. Point to the half notes (♩) when you hear them. **Sing** the song.

Eh Soom Boo Kawaya

MAP
UNITED STATES
NIGERIA

Nigerian Boat Song

CD 3:11

Nigerian Song

Vocables: Eh soom boo ka - wa - ya ke - dou ka - dee.

Eh soom boo ka - wa - ya ke - dou ka - dee.

Ke - dou ka - dee ke - dou ka - dee.

Read these rhythms. **Clap** and say *light* for each quarter note (♩). Clap and say *mornin'* for each pair of eighth notes (♫). Brush one hand down the other arm and say the word *world* for each half note (♪).

Now add pitch. **Sing** these rhythms with pitch names.

do   mi   so so mi so   la   do   mi   do   so   do

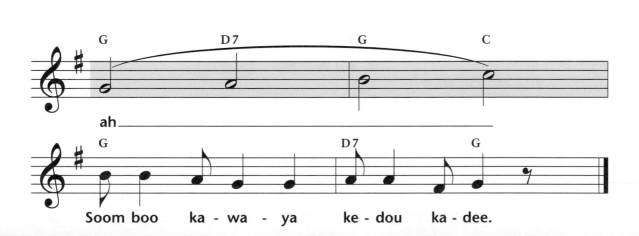

Soom boo   ka - wa - ya   ke - dou   ka - dee.

Countermelody

Listen to "Sun Don't Set in the Mornin'." This song has a **countermelody**. A countermelody is a separate melody that fits with the main melody. Both the main melody and the countermelody are performed at the same time. **Sing** this countermelody.

Sun Don't Set in the Mornin'

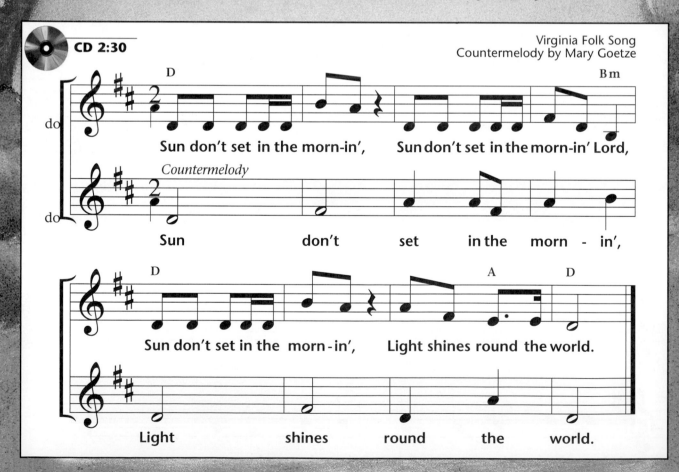

CD 2:30

Virginia Folk Song
Countermelody by Mary Goetze

Sun don't set in the morn-in', Sun don't set in the morn-in' Lord,

Countermelody

Sun don't set in the morn - in',

Sun don't set in the morn-in', Light shines round the world.

Light shines round the world.

Find the half notes (♩) in the countermelody. How many half notes (♩) are there? Are there any half notes in the melody?

To sing this song, two groups of singers are needed. One group sings the melody. Another group sings the countermelody. Both groups sing at the same time.

Sing "Sun Don't Set in the Mornin'" with the countermelody.

Playalong

Play this part on pitched instruments. Then form three groups. One group can play the instrument part. One group can sing the melody. A third group can sing the countermelody. Now there are three groups performing at the same time!

LESSON 5

CONCEPT
DYNAMICS
SKILLS
SING, LISTEN
LINKS
READING,
CULTURES

The Nature of Sound

Some people celebrate things that happen in nature each year. The Japanese people have the Tanabata (Seven Evenings) Festival. This festival grew out of a story about two stars in the sky that come together each year on the night of July 7. Japanese children hope for clear weather that night. If it rains, the stars cannot meet until the next year! **Listen** to the Japanese song "Tanabata."

Sing the song twice. The first time sing loudly. The second time sing softly.

MAP

UNITED STATES   JAPAN

Tanabata

Seven Evenings

CD 3:15

Music by K. Shimousa
Words by H. Gonda and R. Hayashi

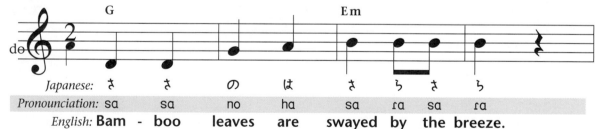

Japanese:	さ	さ	の	は	さ	ら	さ	ら
Pronounciation:	sa	sa	no	ha	sa	ɾa	sa	ɾa
English:	Bam -	boo	leaves	are	swayed	by	the	breeze.

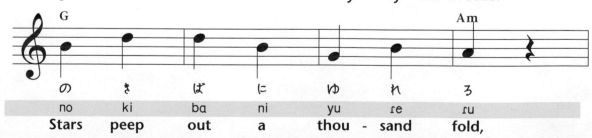

の	き	ば	に	ゆ	れ	る
no	ki	ba	ni	yu	ɾe	ɾu
Stars	peep	out	a	thou -	sand	fold,

THINK!
Think about the lyrics as you sing the song loudly and softly. Which way sounds better? Why?

In music, the word for loud is **forte**. The word for soft is *piano*. When you sang "Tanabata," you sang it first *forte*, then *piano*. You changed the volume. The word for volume in music is **dynamics**. Dynamics make the music more interesting and exciting!

o ho shi sa ma ki ɾa ki ɾa
Stars shin-ing bright-ly o - ver the trees,

ki ɳ gi ɳ su na go
Stars of sil - ver, stars of gold.

Dynamic Sounds

Dynamics make the overture from the opera *William Tell* very exciting. Its composer, Gioacchino Rossini, composed this music to describe a thunder and lightning storm. **Listen** to hear the sounds of the storm. Do you think thunder sounds should be *piano* or *forte*?

Follow the map as you listen to the *William Tell* Overture.

Use *Orchestral Instruments* **CD-ROM** to learn more about the instruments of the orchestra.

LISTENING   CD 3:19

Overture (excerpt) from *William Tell*
by Gioacchino Rossini

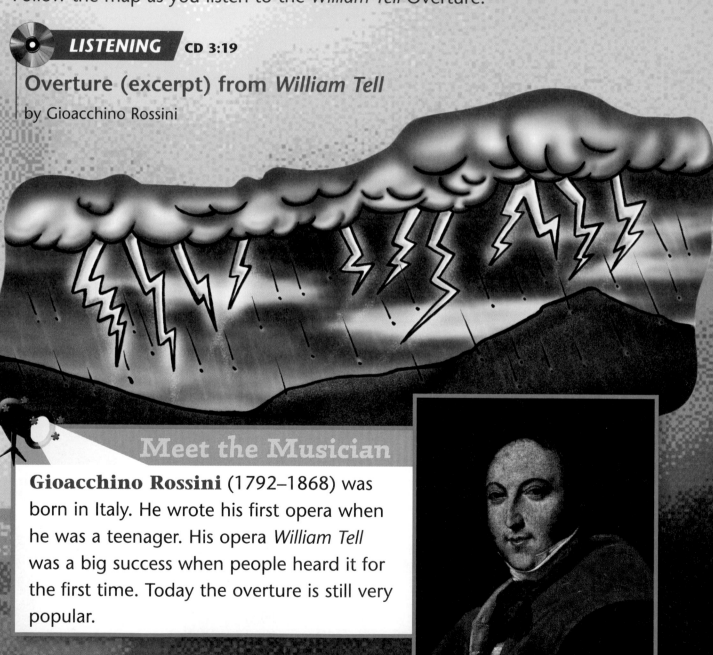

Meet the Musician

Gioacchino Rossini (1792–1868) was born in Italy. He wrote his first opera when he was a teenager. His opera *William Tell* was a big success when people heard it for the first time. Today the overture is still very popular.

Listening Map for *William Tell* (Overture) (excerpt)

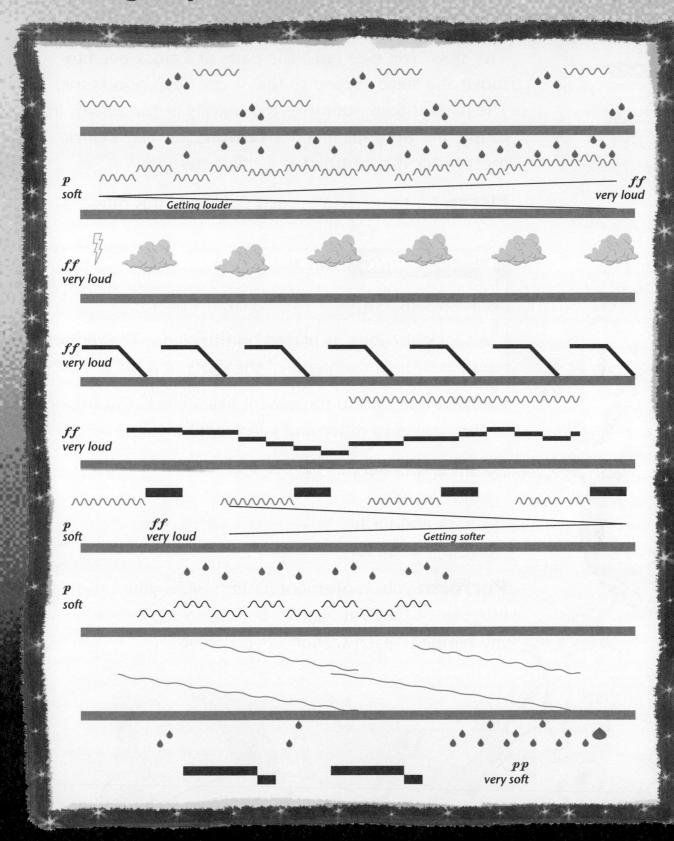

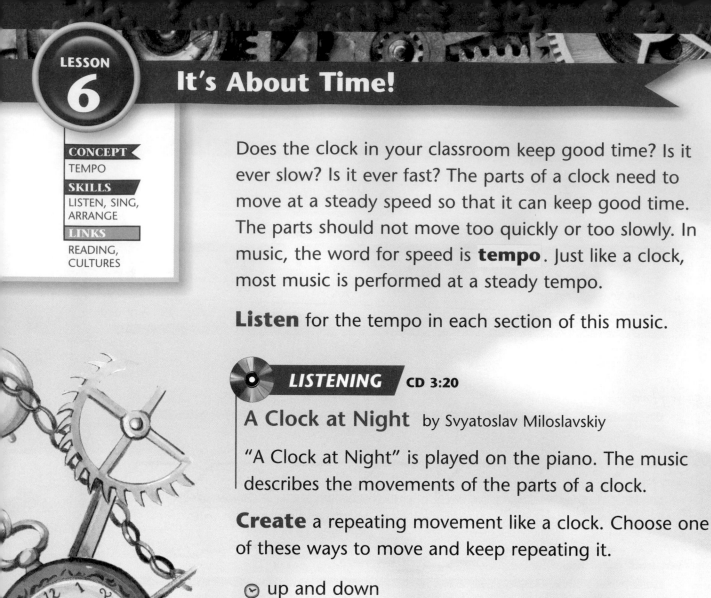

CONCEPT
TEMPO
SKILLS
LISTEN, SING, ARRANGE
LINKS
READING, CULTURES

Does the clock in your classroom keep good time? Is it ever slow? Is it ever fast? The parts of a clock need to move at a steady speed so that it can keep good time. The parts should not move too quickly or too slowly. In music, the word for speed is **tempo**. Just like a clock, most music is performed at a steady tempo.

Listen for the tempo in each section of this music.

LISTENING CD 3:20

A Clock at Night by Svyatoslav Miloslavskiy

"A Clock at Night" is played on the piano. The music describes the movements of the parts of a clock.

Create a repeating movement like a clock. Choose one of these ways to move and keep repeating it.

- up and down
- side to side
- back and forth
- round and round

Perform your movement pattern while you listen to "A Clock at Night." Be sure to show the tempo of each section as you move.

Here is more music about a clock. **Sing** this song from France. Make sure you keep a steady tempo.

MAP

UNITED STATES

FRANCE

La cloche

The Clock

CD 3:21

French Round

French: **Din,   don,   din,   don,   C'est la clo-che   du ma-tin,**
Pronounciation: dɛ̃   dõ   dɛ̃   dõ   sɛ   la   klɔ   ʃə   dü   ma   tɛ̃

Qui sonne au   le - ver du jour: Bon - jour,   bon - jour!
ki   sɔ   no   lə   ve   dü   ʒuʀ   bõ   ʒuʀ   bõ   ʒuʀ

Largo is the word for a slow tempo. **Allegro** is the word for a fast tempo. At what tempo would you sing "La cloche"?

Turn on the Tempo

"John Jacob Jingleheimer Schmidt" is a song all about tempo and dynamics. The tempo of each verse is steady, but each time the song repeats, the song gets faster. How quickly can you sing this song and keep the tempo steady?

John Jacob Jingleheimer Schmidt

CD 3:25

American Camp Song

John Ja - cob Jing - le - heim - er Schmidt,

His name is my name too.

When - ev - er I go out, the peo - ple al - ways shout,

"There goes John Ja - cob Jing - le - heim - er

Schmidt," Da da da da da da da da.

Last time only

With your class, decide if you will use your singing voice, shouting voice, or whispering voice on the words *Da da da da da da da da*. Change the voice you use every time you sing the verse again.

With your class, decide where to sing *piano* and where to sing *forte*.

Put it all together. **Sing** the song. Remember to change the tempo every time you repeat the verse.

Remember which voice to use on the words *Da da da da da da da da*.

Don't forget where to sing *piano* and *forte*. Good luck!

THINK!

How would you change the tempo from the first time you sing "John Jacob Jingleheimer Schmidt" if you wanted to sing it through many times? Remember that each time you sing the song, it gets faster.

LESSON
7

CONCEPT
RHYTHM
SKILLS
LISTEN, ANALYZE,
COMPOSE
LINKS
CULTURES,
DANCE

What's the Connection?

Look at these dancers. They are showing one way to connect a circle. Many dances are done in a circle. "Nigun Atik" on p. 47 is an Israeli dance done in a circle. When you do the first five steps in the A section of "Nigun Atik," use this handheld position.

Perform the dance to the A section.

Listen to the music again. Clap this rhythm to the B section.

Notes can be connected with a **tie**. A tie is a curved line that connects two notes of the same pitch. It means that the sound of the first note should be held for the length of both notes.

These two quarter notes (♩ ♩) are tied together. Another way to show a sound that lasts two beats is ♩ ♩

Clap this rhythm with the B section. Make a two-beat brushing motion down your arm for the tied quarter notes.

Half notes (♩) are also held for two beats. **Clap** this rhythm with the B section.

Make a two-beat brushing motion down your arm for the tied quarter notes and half notes. Both ♩♩ and ♩ will sound the same when you perform them.

Clap this rhythm. Now play this rhythm using instruments. Tapping a metal instrument like the triangle will produce a long, ringing sound. Tapping a drum produces a much shorter sound. **Play** along with the B section of "Nigun Atik."

Israeli men dancing

? THINK! What other rhythm instrument would be a good choice to make sounds that last two beats?

Rattle, Chirp, and Scratch!

Listen for tempo changes in this song from Kentucky.
Sing the song.

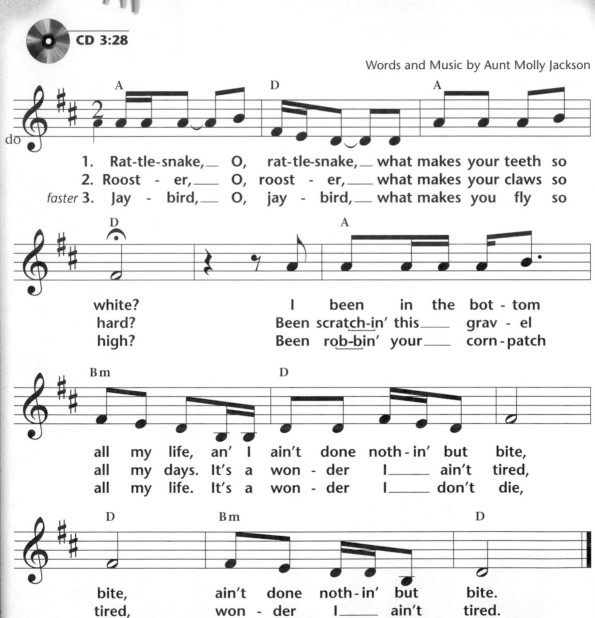

CD 3:28

Words and Music by Aunt Molly Jackson

1. Rat-tle-snake,___ O, rat-tle-snake,___ what makes your teeth so
2. Roost - er,___ O, roost - er,___ what makes your claws so
faster 3. Jay - bird,___ O, jay - bird,___ what makes you fly so

white? I been in the bot - tom
hard? Been scratch-in' this___ grav - el
high? Been rob-bin' your___ corn - patch

all my life, an' I ain't done noth-in' but bite,
all my days. It's a won - der I___ ain't tired,
all my life. It's a won - der I___ don't die,

bite, ain't done noth-in' but bite.
tired, won - der I___ ain't tired.
die, won - der I___ don't die.

Identify the words in each verse that are always sung for two beats.

Create an 8-beat rhythm with a partner.

Say *rattle* and clap for eighth notes (♫).

Say *chirp* and clap for quarter notes (♩).

Say *scratch* and brush for half notes (♩).

Arrange your rhythm different ways. Say your rhythm with a steady tempo. **Perform** your 8-beat rhythm for the class.

CONCEPT
FORM
SKILLS
SING, ANALYZE, DESCRIBE
LINKS
READING, ART

Read this poem about sounds you hear in the city.

City Music

Snap your fingers.
Tap your feet.
Step out a rhythm
down the street.

Rap on the litter bin.
Stamp on the ground.
City music
is all around.

Beep says motor-car.
Ding says bike.
City music
is what we like.

—Tony Mitton

A crowing rooster is usually heard on a farm. **Sing** a song about a rooster on the next page. It uses the same idea more than once. This is called **repetition**. One idea combined with a different idea is called **contrast**. Repetition and contrast make music more interesting.

Kum Bachur

CD 3:31   The Rooster

Israeli Folk Song

1 C   G7   C

Hebrew: קוּם בַּ חוּר עֲ לֵ אֶ וְ אֶ לֵ עֲ בוֹ דָה

Pronunciation: kum bɑ xuʁ a tsel vʼɛ tse lɑ a vo dɑ

English: **Now the roost-er's crow - ing, He crows to greet the day.**

C   G7   C

קוּם בַּ חוּר עֲ לֵ אֶ וְ אֶ לֵ עֲ בוֹ דָה

kum bɑ xuʁ a tsel vʼɛ tse lɑ a vo dɑ

Now the roost-er's crow - ing, He crows to greet the day.

2 C   G7   C

קוּם קוּם יִ אֶ לֵ עֲ בוֹ דָה

kum kum vɛ tse lɑ a vo dɑ

Rise, get up, it's time for work and play.

C   G7   C

קוּם קוּם יִ אֶ לֵ עֲ בוֹ דָה

kum kum vɛ tse lɑ a vo dɑ

Rise, get up, it's time for work and play.

3 C   G7   C

קֻ קֻ רִ קֻ קֻ קֻ רִ קֻ תַּר נֶ גוֹל קָ רֵא

ku ku ʁi ku ku ku ʁi ku taʁ nɛ gol kɑ ʁɑ

Ku - ku - ri - ku, ku - ku - ri - ku, That's what roost - ers say,

C   G7   C

קֻ קֻ רִ קֻ קֻ קֻ רִ קֻ תַּר נֶ גוֹל קָ רֵא

ku ku ʁi ku ku ku ʁi ku taʁ nɛ gol kɑ ʁɑ

Ku - ku - ri - ku, ku - ku - ri - ku, That's what roost - ers say.

Finding Form

Listen for repetition and contrast as you follow the map.

 LISTENING CD 3:35

Ballet of the Unhatched Chicks
from *Pictures at an Exhibition* by Modest Mussorgsky

The form of "Ballet of the Unhatched Chicks" is AABA. The A section repeats, and then the B section makes a contrast. The A section comes back to finish the piece.

Listening Map for Ballet of the Unhatched Chicks

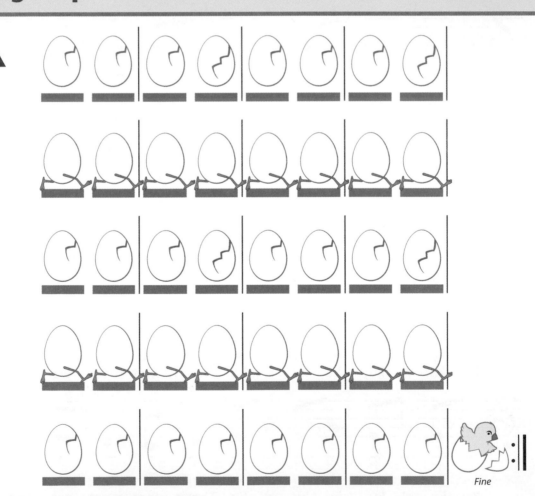

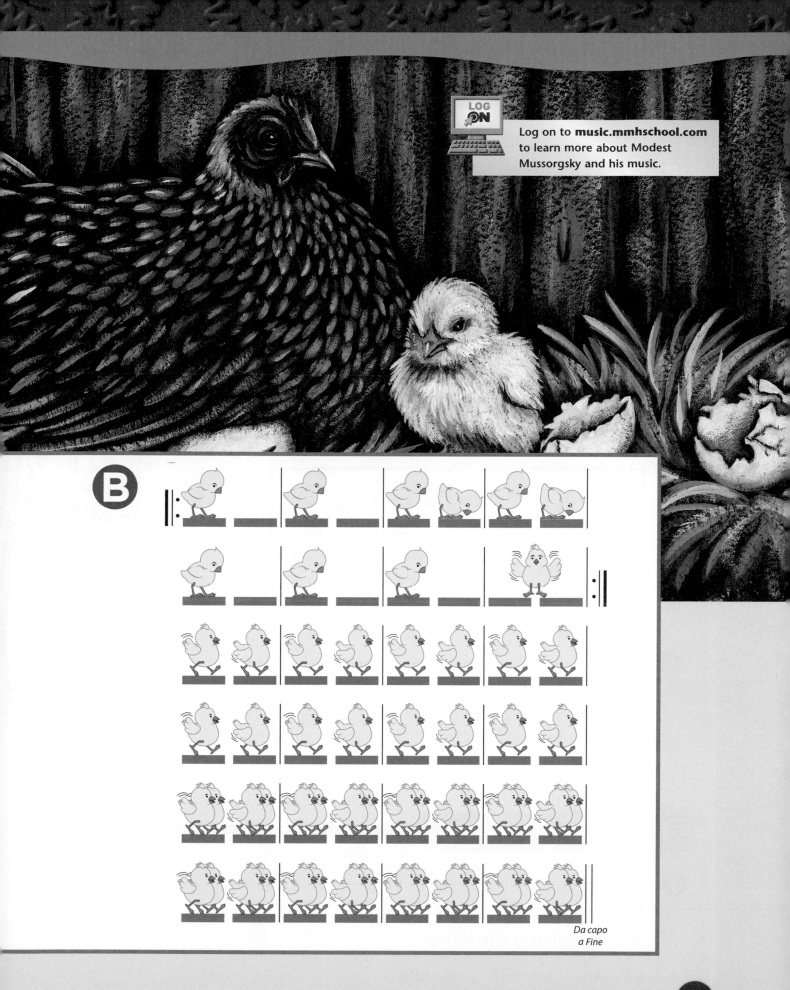

Log on to **music.mmhschool.com** to learn more about Modest Mussorgsky and his music.

Da capo
a Fine

Spotlight Your Success!

REVIEW

1 Which pattern has half notes in it?

a.

b.

c.

d.

2 The first pitch is *do*. Where is *la*?

   a. first space

   b. second space

   c. third line

3 Why are some sections of music called B?

   a. The B section is just like the A section.

   b. The B section is different from the A section.

   c. The B section is a big section.

READ AND LISTEN

CD 3:36

1 **Listen** to a melody with three sections. Close your eyes. Raise your hand each time you hear the A section. Fold your arms for each B section. What is the form?

   a. AAB   **b.** ABB   **c.** ABA

2 **Read** these melodies. Then listen. Which melody do you hear?

a.

b.

c.

THINK!

1 What is the difference between *piano* and *forte*?

2 When you are learning to sing a new piece, what tempo would you choose?

3 What would the form be if only contrast were used in a three-section piece of music?

4 **Write** about how dynamics change the feeling of a song.

CREATE AND PERFORM

Create a rhythm with ABA as the form.

1 Use 𝄴 for your meter signature.

2 Make each section eight beats long.

3 Use at least one ♩ in each section.

4 Write your rhythm on a piece of paper.
Hint: your rhythm should be six measures long.

Play your rhythm.

Meet the Musician
ON NATIONAL RADIO!

Name: Randall Brown
Age: 18
Instrument: Saxophone
Hometown: Twin Falls, Idaho

The first time Randall Brown saw a musician playing a saxophone, he decided he wanted to play one, too. "How can I get one of those?" he thought.

Randall came up with a plan. He placed a big jar on the counter and labeled it "The Randall Brown Saxophone Fund." Each day, members of his family threw their spare change into the jar. Soon, over $300 had been collected!

"My parents finally saw how serious I was about playing the saxophone," says Randall. On his next birthday, Randall received a shiny new saxophone!

When he's not playing saxophone, Randall enjoys learning magic tricks, playing golf and basketball, in-line skating, and playing computer games with his brothers.

LISTENING　CD 4:1–2　**RECORDED INTERVIEW**

Sigh of the Soul for Alyscamp from *Tableaux de Provence* (Fourth Movement)
by Paule Maurice

Listen to Randall's performance and interview on the national radio progam From the Top.

A Tip From the Top!
"Make a Plan."
If you're serious about accomplishing something, make a plan. Randall Brown came up with an idea for how he could get a saxophone, and he helped make it happen.

Spotlight on the English Horn

Did You Know?

The English horn, or *cor anglais*, is a double-reed instrument.

The name "English horn" is something of a mystery. Some think that the word *anglias*, for angels, was misspelled as *anglais*, the French word for English, and the name stuck.

An English horn has a curved bocal, the short metal tube that connects the reed to the instrument. On an oboe, the reed is inserted directly into the top of the instrument. An English horn's bell is pear-shaped, but the bell of an oboe flares out.

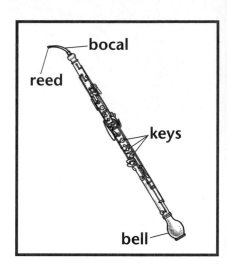

 LISTENING CD 4:3–4

Symphony No. 9 ("From the New World"), Largo (excerpt)

by Antonín Dvořák

Polovtsian Dances (excerpt) from *Prince Igor*

by Alexander Borodin

Listen to these beautiful English horn melodies. The first is reminiscent of the African American spirituals Dvořák heard when he visited America. In the dance by Borodin, you will first hear the oboe, the smaller, higher-pitched cousin of the English horn. Then listen for the English horn, which has a deeper, more mellow sound.

Tunes, Tales, and Traditions

People around the world share songs and stories with each other. Sharing helps people become a larger community. Your class is a community. What songs and stories do you share in your class?

Coming Attractions

Sing songs and play games from around the world.

Sing a song from the movie *Pocahontas.*

Learn how to conduct music.

Everyone shares our planet. We are all part of the world community. In the song "Colors of the Wind," Pocahontas teaches respect for everybody and everything. **Sing** "Colors of the Wind."

Colors of the Wind

from the movie *Pocahontas*

CD 4:5

Music by Alan Menken
Lyrics by Stephen Schwartz

1. You think you own what-ev-er land you land on;
   think the on-ly peo-ple who are peo-ple

the earth is just a dead thing you can claim;
are the peo-ple___ who look and think like you,

but I know ev-'ry rock and tree and crea-ture
but if you walk the foot-steps of a strang-er,

has a life, has a spir-it, has a name. 2. You
you'll learn

things you nev-er knew___ you nev-er knew.

Have you ev-er heard the wolf cry to the blue corn moon, or

asked the grin-ning bob-cat why he grinned?

Can you sing with all the voic-es of the moun-tain?

Can you paint with all the col-ors of the wind?

Can you paint with all the col-ors of the wind?

mountain

wind

sing

Treasure Your Tradition

CONCEPT
RHYTHM
SKILLS
DESCRIBE,
SING, MOVE
LINKS
DANCE,
CULTURES,
HISTORY

Music is one way that people pass down stories and customs. Sometimes music tells a story with words. Sometimes it tells a story by using the sounds of different instruments.

Look at the pictures of these groups on this page. **Describe** how music is used to tell their stories.

Carnaval, Brazil

Gospel singers, Brooklyn, New York

Chilkat dance troupe, Port Chilkoot, Alaska

Many groups of people use dance to tell stories. "Raccoon Dance Song" is a Native American song and dance from the Ottawa nation. It honors the raccoon and is usually performed by children.

Raccoon Dance Song

CD 4:8

Ottawa Native American

Ottawa: **Es - si bon_ nin - di - go___ Es - si bon_ nin - di - go___**

be - ba - ma - da se - a - ni_____ Sa - sa sa - sa

Go back to the beginning

sa - sa sa - sa i hi hi___ i i___ hi

Gallop and Step!

Sometimes a group uses the same instruments to play most of their music. In Scotland, bagpipes and drums are often used to play music.

Listen for the sounds of the Scottish bagpipes and bodhrán (drum) in "Gi'Me Elbow Room."

Sing this song from Scotland.

Scottish bagpipe players

Gi'Me Elbow Room

MAP

UNITED STATES — SCOTLAND

CD 4:12

Scottish Folk Song

D   Bm7   F#m

Cam'-ron he came in-to town and all he want-ed was

A7   1.   2.

el - bow room.   (clap)

Bm7

Oh gi' me el-bow room.___ Oh gi' me el-bow room.

Bm7   A7   D   (for repeat)

Gi' me el-bow room.___ Oh gi' me el-bow room.   Oh

Whisper *gi'me, gi'me* to match the rhythm of your feet as you gallop. First move sideways to the right and then sideways to the left.

Listen to the rhythm of your feet as you step-hop and gallop. Stepping has a different rhythm than galloping.

Log on to **music.mmhschool.com** to learn more about the bagpipes.

When you step-hop on each beat, the rhythm looks like this:

▬▬ ▬

step - hop

When you gallop on each beat, the rhythm looks like this:

▬▬ ▪

gal - lop

THINK!

Which rhythm is equal?

Which rhythm is unequal? Why?

Fiddling with Phrases

CONCEPT
MELODY
SKILLS
SING, MOVE, DESCRIBE
LINKS
FINE ART, CULTURES, DANCE

Many times the things you treasure are not things that you can buy. Maybe your treasures are things that you cannot even see!

Treasure Chests

CD 4:15

Words and Music by Minnie O'Leary

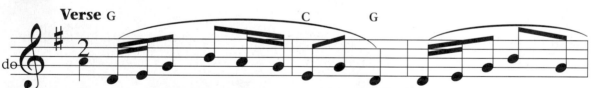

1. Some of us come from a dis-tant land, Some of us from near-
2. Hol - i-days, games and ___ stor - ies, Lan-gua-ges and ___

by, But all of us car - ry a treas-ure chest With
songs; ___ Faith ___ and cour - age and wis - dom, And

things that gold can't buy; with things that gold can't buy.
ways to get a - long; and ways to get a - long.

This song has two sections: a **verse** and a **refrain**. The words in the verses are different. The words in the refrain stay the same. **Tap** the beat on your knees with both hands during the verse. Tap the beat on your knees one hand at a time during the refrain. Look at the pictures to learn this pattern.

Sing the song and perform the movement.

Look at the arched lines over the melody. These lines are called phrase marks and go over a **phrase**. A phrase is a short section of music that is one musical thought. How many phrases are in this song?

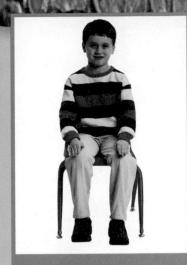

verse

refrain

Refrain C   G

And when we share our treas-ure chests we

C   D   C   G

all grow rich, you see. The rich-es in that treas-ure chest are

Am   D7   C   D7   G

what makes you and me;   are what makes you and me.

Unit 3 Tunes, Tales, and Traditions   **91**

Trace the Phrase

Some phrases are longer than others. "Les saluts," a French Canadian folk dance, has a melody with phrases of different lengths. The A section has two phrases that are each sixteen beats long. The B section has four phrases that are each four beats long.

 LISTENING CD 4:18

Les saluts French Canadian Folk dance

Listen to this folk dance. Trace an arc over your head for each phrase as you listen to the music.

 Art Gallery

Fiddler and Boy Doing Jig

Cornelius Krieghoff (1815–1872) created this oil painting on canvas in 1852. It shows a boy dancing to the music that the man is playing on the fiddle.

One of the instruments you heard playing the melody of "Les saluts" was the violin. When settlers from Europe and the British Isles came to North America, the violin was often the only instrument they had to play as they sang and danced.

A violin is made of wood. It has four strings and is played by pulling a bow across the strings to make them vibrate. The strings can also be plucked.

Listen to "Les saluts" again.

Describe the sound the violin makes when it plays.

tuning pegs

bow

strings

bridge

chin rest

CD-ROM

Use *Orchestral Instruments* **CD-ROM** to learn more about the violin.

Step in Time

CONCEPT
RHYTHM
SKILLS
READ, SING, MOVE
LINKS
HISTORY, DANCE

Say the nursery rhyme "Humpty Dumpty" and clap your hands to the rhythm of the words. "Throw It Out the Window" uses the words of different nursery rhymes. **Sing** the song while tapping the beat on your knee.

Throw It Out the Window

CD 4:19

Nursery Rhyme Parody

1. Old Moth - er Hub - bard___ went to the cup-board to
2. Old____ King Cole was a mer - ry old soul, and a
3. Lit - tle Bo Peep___ has lost___ her sheep,_ and
4. Where,_ oh, where has my lit - tle dog gone?___ Oh,
5. Yan - kee Doo - dle went___ to town___ a -

fetch her poor dog a bone.___ But when she got there, the
mer - ry old soul was he.____ He called for his pipe, and he
does-n't know where to find them. But leave them a - lone; when
where,_ oh, where can he be?____ With his ears___ cut short and his
rid - ing on a po - ny; He stuck___ a fea - ther

cup - board was bare, so she threw it
called for his bowl, and___ threw them
they____ come home she'll_ throw them } out the win - dow, the
tail____ cut long. I'll___ throw him
in_____ his cap and_ threw it

Name another nursery rhyme that would fit this song.
Sing this song using the new nursery rhyme.

Read these rhythms. Say *throw it* for ♩♪ and *out* for ♩.

THINK!

What movement would fit this song the best: step–hop or gallop? Why?

win-dow, the sec-ond sto-ry win-dow.

> But when she got there,   the
> He called for his pipe, and he
> But leave them a - lone; when
> With his ears   cut short and his
> He stuck   a fea - ther

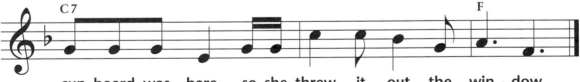

cup-board	was	bare,	so she	threw	it	out	the	win - dow.
called for	his	bowl,	and	threw	them	out	the	win - dow.
they	come home,	she'll	throw	them	out	the	win - dow.
tail	cut	long,	I'll	throw	him	out	the	win - dow.
in	his	cap	and	threw	it	out	the	win - dow.

6. A-tisket, a-tasket,
   a green and yellow basket,
   I wrote a letter to my love
   and threw it out the window.
   The window, the second story window,
   I wrote a letter to my love
   and threw it out the window.

Compare These Rhythms

When you dance, you listen to the rhythm of the music to know how to move. "Bransle de Champaigne" is a French dance that was popular almost 500 years ago. **Listen** to this dance. Think about what movements you would do to the music.

 LISTENING CD 4:22

Bransle de Champaigne by Claude Gervaise

"Bransle de Champaigne" has two sections. Listen to the dance again. Look at the rhythms. How many times do you hear the A section? How many times do you hear the B section?

Look at the end of the first A section and the B section. There is a repeat sign at the end of each section. This sign is called a **repeat sign**. It tells you to perform that section twice. Because of the repeat signs, the form of "Bransle de Champaigne" is AABBA.

Jogging movements are good to use in "Bransle de Champaigne" because there are two equal sounds to each beat (♪♪ ♪♪). Galloping is a good movement for "Throw It Out the Window" because the rhythm is made up of unequal sounds. The long-short, long-short rhythm can be written as:

$\frac{2}{\text{♩.}}$ ♩ ♪♪ ♪♩ ♪♪ ♩ ♪ ‖

gal - lop   gal - lop   gal - lop   gal - lop

Look at the table to see how the rhythms are different for equal and unequal sounds.

Meter sign	$\frac{2}{\text{♩}}$	$\frac{2}{\text{♩.}}$
One sound to a beat	♩	♩.
Two sounds to a beat	♫	♩♪

CONCEPT
MELODY
SKILLS
READ, IDENTIFY,
PLAY
LINKS
HISTORY,
LANGUAGE
ARTS, READING

The song "Cumberland Gap" tells the story of pioneers making the long journey through a mountain pass.

Listen to two phrases of the song "Cumberland Gap." How are the phrases different? With your finger, trace the shape of the melody in the air as you listen again.

Sing the blue highlight section using pitch names. **Hum** the tan highlight phrase to find the two mystery pitches. Are these pitches higher or lower than the other pitches in the song? The names of the new pitches are **low so** and **low la**. Look at the staff below. Is low *la* in a space or on a line? What about low *so*?

so₁   la₁   do   re   mi   so   la

Sing the second phrase of the verse of "Cumberland Gap" using pitch names.

Art Gallery

Daniel Boone Leading Settlers Through the Cumberland Gap

This painting was created by George Caleb Bingham in 1851. It shows pioneer Daniel Boone guiding settlers to Kentucky through the Cumberland Gap. Pioneers are people that find new places to live. As Americans moved west, the Cumberland Gap became an important passageway for explorers through the Appalachian Mountains.

Cumberland Gap

CD 4:23

Southern Appalachian Folk Song

Verse

1.,3.,5.   Me and my   wife   and my wife's   grand - pap
2.   Cum-ber-land   Gap   with it's   cliffs   and   rocks,
4.   Cum-ber-land   Gap   is   a   mighty   fine   place.

all   go - in'   down   to   Cum - ber - land   Gap.
home   of   the   pan - ther,   bear   and   fox.
Three kinds of   wa - ter to   wash   your   face.

Refrain

Cum-ber-land   Gap,   Cum-ber-land   Gap.

(pat)   (clap)   (snap)   (whoo!)

Way   down___   yon-der   in   Cum-ber-land   Gap.

(hum) _____

Mapping out the Music

You have learned about Daniel Boone and the pioneers in the United States. Now you will learn about the *voyageurs* in Canada. *Voyageurs* is a French word for "travelers." These travelers explored Canada in canoes hundreds of years ago. To help them keep a steady beat in their paddling, *voyageurs* sang songs like "En roulant ma boule."

The music has been organized with repeat signs, **first endings**, and **second endings**. This makes the music easier to read and takes less space. **Sing** the song and follow the directions on the music.

En roulant ma boule
As I Roll My Ball

CD 4:26

French Canadian Folk Song

French: En rou-lant ma bou-le rou-lant, En rou-lant ma bou - le,
Pronunciation: ã ɾu lã ma bu lə ɾu lã ã ɾu lã ma bu lə
English: En rou-lant ma bou-le rou-lant, En rou-lant ma bou - le,

bou - le, Der - riér' chez nous, ya - t'un é - tang, En rou-lant ma
bu lə de ɾyeɾ she nu ya tœ e tã ã ɾu lã ma
bou - le. Be - hind our house there is a pond. En rou-lant ma

Listen to "En roulant ma boule." Sing the pitch syllables of the Playalong as you listen.

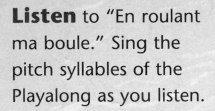

do la₁ so₁

Play the notes through the second ending on a pitched instrument.

Playalong

do so₁ la₁ so₁ do so₁ la₁ do

bou - le, Der - bou - le, Trois beaux ca - nards s'en
bu lə de bu lə tɾwa bo ka naɾ sã
bou - le. Be - bou - le. Three pret - ty ducks are

vont baign-ant, Rou - li, rou-lant, ma bou - le rou-lant,
võ bɛ hã ɾu li ɾu lã ma bu lə ɾu lã
bath - ing there. Rou - li, rou-lant, ma bou - le rou-lant.

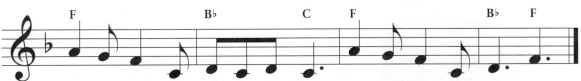

En rou-lant ma bou - le rou-lant, En rou-lant ma bou - le.
ã ɾu lã ma bu lə ɾu lã ã ɾu lã ma bu lə
En rou-lant ma bou - le rou-lant, En rou-lant ma bou - le.

CONCEPT
BACKGROUND
SKILLS
LISTEN, SING,
DESCRIBE
LINKS
SOCIAL STUDIES,
CULTURES,
READING

Global Voices

"Afrakakraba" is a game song from Ghana, a country in West Africa. It is a singing game about comforting a crying baby. **Listen** to the song.

 LISTENING CD 5:1

Afrakakraba Akan Folk Song from Ghana

Afrakakraba afrakakraba afrakakraba kotuwim
A little child sits in the sun crying all day.

Afra chawuhu chawuhu chawuhu
Child, turn around

Afra kofa wudofu
And go to your loved one.

drums from
Ghana

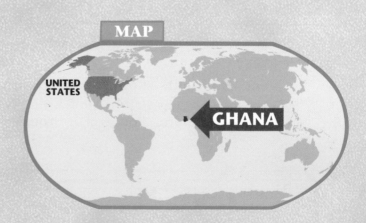

MAP

UNITED
STATES

GHANA

Ghanaian art objects

In the game for "Afrakakraba," there are no winners or losers. Everyone gets a turn!

Stories and Games

This story has been told for many years by the Ashanti people in Ghana. It is called "Anansi the Spider." It is the tale of how the world began. **Read** the story.

Anansi

Anansi the spider had six sons: See Trouble, Road Builder, River Drinker, Game Skinner, Stone Thrower, and Cushion. One day Anansi went a long way from home, got lost, and fell into trouble. Back at home, See Trouble cried "Father is in danger!" to the other sons. Then Road Builder built a road and said, "Follow me!" They came upon a river. "A fish has swallowed him!" one son cried. Then River Drinker took a big drink and swallowed all of the river. Game Skinner went and split open the fish. Then a falcon took Anansi up in the sky. Stone Thrower threw a stone at the falcon. Anansi fell from the sky as Cushion ran to help his father. Anansi landed softly. Later, Anansi wanted to reward his sons with a great globe of light that he found. He could not decide which son to give it to. He asked Nyame, the God of All Things, to hold the globe while he chose which son to give it to. He could not decide, so Nyame took the beautiful white light up into the sky. He keeps it there for all to see, even to this day.

—Ashanti Folk Tale

The game for the African American song, "Little Sally Walker," is almost the same as the game for "Afrakakraba."

Sing "Little Sally Walker" and play the game.

CD 5:2

African American Game

Lit - tle Sal - ly Walk - er sit - ting in a sauc - er

weep-ing and a - moan-ing o - ver all she's done.

Rise, Sal - ly, rise. Wipe your weep-ing eyes. Put your

hands on your hips and let your back-bone slip.

Swing it to the east. Swing it to the west.

Swing it to the ver - y one that you like best.

Conduct Your Own Investigation!

CONCEPT
FORM
SKILLS
LISTEN, MOVE,
DESCRIBE
LINKS
CULTURES

Sometimes a **conductor** leads a band or choir as they perform music. The conductor makes sure that the beat is steady and that all the musicians use the same tempo. A conductor uses special patterns of arm movements to show the musicians how to perform the music. The **meter** of the music tells the conductor what arm pattern to use.

Listen to this African American song. If you were conducting this piece, what tempo would you choose?

Point to the meter in "Crawdad Song." There are two beats in the measure. This is the conducting pattern for every measure.

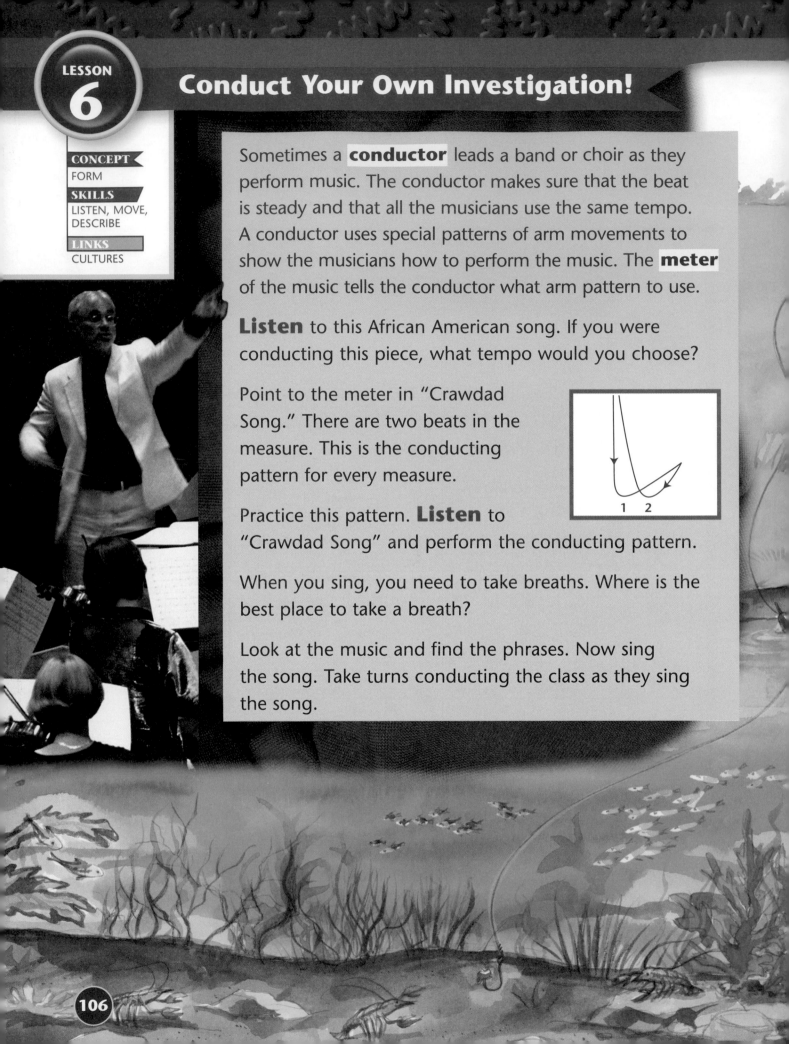

Practice this pattern. **Listen** to "Crawdad Song" and perform the conducting pattern.

When you sing, you need to take breaths. Where is the best place to take a breath?

Look at the music and find the phrases. Now sing the song. Take turns conducting the class as they sing the song.

Crawdad Song

African American

Eb

1. You get a line, and I'll get a pole,__ hon-ey._____
2. Get up old__ man, you slept too__ late,__ hon-ey._____
3. Get up old__ wom-an you slept too__ late,__ hon-ey._____
4. A - long come a man with a sack on his back,__ hon-ey._____A-
5. What you gon - na do when the lake goes_ dry,__ hon-ey._____

Eb   Bb   Bb7

You get a line, and I'll get a pole,__ babe._____
Get up old__ man, you slept too__ late,__ babe._____
Get up old__ wom-an you slept too__ late,__ babe._____
long come a man with a sack on his back,__ babe._____A-
What you gon - na do when the lake goes_ dry,__ babe?_____

Eb   Eb7

You get a line, and I'll get a pole, and
Get up old____ man, you slept too__ late;____
Get up old____ wom-an you slept too__ late;____
long come a man with a sack on his back, pack-in'
What you gon - na do when the lake goes__ dry? Sit

Ab   Bb7

we'll go down to the craw - dad hole,____
last piece of craw - dad's__ on your plate,____
craw - dad man done__ passed your gate,____
all the craw - dads__ he can pack,____
on the bank and watch the craw - dads die,____

Eb   Bb7   Eb

hon - ey,____ su - gar ba - by, mine.____

Unit 3 Tunes, Tales, and Traditions

107

Lullaby Time

"Crawdad Song" is a fun song. "Duerme Negrito" is a very different type of song. It is a lullaby. Lullabies are sung to calm and soothe people to sleep. This song is in $\frac{4}{4}$ meter. The conducting pattern for $\frac{4}{4}$ looks like this:

Practice this pattern. **Listen** to "Duerme Negrito." When the percussion begins, try to conduct $\frac{4}{4}$ or move to the beat.

 LISTENING CD 5:8

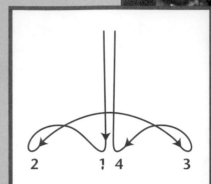

Duerme Negrito by Atahualpa Yupanqui
This lullaby is sung in Argentina. What do you find calm and soothing about it?

Meet the Musician

Atahualpa Yupanqui (1908–1992) wrote "Duerme Negrito," and was born in Buenos Aires, Argentina. He was a composer, guitarist, and singer. When he was young, he rode around Argentina on horseback learning the songs of the people. Later, he traveled throughout South America learning more songs and stories. He performed these songs all over the world.

Mercedes Sosa
(1935–2009) was born in
Tucuman, Argentina. She is
known for her songs about
the struggles and dreams
of people in Latin America.
The United Nations and
many governments around
the world have honored
her for her musical
message of human rights.

Log on to **music.mmhschool.com**
to learn more about Mercedes Sosa.

Move to the Rhythm

CONCEPT
RHYTHM
SKILLS
LISTEN, CREATE, PERFORM
LINKS
CULTURES, DANCE, LANGUAGE ARTS

When people sing, they often find ways to move, like in "Little Sally Walker." **Listen** to this song from Mexico, and look at the words while you listen. What is the song about? How could you move to this song?

MAP

UNITED STATES → MEXICO

La mar

The Sea

CD 5:9

Mexican Folk Song

Spanish: La mar es - ta - ba se - re - na, se -
Pronunciation: la mar es ta βa se ɾe na se

re - na es - ta - be la mar._____ La
ɾe na es ta βa la mar la

mar es - ta - ba se - re - na, se -
mar es ta βa se ɾe na se

re - na es - ta - ba la mar.
ɾe na es ta βa la mar

Listen to the song again and create some ways to move. **Sing** the song and add the movements.

When you dance, you are moving your body to the music. Some music has its very own movements. The **zamba**, from Argentina, has its own special movements. When people dance the zamba, they are showing how much they enjoy the music!

 LISTENING CD 5:13

Medley Polleritas by M.J. Castilla, Julio Espinoza, Gustavo Leguizamón, and Raul Shaw Moreno

Listening Map for Medley Polleritas

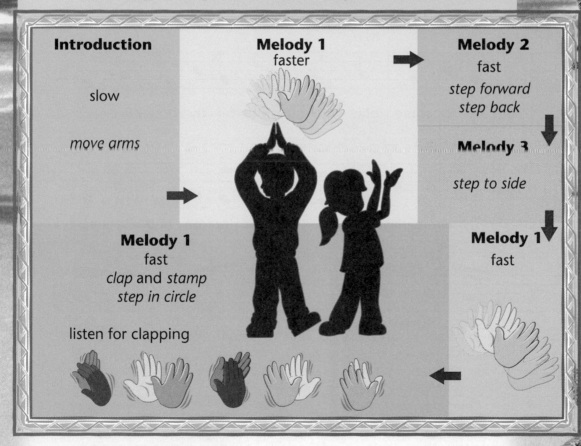

Introduction

slow

move arms

Melody 1
faster

Melody 2
fast
step forward
step back

Melody 3

step to side

Melody 1
fast
clap and *stamp*
step in circle

listen for clapping

Melody 1
fast

What kind of movements would go with the rhythm of this music? **Create** movements using different parts of your body.

Creating Movements

A person who creates a pattern of movements to go with music is called a **choreographer**. The **choreography** is the pattern of dance movements. When dancers learn the choreography to a song or dance, they practice the movements in the same order each time.

Sing this song. It is in two sections, AB. Then choreograph your own movements.

Butterfly Come Play with Me

CD 5:14

Words and Music by
Mary Ellen Pinzino

But-ter-fly come play with me. But-ter-fly come here._____

But-ter-fly come play with me. But-ter-fly can you hear?

We will laugh and dance and sing and play. We will

fly through the air. We will laugh and dance and

sing and play and fly ev'-ry-where.

Create your own choreography for the A section. Decide the order to perform your movement choices.

Practice the choreography already created for the B section. Now perform the piece.

Perform your choreography for the class.

CONCEPT
MELODY
SKILLS
SING, READ,
COMPOSE
LINKS
SOCIAL STUDIES

"Lukey's Boat" is a sea chantey from Newfoundland, Canada. Many sea chanteys come from the island of Newfoundland. **Listen** to "Lukey's Boat," and follow the music. The song uses low *so* and low *la*. Point to low *so* and low *la* in the music.

Sing the song.

MAP

UNITED
STATES NEWFOUNDLAND

Lukey's Boat

CD 5:17

Newfoundland Folk Song

do

1. Oh, Lu - key's boat is paint - ed green, { Ah -
2. Oh, Lu - key's boat got a fine fore cut-ty, {

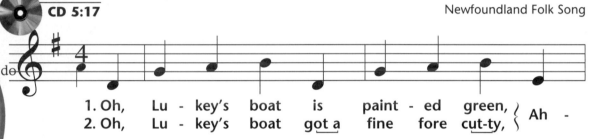

ha, me b'ys! { Oh, Lu - key's boat is paint - ed green, the
                { Oh, Lu - key's boat got a fine fore cut-ty, and

fin - est boat you've ev - er seen. { Ah - ha, me rid-dle - i - day!
ev' - ry seam is chinked with put-ty, {

3. Oh, Lukey's boat got a high stopped jib,
   Ah-ha, me b'ys!
   Oh, Lukey's boat got a high stopped jib
   and a patent block to her foremast head,
   Ah-ha, me riddle-i-day!

4. Oh, Lukey's boat got cotton sails,
   A-ha, me b'ys!
   Oh, Lukey's boat got cotton sails
   and planks put on with galvanized nails,
   Ah-ha, me riddle-i-day!

5. Oh, Lukey's rolling out his grub,
   Ah-ha, me b'ys!
   Oh, Lukey's rolling out his grub
   a barrel, a bag, and a ten-pound tub,
   Ah-ha, me riddle-i-day!

6. Oh, Lukey he sailed down the shore,
   Ah-ha, me b'ys!
   Oh, Lukey he sailed down the shore
   To catch some fish from Labrador,
   Ah-ha, me riddle-i-day!

Some of these patterns also have low *so* and low *la* in them.

Sing these short patterns with pitch names.
Match them with the notated patterns below.

1 *do re do*   **3** *do la so*

2 *mi re do*   **4** *so la do*

Choose two patterns to put together.
Sing them one after the other.

This school of fish
swims in a pattern.

Pitch of the Day

Clap the rhythm patterns.

Sing the patterns in the big colored fish. Pick a pattern from each fish. Put all three patterns together to create a larger pattern. Sing your pattern in the color order of the small fish in the box.

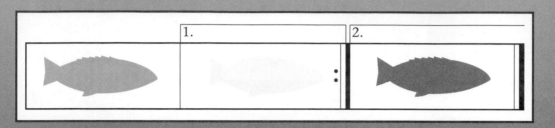

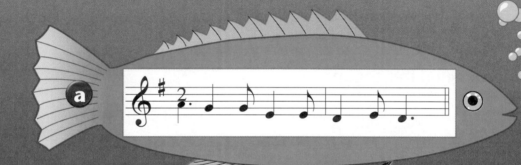

Spotlight Your Success!

1 Compare these two phrases from "Cumberland Gap." Choose the answer that best describes the two phrases.

a. same length, same rhythm, different pitches

b. same length, different rhythm, different pitches

c. different length, different rhythm, different pitches

2 Which song does not have low *so* and low *la* in it?

a. "Butterfly, Come Play with Me"

b. "Gi'Me Elbow Room"

c. "Lukey's Boat"

3 Which one of these is a conducting pattern?

a.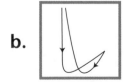

b.

c. ostinato

READ AND LISTEN

CD 5:20

1 Which rhythm do you hear?

a. 𝄴 𝅗𝅭 𝅗𝅭 | 𝅗 𝅘𝅥 𝅗𝅭 ‖

b. 𝄴 𝅘𝅥 𝅘𝅥𝅮𝅘𝅥𝅮 𝅘𝅥𝅮𝅘𝅥𝅮 | 𝅗𝅭 𝅗𝅭 ‖

c. 𝄴 𝅘𝅥 𝅘𝅥𝅮𝅘𝅥𝅮𝅭 | 𝅗 𝅘𝅥𝅮 𝅗𝅭 ‖

d. 𝄴 𝅗𝅭 𝅗𝅭 | 𝅗𝅭 𝄽 ‖

THINK!

1 How is a musical phrase in a song like a sentence in a paragraph?

2 How can you tell when one phrase ends and a new one starts?

3 **Write** about a song or dance from another country that you liked. Why did you like it?

CREATE AND PERFORM

1 **Create** a rhythm pattern in 𝄴 meter.

2 Your pattern should be 4 measures long.

3 Use 𝅗𝅭 and 𝅘𝅥 𝅘𝅥𝅮 in your pattern.

4 End your pattern with 𝅗𝅭 𝅘𝅥𝅮 𝄽.

5 **Perform** your pattern on an unpitched instrument.

Meet the Musician
ON NATIONAL RADIO!

Barbara Vante
Age: 13
Instrument: Viola
Hometown: Boston, Massachusetts

Thirteen-year-old Barbara Vante has a wonderful way of describing the sound made by her favorite instrument. "The viola has a chocolaty creamy sound that is nice and melting and has flavor!" she says.

Before taking up the viola, Barbara played the violin, which she thinks has a "strawberry cream" sound. She likes the deep, rich sound of the viola more, though.

Barbara also prefers the viola's larger size. "The viola suits me because I have big fingers!" she explains. "I can grab it more easily than the violin."

 LISTENING CD 5:21–22 **RECORDED INTERVIEW**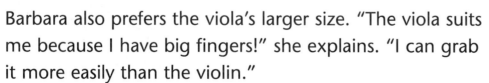

Concerto in B Minor, Second Movement (Andante ma non troppo)
by George Frideric Handel (Casadesus)

Listen to Barbara's performance and interview on the national radio program **From the Top**.

Spotlight on the Brass Quintet

Did You Know?

A brass quintet consists of five musicians: two trumpets, a French horn, a trombone, and a tuba.

The players in a brass quintet sit in a semicircle. Because there is no conductor to keep everyone together, they need to see each other to carry on their musical conversations.

Each instrument in a brass quintet plays its own separate part. At any time, each instrument may be called on to play the main melody or an accompanying role.

The brass quintet and the wind quintet have one instrument in common: the French horn.

 LISTENING CD 5:23–24

Volta from *Dances from Terpsichore*

by Michael Praetorius

Sonatine for Brass Quintet, First Movement (excerpt) by Eugène Bozza

Listen to these two pieces for brass quintet. In the piece by Praetorius, written over 400 years ago, the instruments sound like they are dancing. The more modern piece by Bozza is written for the same five instruments.

Music on the Go!

People are on the go everywhere you look! Some people are on their way to work. Some people are rushing to catch a plane to a faraway place. Some people just want to enjoy the sunshine! Where do you have to go today? Whether you are off to look for adventure across the globe or across the street, music can go right along with you!

Coming Attractions

Sing songs in canon.

Hear and learn about an ancient Chinese instrument.

Create your own rhythm conversation.

ONE PUSH RECORDING

"Movin' Right Along" is a song from *The Muppet Movie.* It has two sections, which we call A and B. The words and melodies in the A and B sections are different. **Sing** the song and see where the A and B sections are.

from *The Muppet Movie*

CD 6:1

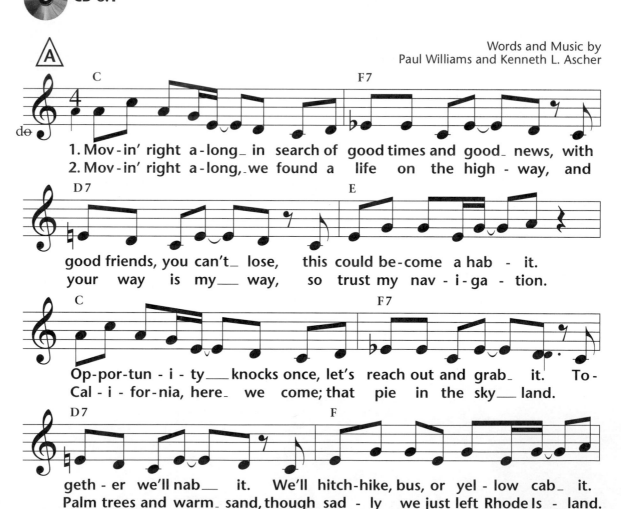

Words and Music by
Paul Williams and Kenneth L. Ascher

1. Mov-in' right a-long_ in search of good times and good_ news, with
2. Mov-in' right a-long,_we found a life on the high-way, and

good friends, you can't_ lose, this could be-come a hab - it.
your way is my__ way, so trust my nav-i-ga - tion.

Op-por-tun - i - ty__knocks once, let's reach out and grab_ it. To-
Cal - i - for-nia, here_ we come; that pie in the sky__ land.

geth - er we'll nab__ it. We'll hitch-hike, bus, or yel-low cab_ it.
Palm trees and warm_ sand, though sad - ly we just left Rhode Is - land.

CONCEPT
FORM
SKILLS
LISTEN, COMPARE,
IDENTIFY
LINKS
SOCIAL
STUDIES

Travel Phrases

When you plan a trip, one of the things that you have to decide is how you will get where you want to go. There are many ways to get around. You can take a bus, a car, or a train. What other types of transportation can you think of?

Listen to "Stevedore's Song." A *stevedore* is a worker who loads and unloads cargo from ships. Does the stevedore in this song enjoy his job?

Sing "Stevedore's Song."

Stevedore's Song

CD 6:4

Calypso Melody

1. Get up in the morn-ing at the crack of dawn,
2. Wish I was a sail-or that put out to sea.
3. Then I get to think-ing of a sail-or's life:

work-ing in the sun the whole day long,
That's the kind of life, the life for me:
hard-ly ev-er sees his chil-dren and wife;

load-ing all the freight piled on the dock,
'stead of get-ting up at the crack of dawn,
when I'm load-ing ships down at the dock,

might-y glad to quit at five o'-clock.
work-ing in the sun the whole day long.
home for sup-per-time at six o'-clock.

"Stevedore's Song" has four short phrases in each verse.
Trace the phrases in the air with your finger as you sing the song.

Are the phrases the same or different?

Spinning a Phrase

"Spinning Song," by A. Ellmenreich, is about the motion of a spinning wheel. A spinning wheel was used many years ago to make yarn or thread. Tapping the treadle (foot pedal) with a steady beat kept the wheel turning.

 LISTENING CD 6:7

Spinning Song by A. Ellmenreich

The "a" section of "Spinning Song" has four short phrases. Some of the phrases are **identical**, or exactly the same. Some are described as **similar**, because they begin the same but end differently.

Listen for the similar and identical phrases in the "a" section of "Spinning Song."

Listening Map for Spinning Song

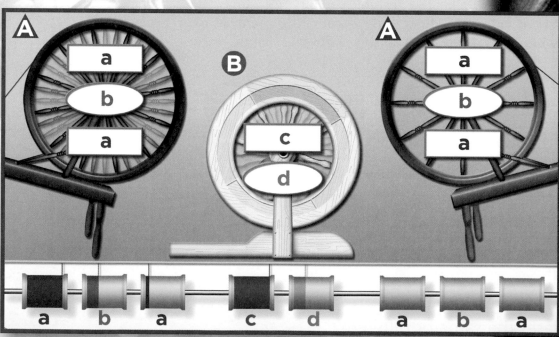

Here is another song about something else a-turnin'!
Listen to the four phrases in this song.

There's a Little Wheel A-Turnin' in My Heart

CD 6:9

African American Folk Song

There's a lit-tle wheel a-turn-in' in my heart. There's a
lit-tle wheel a-turn-in' in my heart. In my heart,___ in my
heart,___ there's a lit-tle wheel a-turn-in' in my heart.

Sing and pat the rhythm of each of these pairs of phrases from "There's a Little Wheel A-Turnin' in My Heart." Then point to the word to the right that describes them:

- Phrases 1 and 2
- Phrases 3 and 4
- Phrases 2 and 4
- Phrases 1 and 3

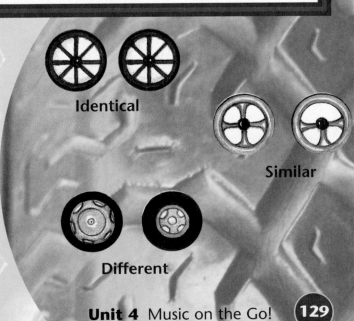

Identical

Similar

Different

CONCEPT
RHYTHM
SKILLS
SING, IDENTIFY, PLAY
LINKS
FINE ARTS

One Beat, Four Sounds

Before cars were invented, people rode horses to get where they wanted to go. Sometimes a carriage called a buggy was attached to the horse. When the automobile was invented, it was sometimes called a horseless carriage. Have you ever been on a buggy ride? Listen to "Riding in the Buggy" while you look at the picture of the horse-drawn buggies.

 ## Art Gallery

Deep Snow, by Grandma Moses
The woman who painted this painting was called "Grandma" becase she lived until she was 101 years old!

Sing the song while patting the beat on your lap.

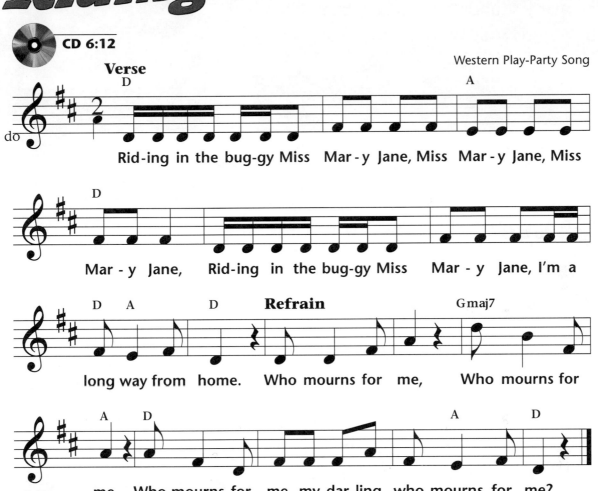

CD 6:12

Verse

Western Play-Party Song

D   A

Rid-ing in the bug-gy Miss   Mar-y Jane, Miss   Mar-y Jane, Miss

D

Mar-y   Jane,   Rid-ing in the bug-gy Miss   Mar-y   Jane, I'm a

D   A   D   **Refrain**   Gmaj7

long way from   home.   Who mourns for   me,   Who mourns for

A   D   A   D

me,   Who mourns for   me, my dar-ling, who mourns for   me?

Ostinato is the Italian word for stubborn. In music, an ostinato is a pattern that repeats without changing. **Perform** this ostinato as an accompaniment for "Riding in the Buggy."

Hop   on   in.   Take a bug-gy ride!

Clap the rhythm as you speak the pattern. How many sounds occur on each of the four beats?

Unit 4 Music on the Go!   **131**

The Beat Goes On

"Polly Wolly Doodle" is from the southern part of the United States. The words *polly wolly doodle* are nonsense words. As you sing the song, listen to how many sounds are on each beat when you sing the words *polly wolly doodle all the.*

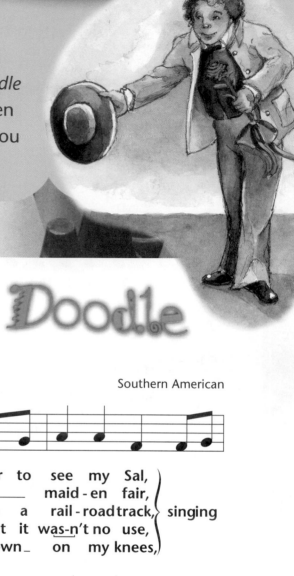

Polly Wolly Doodle

CD 6:15

Southern American

Verse

1. Oh, I went down South for to see my Sal,
2. Oh, my Sal she is a_____ maid-en fair,
3. Oh, a grass-hop-per sit-tin' on a rail-road track, } singing
4. Oh, I went to bed, but it was-n't no use,
5. Be - hind the barn, down_ on my knees,

pol-ly-wol-ly-doo-dle all the day.

My_____ Sal, she is a
With_____ curl-y eyes and
A_____ pick-in' his teeth with a
My_____ feet stuck out like a
I_____ thought I heard a

spunk - y gal,
laugh - ing hair,
car - pet tack, } sing-ing pol-ly-wol-ly-doo-dle all the
chick - en roost,
chick - en sneeze,

132

Do the words *polly wolly doodle all the* have the same rhythm? How many sounds are there on each beat when you sing those words?

mi   re   do

Listen to "Polly Wolly Doodle."
Sing the pitch syllables of the playalong as you listen to the refrain.
Play the pitch syllables on a pitched instrument during the refrain.

Playalong

Refrain

do

mi   mi   mi   mi   mi   mi   re   re

re   re   re   re   re   re   do   do

F   **Refrain**

day.   Fare thee well,   fare thee well,   fare thee

F   C 7

well, my fair - y   fay,   for I'm goin' to Lou'-si - an - a for to

C 7   F

see my Su - zi - an-na, sing-ing pol - ly-wol-ly-doo-dle all the day.

Round Goes the Windmill

CONCEPT
RHYTHM

SKILLS
SING, IDENTIFY, READ

LINKS
FINE ART, LANGUAGE ARTS

Windmills can still be seen today on hillsides in Europe, the United States, and South Africa. Windmills have been used for centuries to grind corn and wheat. Windmills can also produce electric power by pumping water. Today, many people are still interested in the history and beauty of these buildings.

Art Gallery

A Field of Tulips in Holland, by Claude Monet Holland, also called The Netherlands, is famous for the tulip flower. The field in this painting is full of them.

When the wind blows, the turning sails of an old windmill make a sound that can be heard over and over. The words *tique tique taque* imitate that sound in this song. **Listen** to "I Hear the Windmill."

Sing the song. **Pat** the rhythm each time you hear *tique tique taque.*

J'entends le moulin
I Hear the Windmill

 CD 6:18

French Canadian Folk Song

French: J'en-tends le mou-lin, ti-que ti-que ta-que. J'en-tends le mou-lin,
Pronunciation: ʒɑ̃ tɑ̃ lə mu lɛ̃ ti kə ti kə ta kə ʒɑ̃ tɑ̃ lə mu lɛ̃
English: I hear the wind-mill, tee-kah tee-kah tack-ah. I hear the wind-mill,

ta - que. J'en-tends le mou-lin, ti - que ti - que ta - que.
ta kə ʒɑ̃ tɑ̃ lə mu lɛ̃ ti kə ti kə ta kə
tack - ah. I hear the wind-mill, tee-kah tee-kah tack - ah.

J'en-tends le mou-lin, ta - que. Mon père a fait bâ -
ʒɑ̃ tɑ̃ lə mu lɛ̃ ta kə mɔ̃ pɛ ʁa fɛ ba
I hear the wind-mill, tack - ah. My fa-ther had a

tir mai-son, ti-que ti-que ti-que ta-que. J'en-tends le mou-lin,
tiʁ mɛ zɔ̃ ti kə ti kə ti kə ta kə ʒɑ̃ tɑ̃ lə mu lɛ̃
fine house built, tee-kah tee-kah tee-kah tack-ah. I hear the wind-mill,

ti - que ti - que ta - que. J'en - tends le mou - lin, ta - que.
ti kə ti kə ta kə ʒɑ̃ tɑ̃ lə mu lɛ̃ ta kə
tee-kah tee-kah tack - ah. I hear the wind-mill, tack - ah.

Unit 4 Music on the Go!

135

Wheels of Rhythm

In "J'entends le moulin," you hear
four sounds on one beat when you
sing the words *tique tique.*

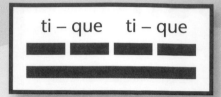

In music, four sounds on one beat can look
like this:

 or

These are called
sixteenth notes.

Look at the melodic
ostinato of "There's a Little Wheel A-Turnin'
in My Heart" on the next page. **Identify**
the beats with four sixteenth notes.

Sing this ostinato with "There's a Little Wheel A-Turnin' in My Heart" on p. 129.

CONCEPT
MELODY
SKILLS
LISTEN, SING, IDENTIFY
LINKS
READING, CULTURES

What better way is there to start the day than with a song? **Listen** to "Rise Up Singin'." Does the first leap in the melody go up or down?

Rise Up Singin'

CD 6:22

Words and Music by Mary Goetze

When I rise up sing-in' in the morn-in',

then I will be sing-in' all the day.

Sing-in' at my work and sing-in' at my play,

spread-in' joy to all a-long my way!

Do can be on any line or space of the staff. Sing the names of the pitches on this staff, beginning with *do.*

Sing the last phrase of "Rise Up Singin'" using pitch syllables.

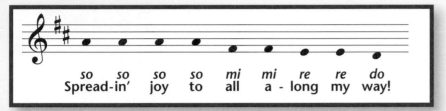

| so | so | so | so | mi | mi | re | re | do |
| Spread-in' | joy | to | all | a - long | | my | way! |

Now sing the pitch names for the melody of *When I rise up sing-in' in the mornin'.* Hum the pitch when you see the question mark.

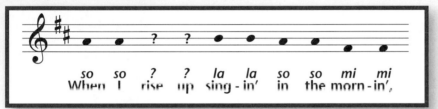

| so | so | ? | ? | la | la | so | so | mi | mi |
| When | I | rise | up | sing - in' | | in | the | morn - in', |

Is the ? pitch higher or lower than *la?*
This pitch is called **high *do***, or *do¹.*

Sing the song, and raise your hand in the air whenever you sing high *do.*

Do can be on different lines and spaces of the staff, but the order of pitches is always the same. The order of the pitches is shown on the pitch stairs.

Find high *do* on the pitch stairs.

do¹
la
so
mi
re
do
la₁
so₁

Playing Up the Scale

Songs that have melodies only containing the pitches *do*, *re*, *mi*, *so* and *la* are called **pentatonic** songs. The word *penta* is the Greek word for "five." Tonic is another word for "tone" or pitch.

Even if a song uses low *la*, low *so*, and high *do*, the song is still pentatonic if it uses only five pitch names (*do*, *re*, *mi*, *so*, and *la*).

Look at the music for "Rise Up Singin'." Is it a pentatonic song?

When all eight pitches are placed in order from *do* to *do'*, it is a scale. A **scale** is a group of pitches in order from lowest to highest.

Sing or play the pitch syllables used in "Rise Up Singing" in order from the lowest to the highest.

You just performed a pentatonic scale!

D	E	F#		A	B		D
do	*re*	*mi*		*so*	*la*		*do'*

A **canon**, or **round**, is a song with a melody that can be sung by two or more groups, each starting at a different time. Listen to "Shalom Chaveyrim."

Sing the song in **unison**. To sing in unison means to sing the melody with others. There is only one part in unison singing. Now sing the song as a canon.

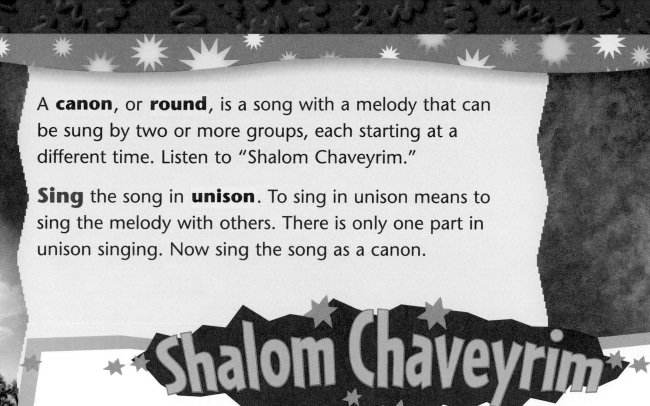

Shalom Chaveyrim

Shalom, My Friends

CD 6:25

Israeli Folk Song

Hebrew: שָׁ - לוֹם חַ - בֵּ - רִים שָׁ - לוֹם חַ - בֵּ - רִים שָׁ - לוֹם שָׁ -

Pronunciation: sha lom xa ve rim sha lom xa ve rim sha lom sha

English: **Sha - lom my____ friends, sha-lom, my____ friends, sha-lom, sha-**

לוֹם - שָׁ לוֹם - שָׁ אוֹת - רַ - הִתְ - לְ אוֹת - רַ - הִתְ - לְ לוֹם

lom lɛ hit ra ot lɛ hit ra ot sha lom sha lom

lom. We'll meet a - gain, we'll meet a - gain, sha-lom, sha - lom.

CONCEPT
FORM

SKILLS
LISTEN, SING,
COMPARE

LINKS
CULTURES,
LANGUAGE ARTS,
SOCIAL STUDIES

Global Voices

In Norwegian folk music, singing and dancing go together. "Her kommer vennen min" is a folk song from Norway. There is also a dance that goes with the song. **Listen** to the song.

LISTENING CD 6:29

MAP

UNITED STATES   NORWAY

Her kommer vennen min Norwegian folk song

This is a well-known folk song. It is performed throughout Norway by folk music groups.

Her kommer vennen min og her kommer jeg
Here comes my friend and here I come.

Tra la la, tra la la

Her kommer vennen min og her kommer jeg
Here comes my friend and here I come.

Tra la la, tra la la

Nei du så bukker jeg
You curtsy, then I will bow

Nei du så bukker jeg
You curtsy, then I will bow

Akta deg; du får meg
Watch out for me,

ellers tar jeg deg
or I will take you!

Art Gallery

Motive from the County of Nordland

Adelsteen Normann (1848–1918) often painted images of fjords. A fjord is a long and narrow strip of sea between tall, steep slopes.

Norwegian Memories

"Oleanna" is a Norwegian emigrant song. People from Norway who came to live in the United States sang this song. It brought back memories of Norway.

Sing "Oleanna." How many different sections are there? Are the sections the same or different?

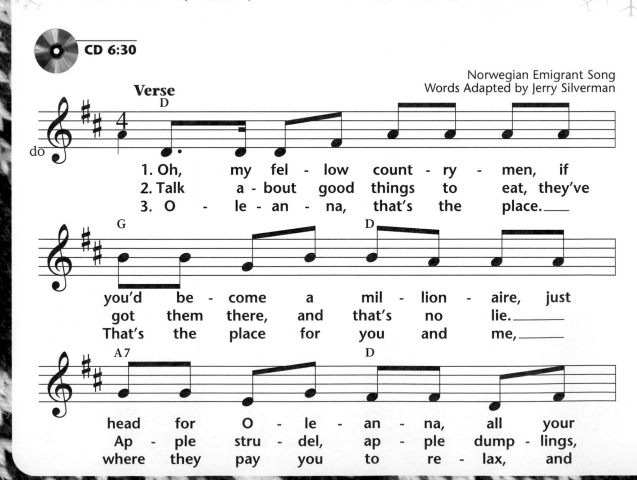

OLEANNA

CD 6:30

Norwegian Emigrant Song
Words Adapted by Jerry Silverman

Verse

1. Oh, my fel - low coun - try - men, if you'd be - come a mil - lion - aire, just head for O - le - an - na, all your
2. Talk a - bout good things to eat, they've got them there, and that's no lie. Ap - ple stru - del, ap - ple dump - lings,
3. O - le - an - na, that's the place. That's the place for you and me, where they pay you to re - lax, and

144

Listen to this dance by Edvard Grieg.

LISTENING CD 6:33

Norwegian Dance, Op. 35, No. 2 by Edvard Grieg

Edvard Grieg was a famous composer from Norway. Most of his music was based on familiar Norwegian folk songs.

How many times does the A section repeat? How is the A section different from the B section?

Log on to **music.mmhschool.com** to learn more about Edvard Grieg.

Viking animal-shaped bronze brooch from Norway

A .... D

fond - est dreams will all be there.
ap - ple sauce, and ap - ple pie.
when you sleep, it's doub - le fee.

Refrain

D .... G .... D

O - le, O - le - an - na, O - le, O - le - an - na,

A7 .... D .... A .... D

O - le, O - le, O - le, O - le, O - le, O - le - an - na.

Melodies in Motion

CONCEPT
MELODY
SKILLS
SING, DESCRIBE, COMPARE
LINKS
CULTURES, LANGUAGE ARTS, SOCIAL STUDIES

"Jasmine Flower" is a folk song from China. It is about the beauty and lovely scent of the jasmine flower.
Sing "Jasmine Flower."

MAP

UNITED STATES — CHINA

Jasmine Flower

 CD 7:1

Chinese Folk Song
Collected and Transcribed by Kathy Sorensen

do

Mandarin: 好 一 朵 美 麗 的 茉 莉 花 好 一 朵 美 麗 的
Pronunciation: hɑo yi dwɔmei li də mo li xwɑ hɑo yi dwɔmei li də
English: Oh, what a love - ly___ Jas - mine_ flow-er. Oh, what a love - ly___

茉 莉 花 芬 芳 美 麗 滿 枝 椏
mo li xwɑ fɛn fɑng mei li mɑn ʒɛ yɑ
Jas - mine_ flow-er. El - e - gance and_ sweet per - fume.

又 香 又 白 人 人 誇
yo shyɑng yo bɑi rɛn rɛn kwɑ
Cher - ished_ flow-er all___ snow - y___ white.

Learn About the Erhu

The *erhu* is a two-stringed instrument from China. It has two strings and two tuning pegs at the top. It rests on the player's knee and is played with a bow. The *erhu* is one of the most popular folk instruments in China. It has been played for over one thousand years.

Playalong

Alto Metallophone

(Repeat 6 times)

讓　我　來　將　你　摘　下
rang　wo　lai　jyang　ni　tsai　shya
Let___　me___　gen - tly　pick　you___　now,

Em　　　　　　　　　　　　　　　　D
送　給　別　人　家
song　gei　byɛ　rɛn　jya
Send　you___　to___　my___　love.

Em　D
茉　莉　花　　　茉　莉　花
mo　li　xwa　　　mo　li　xwa
Jas - mine　flow-er,　oh,　Jas - mine___　flow-er.

THINK!

Describe the sound of the *erhu*. How is the sound like the sound of the violin?

Which Way Did It Go?

Melodies can move in four different ways:
by **repeating** the same pitch,

by moving in **steps** from one pitch to the very
next higher or lower pitch,

by **skipping** from one pitch on a line to the very
next higher or lower pitch on a line, or by skipping
from one pitch on a space to the very next higher or
lower pitch on a space,

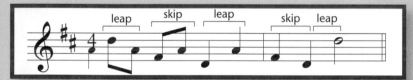

or by **leaping**, higher or lower, by jumping over
more than one pitch.

"Pay Me My Money Down" is a song from the
Georgia Sea Islands. It is about workers who load
cargo ships. The melody is made up of repeated
notes, steps, and leaps. **Listen** to the song and
sing the response each time it comes.

Sing the whole song on the next page.

Use what you have learned about repeated notes,
steps, and leaps to point to each and identify them.

Pay Me My Money Down

CD 7:5

African American Work Song
from the Georgia Sea Islands
Collected and Adapted by Lydia A. Parrish

Verse

Call   C

1. I thought I heard the cap-tain say, —

C *Response*   G 7   *Call*

"Pay me my mon-ey down." — To-mor-row is our

G 7   *Response*   C

sail - ing day, — "Pay me my mon-ey down." —

Refrain

C *All*   G 7

"Pay— me,— oh, pay— me,— Pay me my mon-ey down. —

G 7   C

Pay me or go to jail, — Pay me my mon-ey down." —

2. As soon as the boat was clear of the bar,
   "Pay me my money down."
   He knocked my down with the end of a spar,
   "Pay me my money down."

3. Well, I wish I was Mister Steven's son,
   "Pay me my money down."
   I'd sit on the bank and watch the work done,
   "Pay me my money down."

Playin' on the Old Banjo

CONCEPT
RHYTHM
SKILLS
LISTEN,
COMPARE,
COMPOSE
LINKS
VISUAL ARTS

CD-ROM

Use *World
Instruments*
CD-ROM to
learn more
about North
American
instruments.

Folk songs are a way that people can tell family and friends about good times through music. Some folk songs tell stories. Some are just for fun! "Dinah" is an American folk song. You can hear a banjo playing in this song. A banjo has five strings that are strummed or plucked. **Listen** for the banjo in the song "Dinah." Does the song tell a story, or is it just for fun?

Del McCoury Band

Dinah

CD 7:8

Minstrel Song

No one in the house but Di - nah, Di - nah,

no one in the house I know, I know; no one in the house but

Di - nah, Di - nah, play-in' on the old ban - jo.

Look at the rhythm of "Dinah." Which measures in green and red have the same rhythm? Which measures in the green and red have different rhythms?

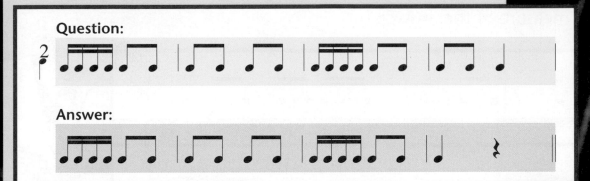

These two lines are a musical conversation. The green line is the question, and the red line is the answer. When you and a friend have a conversation, you ask each other questions and give each other answers. A good answer always has something to do with the question. An answer is also different from a question. It always comes after the question and usually feels like an ending.

Art Gallery

The Banjo Lesson
This was painted by Henry Ossawa Tanner (1859–1937), an African American artist. It shows a man teaching his grandson how to play the banjo.

Rhythmic Conversations

Clap each of these rhythmic questions and then pat a rhythmic answer for it. Use part of the question in the answer, and remember to finish with a quarter note on the last measure of the answer.

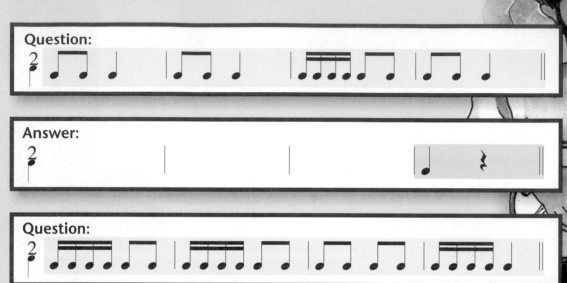

Perform one of these question and answer pairs with a partner during the instrumental sections of "Dinah."

THINK! Would you call these questions and answers identical, similar, or different? Why?

The American song "Oh, Susanna" also uses the banjo. Does this song tell a story or is it just for fun? **Listen** for the banjo playing in the interlude. **Sing** the song.

Oh, Susanna

CD 7:11

Words and Music by Stephen Foster

Verse

1. I___ come from Al - a - bam - a with my ban-jo on my knee.
2. I___ had a dream the oth-er night, when ev'-ry-thing was still.

I'm_ going to Loui - si - an - a, my___ true love for to see.
I___ thought I saw Su-san - na a - com-ing down the hill.

It___ rained all night the day I left, the weath-er it was dry,
The_ buck-wheat cake was in her mouth, the tear was in her eye.

The_ sun so hot I froze to death, Su - san-na, don't you cry.
Says_ I, "I'm com-ing from the South, Su - san-na, don't you cry."

Refrain

Oh, Su - san-na, oh, don't you cry for me.

I___ come from Al - a-bam-a with my ban-jo on my knee.

Rondo a Round

CONCEPT
FORM
SKILLS
LISTEN, IDENTIFY,
CREATE
LINKS
FINE ARTS,
CULTURES

You are on the move every day. You go to school. You play with friends. You have hobbies. No matter how far you go or how long you are gone, you can always come back to the place you call home.

A piece of music where the A section always returns is called a **rondo**. The sections in between are different. The name rondo comes from the French word rondeau, which means "to come back around." A rondo form looks like this: ABACA.

Listen to "Gypsy Rondo." How many times does the A section return?

 LISTENING CD 7:14

Trio for Piano, Violin and Cello No. 39, Finale ("Gypsy Rondo")

by Franz Joseph Haydn

The form of this rondo is ABACA *Coda.* A short section added to the end of a song is called a **coda**. *Coda* is the Italian word for "tail."

 THINK! If you added another contrasting section of music to this rondo, what letter would you use?

Meet the Musician

Franz Joseph Haydn (1732–1809) is considered the father of the symphony and the string quartet. He wrote so much music during his lifetime that some of it has never even been performed.

Sad to Say I'm on My Way

Even when you have had a lot of fun on a trip, there comes a time to say farewell. **Sing** "Jamaica Farewell."

MAP
UNITED STATES
JAMAICA

Jamaica Farewell

CD 7:17

Words and Music by Irving Burgie

Verse

C   F

1. Down the way where the nights are gay___ and the

G7   C

sun shines dail - y on the moun - tain - top,

C   F

I took a trip on a sail - ing ship___ and when I

G7   C

reached Ja - mai - ca, I made a stop.___ But I'm

Refrain

C   Dm7   G

sad to say I'm on my way.___ Won't be back for

C

man - y a day.___ My heart is down,___ my head is

156

turn-ing a - round,_ I had to leave a lit-tle girl in

4 **Verse**

King-ston town._ 2. Sounds of laugh-ter

ev' - ry - where_ and the danc-ing girls sway-ing

to and fro. I must de - clare that my

heart is there,_ though I've been from Maine to

Refrain

Mex - i - co.__ But I'm sad to say I'm

on my way._ Won't be back for man-y a day._ My

heart is down,_ my head is turn-ing a-round, I had to

5

leave a lit - tle girl in King-ston town._

Spotlight Your Success!

REVIEW

1 Which song has high *do* in it?

   a. Riding in the Buggy **b.** J'entends le moulin **c.** Dinah

2 Which pair of phrases below can be called similar?

a.

b.

c.

3 Which pair of phrases can be called identical?

4 How does a short musical phrase become an *ostinato*?

   a. The musical phrase stops and starts.

   b. The musical phrase repeats without changing.

   c. The musical phrase is heard only during the second verse.

READ AND LISTEN

CD 7:20

1 Which rhythm do you hear?

2 All of these pitch patterns begin on *so*.
Which pattern do you hear?

a.

b.

c.

THINK!

1 How can you tell if a musical piece is a rondo?

When you look at a melody on the staff, how can you tell leaps from steps?

Write about the two canons you sang in this unit.
What makes these songs canons?

CREATE AND PERFORM

1 **Create** rhythmic answers for the following questions. Form two groups to clap.
Perform the questions and answers.

Meet the Musician
ON NATIONAL RADIO!

Name: Eoghan Conway   **Age: 12**
Instrument: Tin Whistle
Hometown: Somerville, Massachusetts

The tin whistle is a popular instrument in Ireland, where twelve-year-old Eoghan (pronounced Owen) Conway was born. He and his family moved to the United States when he was five.

Eoghan recently traveled back to Ireland to compete in a tin whistle competition. Young musicians from all over the world took part in the contest. Eoghan won first place!

"Many people think of the tin whistle as a toy, but it is a great instrument to learn music on," declares Eoghan. "It is also portable. When I go camping, I can bring my tin whistle and play around the campfire." Eoghan likes to play traditional Irish jigs and tap his feet along with the music.

 LISTENING | CD 7:21–22 | **RECORDED INTERVIEW**

The Gold Ring
Traditional Irish jig

Listen to Eoghan's performance and interview on the national radio program **From the Top**.

Spotlight on the Tuba

Did You Know?

The tuba was invented in Germany in 1865 for use in military bands.

Because of the tuba's big size, tuba players usually hold their instruments in their laps when they perform.

The marching band version of a tuba is designed to rest on the player's shoulders. The mouthpiece is in a different position to make it easier to play while marching.

The largest size tuba is eight feet tall with a tube length of 45 feet.

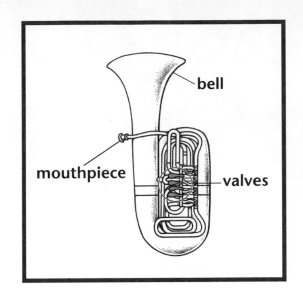

bell

mouthpiece

valves

 LISTENING CD 7:23–24

Daniel in the Lion's Den (excerpt) by Francis McBeth

Sensemayá (excerpt)
by Silvestre Revueltas

Listen to the tuba solos in both of these orchestral pieces. The tuba plays an important role in Revueltas's colorful piece, inspired by the Native American music of Mexico.

Sing a Wish, Dance a Dream

Wish upon a star and hope your dreams come true.

Night
Stars over snow,
    And in the west a planet
Swinging below a star—
    Look for a lovely thing and
    you will find it.
It is not far—
    It never will be far.

—Sara Teasdale

Coming Attractions

Play along on instruments.

Create your own body percussion.

Sing a folk song from China.

Have you ever seen a dog dig for a bone?
Sometimes a little hard work and determination are what
it takes to make a wish come true.

Listen to the ostinato in the first section of "Digga
Digga Dog" and speak the text quietly as you listen.

Sing "Digga Digga Dog."

Digga Digga Dog

from the movie *102 Dalmatians*

CD 7:25

Words and Music by Pamela Phillips Oland,
Mark Brymer, George Clinton, Jr.,
Garry M. Shider, and David L. Spradley

Dig - ga   dig - ga   dog,   dig - ga   dig - ga   dog.

Dig - ga   dig - ga   dog,   dig - ga   dig - ga   dog.

Dig - ga   dig - ga   dog,   dig - ga   dig - ga   dog.   Dog.

CONCEPT
RHYTHM

SKILLS
PERFORM, CREATE, COMPARE

LINKS
CULTURES, LANGUAGE ARTS

Sometimes you dream when you sleep. When you wake, your dreams can become hopes and wishes. What are your hopes and wishes? **Read** this poem about hope.

Hope Is the Thing with Feathers

"Hope" is the thing with feathers—
That perches on the soul—
And sings the tune without the words—
And never stops–at all—

—*Emily Dickinson*

Pat the beat while you listen to the Spanish words in "Cielito lindo."

MAP

UNITED STATES

MEXICO

Cielito lindo

CD 7:28

Mexican Folk Song

Verse

Spanish: De la Sie - rra Mo - re - na, Ci_e - li - to
Pronunciation: de la sye r̄a mo ɾe na sye li to
English: Com - ing down___ from dark moun - tains, Cie - li - to

Lin - do vi_e - nen ba - jan - do_____
lin do βi_e nen ba xan do
Lin - do, you___ come to cheer us.___

166

There are three beats in each measure in "Cielito lindo," and a ♩ gets one beat. The meter of "Cielito lindo" is $\frac{3}{4}$

Create your own 3-beat body percussion pattern to perform as you sing the refrain.

Night Music

Many pieces of music have been written about nighttime. One of the most famous was written by Wolfgang Amadeus Mozart.

Meet the Musician

Wolfgang Amadeus Mozart
(1756–1791) and his older sister, Nannerl, were taught by their father when they were very young children. Wolfgang began composing music when he was only five years old! Their father took them on a tour of Europe. They played for royalty as well as the public in Germany, France, Belgium, England, and Switzerland.

 LISTENING CD 7:32

Eine Kleine Nachtmusik (Serenade No. 13 in G, K. 525) Minuet

by Wolfgang Amadeus Mozart

One of Mozart's best known pieces is *Eine Kleine Nachtmusik,* which means "A Little Night Music." It was written for a string orchestra. Mozart wrote this piece to entertain people in the evening.

This minuet is also in $\frac{3}{4}$. The conducting pattern for $\frac{3}{4}$ is  .
Conduct as you listen.

Listening Map for Minuet from *Eine Kleine Nachtmusik*

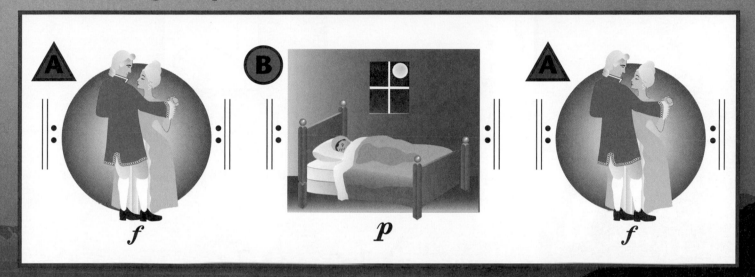

An Upbeat Day!

CONCEPT
RHYTHM
SKILLS
SING, LISTEN, ANALYZE
LINKS
CULTURES, GEOGRAPHY

The beats in "Cielito lindo" on pages 166 and 167 are grouped in threes. The first beat of each group is called the **downbeat**, or strong beat. The downbeat is usually accented. The last beat of each group is called the **upbeat**, or weak beat. The first word in "Cielito lindo" falls on a downbeat.

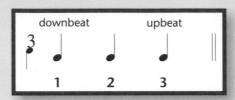

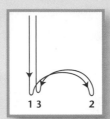

"Boll Weevil" is an American folk song that has its beats in groups of two. As you listen, **tap** on the cotton bolls to show two beats in each measure. **Tap** the first cotton boll on each downbeat.

 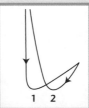

Sing "Boll Weevil."

BOLL WEEVIL

CD 8:1

MIDI

For another activity with "Boll Weevil," see *Spotlight on MIDI*.

Southern Folk Song

Verse

1. The Boll Wee-vil am a lit-tle black bug from
2. The first time I saw Boll Wee-vil,____ He was
3. The Boll Wee-vil to the farm-er said, "You'd
4. The mer-chant took__ half the cot-ton.____ The

Mex - i - co they say. Come all the way to Tex-as Just to
sit - tin' on the square. The next time I saw Boll Wee-vil, He had
bet-ter leave me a - lone. I done eat all your cot-ton, Now I'm
Boll Wee-vil took the rest. He on - ly left the farm-er Just a

Refrain

find a place to stay.
his whole fam' - ly there.   } Just a look-in' for a home.
start - in' on your corn."
sin - gle rag - ged vest.

Just a look - in' for a home.

Just a look - in' for a home.

Just a look - in' for a home.

Flagging the Upbeat Phrases

"Bella bimba" is an Italian song about a pretty girl dancing.

Pat, clap, and snap as you sing "Bella bimba."

MAP

UNITED STATES

ITALY

Bella bimba

Italian Folk Song

 CD 8:4

Pretty Girl

Refrain

Italian: Ma - co - me bal - li bel - la bim - ba, bel - la bim - ba, bel - la

Pronunciation: ma   ko   me   bal   li   bɛl   la   bim   ba   bɛl   la   bim   ba   bɛl   la

English: Now,   see the pret - ty girl   is   danc - ing, she   is   danc - ing, she   is

bim - ba, Ma   co-me bal - li bel-la bim - ba, Co-me bal - li, bal - li ben!

bim   ba   ma   ko   me   bal   li   bɛl   la   bim   ba   ke   me   bal   li   bal   li   bɛn

danc-ing, Now see the pret-ty girl is danc-ing, she is danc-ing oh so well.

Verse

Guar - da   che   pas - sa   La   vi - la - ne - la,

gwaɾ   da   ke   pas   sa   la   vi   la   ne   la

Watch   as   she   pass - es   the   Vi - la - ne - la,

Go back to the beginning and sing to the end.
(Da Capo al Fine)

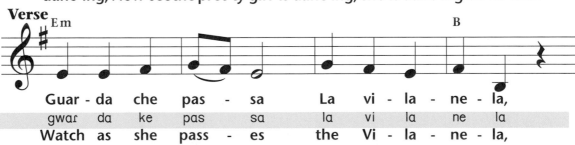

A - gi   le e   snel - la,   Sa - ben   bal - lor!

a   ji   le   snɛl   la   sa   bɛn   bal   loɾ

Grace - ful   and   slen - der,   How   she   can   dance!

"Bella bimba" has a verse and a refrain. The verse begins on the downbeat. The refrain begins on the last beat of a measure, so it begins on an upbeat.

Look at the accompaniment below. Does it begin on the upbeat or a downbeat?

Read the rhythm, then play the accompaniment on instruments during the verse of "Bella bimba":

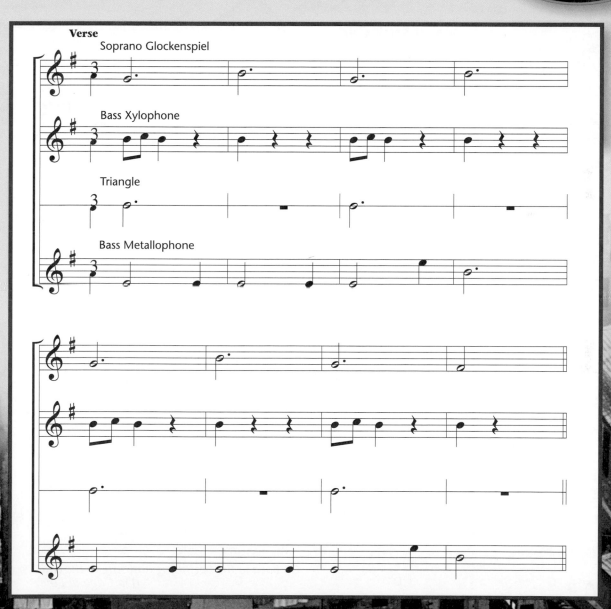

LESSON
3

CONCEPT
RHYTHM
SKILLS
READ, WRITE, ANALYZE
LINKS
CULTURES, DANCE

Three to Get Ready!

"Tititorea" is the name given to Maori games played with rods or sticks. **Tap** the beat as you listen to "Tititorea."

Sing the song.

MAP

UNITED STATES

NEW ZEALAND

Tititorea
Maori Stick Game

CD 8:8

New Zealand Folk Song
Collected and Transcribed by Kathy B. Sorensen

*End
(Fine)*

Maori: **E hi - ne ho - ki mai ra.**
Pronunciation: e hi ne ho ki maɪ ɾa

E pa - pa___ wai - a - ri ta - ku nei___ ma - hi,
e pa pa waɪ a ɾi ta ku neɪ ma hi

ta - ku nei___ ma - hi tu - ku roi - ma ta. Au
ta ku neɪ ma hi tu ku ɾɔɪ ma ta au

e au - e___ ka - ma - te au,
e au e ka ma te au

*Go back to the beginning and sing to the end.
(Da Capo al Fine)*

E hi - ne ho - ki mai ra.
e hi ne ho ki maɪ ɾa

The Maori people are native New Zealanders. *Aotearoa* is the Maori name for their country. Elders, grandmothers, and grandfathers teach Tititorea to children. Stick games help them become strong, quick, and skillful with their hands.

Learn About the Tititorea Stick Game

The short sticks are called tititorea. They perform patterns in time with the beat. The patterns include tapping sticks on the floor or together, to the side or in front. They also flip the sticks from one end to the other. The patterns are performed by partners seated on the floor. They toss sticks back and forth with their partners.

Staying on Track

Listen to this song about being far from home.
Tap the beat softly as you listen. **Sing** the song.

O, The Train's Off the Track

CD 8:12

Virginian Folk Song

1. O, the train's off the track, and I can't get it back, and I
2. If you say___ so___ I'll rail - road no more;___ I'll

can't get a let - ter to my home,
side - track my train and go___ home,

to my home, to my home, and I can't get a let - ter to my home.
go___ home, go___ home,___ I'll side-track my train and go___ home.

Perform a pat-pat-clap-snap pattern (♩ ♩ ♩ ♩) starting on the downbeat.

A sound that lasts one half note plus one quarter note is called a **dotted half note** (𝅗𝅥.).

Find the dotted half notes in the music of "O, The Train's Off the Track." **Sing** the song again, and raise your hand every time you sing a dotted half note (𝅗𝅥.). Now play along with the song.

Tambourine   (Repeat 3 times)

Alto Xylophone

Bass Xylophone

What's the Whole Idea?

LOG
ON

**Log on to
music.mmhschool.com**
to learn more about J.S.
Bach and his music.

The cello is the second largest stringed instrument in the orchestra. It is played with a bow, like the violin. The cello is so large that it rests on the floor.

Listen for the cello in "Gigue" from *Suite No. 1 for Solo Cello in G Major* by Johann Sebastian Bach.

🔵 **LISTENING** **CD 8:15**

Gigue from Suite No. 1 for Cello *in G Major*

by J.S. Bach

Johann Sebastian Bach (1685–1750) was a German composer. He wrote many pieces for different instruments. This is from a group of pieces written especially for the cello.

Conductors help keep members of the orchestra or choir together by showing the meter of the music. The conducting patterns they use are based on the meter of the music.

Here is a two-beat pattern and a three-beat pattern.

Find the downbeat of both patterns. Find the upbeat of both patterns. What beat is the upbeat in the two-beat pattern? In the three-beat pattern?

Conduct the two-beat pattern as you listen to *Gigue from Suite No. 1 for Cello* again.
Here is a four-beat conducting pattern.

Find the downbeat and upbeat in this pattern.

Freedom of Expression

A sound that lasts for four beats is called a **whole note** and is written like this: 𝅝

In $\frac{4}{4}$ meter, one whole note fills a whole measure. If a quarter rest equals one beat of silence, how many beats of silence would a **whole rest** (▬) equal?

How is the whole rest ▬ different from the half rest ▬?

Sing this African American song that contains whole notes.

CD 8:16
Freely

Freedom Song

Call

Response

Woke up this morn-ing with my mind stayed on free - dom.

Call

Response

Woke up this morn-ing with my heart stayed on free - dom.

Call

Response

Woke up this morn-ing with my soul stayed on free - dom.

End (Fine)

Hal-le - lu, hal-le-lu, hal-le - lu, hal-le-lu, hal-le - lu - jah.

How many whole notes are in this song?

Sing the song again. When you sing a whole note, draw a circle in the air during the four beats.

Clap this ostinato with the song. Where is the whole rest?

Play the ostinato on an unpitched instrument.

Playalong

THINK! **How would you describe the feeling or mood of this song?**

I'm gon-na walk, talk,__ sing, shout,_ hal-le-lu___ I got my

mind on free-dom. Walk, talk__ sing, shout,_ clap my hands and keep my

Go to the beginning and sing to the end
(Da Capo al Fine)

mind on free-dom. Walk, talk,_ sing, shout,_ clap my hands.

CONCEPT
FORM
SKILLS
SING, CREATE, PERFORM
LINKS
DANCE, VISUAL ARTS, CULTURES

When you make a wish or daydream about something you would like to do, you may picture it in your mind. **Listen** to this song about an imaginary toy. Try to imagine how the toy moves.

Sing "The Marvelous Toy."

The Marvelous Toy

CD 8:19

Words and Music by Tom Paxton

Verse

1. When I was just a wee lit-tle child full of health and joy, my
2. The first time that I picked it___ up I had a big sur-prise, for

fa - ther home - ward came one night, and gave to me a toy. A
right on it's bot-tom were two big but-tons that looked like big green eyes. I

won - der to be-hold it was, with man-y col-ors bright, and the
first pushed one and then the oth-er, and then I twist-ed its lid, and___

mo - ment I laid eyes on it, it be - came my heart's de - light.
when I set it down a - gain___ here is what it did:

Think of a 4-beat movement ostinato to show how the marvelous toy might move. **Perform** your movement ostinato when you sing the refrain.

Keeping the Baby Happy ...

by Rube Goldberg

How do you think the invention in the picture might work? What sounds might it make? **Rube Goldberg** (1883–1970) was an American cartoonist who drew funny inventions with many moving parts. Some of his cartoon creations might be like the toy in the song "The Marvelous Toy."

Refrain C   G7   C

It went 'zip' when it moved, and 'bop' when it stopped, and 'whirr' when it stood

F   Am   C   G7   C

still.   I   nev-er knew just   what it was, and   I   guess   I   nev-er will.

Unit 5 Sing a Wish, Dance a Dream

Playing with Ostinato

Minahasa is a region in the province of North Sulawesi, in the Republic of Indonesia. Minahasans are the people who live on or come from the northern tip of the island of Sulawesi. "Wéané" is a lullaby. It is a song that the Minahasans sing to put their children to sleep.

Listen to the words of "Wéané."

MAP

UNITED STATES

INDONESIA

CD 8:22

Menadonese Lullaby

Minahasa: O i - nang ni ké - ké, ma - ngé wi - sa - ko?_____
Pronunciation: o i na ni ke ke ma ngi wi sa ko
English: Mo - ther won't you give me just one lit - tle cake?_____

Ma - ngé wa - ki wé - nang, tu mu - lus__ ba - lé - ké_____
ma ngi wa ki we nang tu mu lus ba le ko
Hush my dar - ling you shall have one af - ter__ you a - wake.__

Wé - a - né, wé - a - né, wé - a - né to - jo!_____
we a ni we a ni we a ni to yo
Wé - a - né, wé - a - né, go to sleep my sweet!__

Da - i mau si - a - pa ko - t - ré___ ma - ké - wé.
da i mo si a po ko ta re ma ki we
From the vil - lage I shall bring you some - thing__ nice to eat.

184

Play these ostinato patterns to accompany the verse of "Wéané." Listen to one another as you play together.

Pat ostinato 1 as you whisper the words:

Sleep,   sleep   lit - tle   one.

Practice ostinato 2 this way: Clap the rhythm of the first two measures; snap the rhythm of the last two measures.

Wish for some-thing nice.   Some-thing nice will come.

Play the ostinatos together as a class.

- Play ostinato 1 on metal instruments.
- Play the rhythms that you clapped in ostinato 2 on larger wood instruments.
- Play the rhythms that you snapped in ostinato 2 on smaller wood instruments.

LESSON 6

CONCEPT
MELODY
SKILLS
SING, READ, PERFORM
LINKS
CULTURES

Searching for Pitches

While you sleep at night, a whole world of creatures comes alive. One such creature is the cricket. The German song "Night Song" is about the nighttime song of the cricket. The melody has only three pitches. **Sing** the song.

MAP

UNITED STATES · GERMANY

CD 8:26

German Lullaby

All through the night, The moon is sil - ver bright,

Crick - et sings his ti - ny song. Sings it through the

whole night long. All through the night.

Pitches can be read with pitch syllables such as *do*, *re*, and *mi*. They can also be read using their letter names.

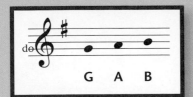

G   A   B

The letter names for the pitches on the staff above are G, A, and B. The **treble clef** (𝄞) at the beginning of a staff is sometimes called the **G clef**. It circles the second line to tell you that it is G.

Sing the melody of "Night Song" using the letter names of the pitches. **Play** the music below.

Name the Notes

This song, "Little Boy of the Sheep," is from the Hebrides Islands off the coast of Scotland. Sheep are raised by many people who live there. The song is about the things a shepherd might do to pass the time while guarding sheep in the fields. **Sing** the song.

Look at the tinted pitches. Sing "Little Boy of the Sheep." Use pitch names in place of the words on the tinted pitches.

The bagpipes are ancient instruments still played today. **Play** this rhythm with "Little Boy of the Sheep."

Bagpipe players at the Cowal Highland Games in Dunoon, Scotland

Playalong

Wish for a Fish!

CONCEPT
TEXTURE
SKILLS
SING, IDENTIFY, PERFORM
LINKS
CULTURES, VISUAL ARTS

"Wang Ü Ger" is a Chinese fishing song. People often have to work together on a fishing boat to carry out tasks such as pulling ropes and nets. They all have to pull at the same speed. To stay at the same speed, workers often sing songs in the same tempo.

Listen to the song and follow the English words. **Sing** the song. **Listen** to the pronunciation of the Chinese words. Practice saying the words.

Sing the song in Chinese and English.

WANG Ü GER

MAP

UNITED STATES   CHINA

Chinese Fishing Song

CD 8:32

Chinese Folk Song
Collected and Transcribed by Kathy B. Sorensen
English Version by MMH

Mandarin:	白	浪	淘	淘	我	不	怕
Pronunciation:	bai	lang	tau	tau	wɔ	bu	pa
English:	Though	the	waves___	run___	high	and	deep,

	掌	穩	舵	兒	往	前	划
	jang	wɛn	duɔ	ər	wang	chiɛn	hwa
	We	sail	on___	the___	course	we	keep.

When someone asks you to accompany them, they are asking you to go with them. Sometimes people sing the melody of songs alone. Other times they may sing the songs with instruments adding sounds to go with, or accompany, the song. An **accompaniment** is a musical background to a melody. Name a song you have sung in class that has an accompaniment.

Some songs, like "Wang Ü Ger," can be accompanied with **chords**. A chord is three or more pitches that sound together.

This Chinese fisherman on ▶ a bamboo boat uses trained birds to fish for him.

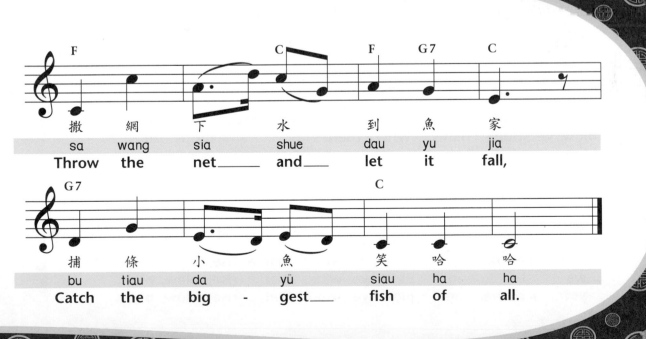

F		C		F	G 7	C
撒	網	下	水	到	魚	家
sa	wang	sia	shue	dau	yu	jia
Throw	**the**	**net___**	**and___**	**let**	**it**	**fall,**

G 7				C		
捕	條	小	魚	笑	哈	哈
bu	tiau	da	yü	siau	ha	ha
Catch	**the**	**big -**	**gest___**	**fish**	**of**	**all.**

Add a Little Harmony

"Blow, Ye Winds, Blow" is another song about the sea. The accompaniment for "Blow, Ye Winds, Blow" uses many different chords. When different pitches sound at the same time, they create **harmony**. Sing the song.

Blow, Ye Winds, Blow

CD 9:1

Massachusetts Sea Shanty

You must make me a fine Hol-land shirt. Blow, blow,
You must wash it in yon-der___ spring. Blow, blow,
You must dry it on yon-der___ thorn. Blow, blow,

blow ye winds___ blow. And not have in it a
blow ye winds___ blow. Where there's not a drop of___
blow ye winds___ blow. Where the sun nev-er

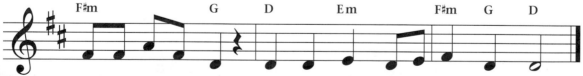

stitch of nee-dle-work. Blow ye winds that a-rise, blow, blow.
wa-ter___ in. Blow ye winds that a-rise, blow, blow.
yet___ shone___ on. Blow ye winds that a-rise, blow, blow.

Use a melody instrument to accompany "Blow, Ye Winds, Blow." **Play** these pitches as you sing the song. Listen to the harmony the accompaniment makes.

Playalong

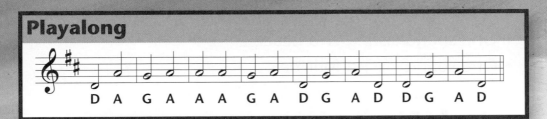

D A G A A A G A D G A D D G A D

THINK! Name an instrument that can play three or more pitches at the same time to make chords.

LISTENING CD 9:33

American Salute by Morton Gould
This piece was written for orchestra.
It features many instruments you know.

Listen for harmony in *American Salute*.
Identify instruments you know in the recording.

CONCEPT
RHYTHM
SKILLS
PERFORM,
READ, SING
LINKS
CULTURES,
DANCE

Keeping Track of Rhythms

Find the name and the notes below that mean:

- One sound on a beat.
- Two sounds on a beat.
- Four sounds on a beat.
- One sound lasting two beats.
- One sound lasting four beats.

Perform each of the note values above using these words and sounds:

- quarter notes—Whisper *patch*.
- eighth notes—Say *pocket*.
- half notes—Say *where* with your voice, starting on a higher pitch and ending by sliding to a lower one.
- sixteenth notes—Say *puttin' puttin'*.

Practice performing these two ostinati using the words *patch, pocket, where,* and *puttin' puttin'*.

Sing this Southern American singing game.

The Paw Paw Patch

CD 9:4

Southern American Singing Game Song

1. Where, oh where, is dear lit-tle Nel-lie?
2. Come on boys, let's go and__ find her,
3. Pick-in' up paw paws, puttin' em in your pock-et,

Where, oh where, is dear lit-tle Nel-lie?
come on, boys, let's go and__ find her,
pick-in' up paw paws, puttin' em in your pock - et,

Where, oh where, is dear lit-tle Nel-lie?
come on, boys, let's go and__ find her,
pick-in' up paw paws, puttin' em in your pock - et,

'Way down yon-der in the paw - paw patch.

Sing the song again and perform the two paw paw patch ostinati.

Dancing Rhythms

People in Israel often dance while singing songs. When they dance, they put the rhythm in their bodies instead of speaking an ostinato as you did in "The Paw Paw Patch." **Sing** "Let's Go Dancing."

Let's Go Dancing

MAP

UNITED STATES

ISRAEL

CD 9:7

Translated by Moshe Jacobson

Let's go danc-ing ev - 'ry one.   Let's go danc-ing, join the fun.

Let's go danc-ing in a ring.   Let's go danc-ing as we sing.

Let's go danc-ing in a ring.   Let's go danc-ing as we sing, "Ya -

lel,_____ ya-lel - li_____ ya-lel, ya - lel_____ ya-lel - li."   (clap)

Let's go danc-ing ev - 'ry one.   Let's go danc-ing, join the fun.

Jerusalem, Israel

Let's go danc-ing in a ring. Let's go danc-ing as we sing.

Let's go danc-ing in a ring. Let's go danc-ing as we sing.

Spotlight Your Success!

REVIEW

1 Which one of these melodies starts on a downbeat?

a.

b.

c.

READ AND LISTEN

 CD 9:10

1 Which rhythm do you hear?

a.

b.

c.

2 Which rhythm do you hear?

a.

b.

c.

3 Which rhythm do you hear?

a. (music notation)

b. (music notation)

c. (music notation)

THINK!

1 Can one recorder play a chord? Can one guitar? Explain why.

2 How can you tell if the song you are listening to has beat groupings of three or four?

3 Describe one way to create harmony to accompany a melody.

4 Which of these instruments can play a whole note— wood block or triangle? Explain why.

5 **Write** about what the conductor's arm movement pattern shows the orchestra besides the tempo. How does this help the orchestra play well together?

CREATE AND PERFORM

Create a 4-measure ostinato for "Bella bimba." **Perform** it for the class while your teacher plays "Bella bimba" on an instrument.

Meet the Musician
ON NATIONAL RADIO!

Name: Heidi Gorton
Age: 17
Instrument: Harp
Hometown: Pittsburgh, Pennsylvania

It is not surprising that seventeen-year-old Heidi Gorton decided to play music. Her parents and grandparents are all professional musicians. She has been surrounded by music her whole life!

Heidi's mother is a harpist. "I used to listen to my mother playing, and I loved the sound," remembers Heidi. "I wanted to play harp, too."

Heidi's parents are members of an orchestra that performs around the world. Heidi joins her parents whenever they travel. "I've gone to Vienna, the Canary Islands, Japan, South America, and France," she says. Heidi feels really lucky to have visited so many different places.

LISTENING   CD 9:11–12   **RECORDED INTERVIEW**

Danse Profane by Claude Debussy

Listen to Heidi's performance and interview on the national radio program **From the Top**.

Gail Boyd wanted to be a lawyer since she was five years old. At twelve, she knew she'd choose entertainment law. Although Ms. Boyd has only recently begun studying the violin, she's always enjoyed the arts. When she'd heard, as a child, how famous singers like Florence Ballard of The Supremes had been cheated by record companies, Ms. Boyd decided she wanted to protect artists.

For thirteen years, Ms. Boyd has managed jazz artists' careers by helping them get performances, recordings, and fair contracts. She has represented the Clayton-Hamilton Jazz Orchestra, a dynamite big band, for over eight years.

"Absolutely the most rewarding part of my career," Ms. Boyd feels, "is helping to keep jazz alive. It's important to build jazz musicians' audiences and keep young people interested in this art form."

Spotlight on the Cymbal

Did You Know?

A cymbal is a thin, plate-shaped metal disk. It is held at the middle so the rest can vibrate freely.

Cymbals can be played individually with drumsticks or small brushes, or used as a pair and struck one against the other.

 LISTENING CD 9:13–14

March (excerpt) from *Love for Three Oranges Suite*
by Sergei Prokofiev

Overture from *La forza del destino*
by Giuseppe Verdi

Listen for the cymbals. A pair of crash cymbals struck against each other makes strong accents. The "whoosh" of the single brushed cymbal creates atmosphere.

UNIT 6

Express Yourself!

Music can make you feel happy, and it can make you feel sad. Music can make you want to move your feet! When you share music, you share all the ways that music makes you feel.

Coming Attractions

Play a counting game in Spanish.

Explore the sounds your voice can make.

Create your own music!

The song "Three Little Birds" was composed by Bob Marley. He was a famous musician and songwriter from Jamaica. The style of this music is called reggae. Read the words to the song and then listen to the music. **Sing** the song.

Three Little Birds

CD 9:15

Words and Music by Bob Marley

Homeward Bound

CONCEPT
MELODY
SKILLS
MOVE, SING, READ
LINKS
CULTURES, DANCE, READING

In baseball, the runner on base always heads for home. In music, the melody always heads for home, too. This home in music is called the **tonal center**. Melodies often begin on the tonal center, move away from it, and then return. The tonal center is usually the last pitch of a melody.

"The Ballad of the Bedbugs and the Beetles" has an ending that sounds final, or complete, because the melody ends on the tonal center.

Sing this song about a very unusual baseball game. **Listen** for the tonal center.

The Ballad of the Bedbugs and the Beetles

CD 9:18

Folk Rhyme
Melody by Carol King

I woke up Sun-day morn-ing and looked up - on the wall.

The bee-tles and the bed-bugs were play-in' a game of ball.

The score was two to noth-ing. The bee-tles were a - head.

The bed-bugs hit a hom-er and knocked me out of bed!

Choose a spot in the classroom to call your home base. As you sing "The Ballad of the Bedbugs and the Beetles," move away from your home base. Move back toward your home base as the melody returns to the tonal center on the last word of the song.

Here are the pitches in the G pentatonic scale.

Use the pitches from the G pentatonic scale to create a melody for the rhythm below. End your melody on G.

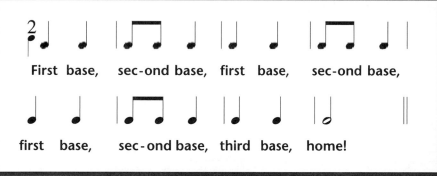

First base, sec-ond base, first base, sec-ond base,

first base, sec-ond base, third base, home!

Home at Last!

"Charlie" is a folk song from the British Isles about Bonnie Prince Charlie. Charlie is happy to be on his way home. The tonal center, or home tone, of "Charlie" is E. This song does not start on the tonal center.

Sing this song and listen for the tonal center.

Charlie

CD 9:21

Adapted from a British Folk Song

Verse

1. Step her to your weev'-ly wheat, and step her to your bar-ley,
2. O-ver and o-ver, ten times o-ver, Char-lie is a ro-ver;

Step her to your weev'-ly wheat to bake a cake for Char-lie.
Take your part-ner by the hands and wring the dish-rag o-ver.

After you sing "Charlie," silently count to ten and then hum the tonal center.

O-ver the riv-er to feed my sheep, O-ver the riv-er, Char - lie!

O-ver the riv-er to feed my sheep, And mea-sure up my bar - ley!

CONCEPT
RHYTHM
SKILLS
SING, MOVE, READ
LINKS
CULTURES, DANCE, READING

"Uno de enero" is a song from Mexico. It names the first seven months of the year. Look at the chart below. **Read** the first seven months, and count from one to seven in Spanish.

uno (one)	**enero** (January)
dos (two)	**febrea** (February)
tres (three)	**marzo** (March)
cuatro (four)	**abril** (April)
cinco (five)	**mayo** (May)
seis (six)	**junio** (June)
siete (seven)	**julio** (July)

Look at the music and find these Spanish words.
Listen to the song and follow along with the music.
Sing "Uno de enero."

MAP

UNITED STATES

MEXICO

UNO DE ENERO

The First of January

 CD 9:24

Mexican Folk Song

Spanish: U - no de e - ne - ro, dos de fe - bre - ra, tres de
Pronunciation: u no ðe ne ɾo ðos ðe fe βɾe ɾa tɾes ðe
English: First___ of Jan-u-a-ry, sec-ond of Feb-ru-a-ry, third of

mar - zo, cua-tro de a - bril. Cin-co de ma - yo, seis de
maɾ so kwa tɾo ðea βɾil sing ko ðe ma yo seis ðe
March,_ fourth_ of A-pril, fifth_ of May,___ sixth of

La raspa Mexican folk dance

"La raspa" is a folk dance from Mexico. The melodies of "Uno de enero" and "La raspa" have three equal sounds on some beats. **Listen** to "La raspa" and raise your hand when you hear three equal sounds on one beat.

Tap this rhythm as you listen to the melody of "La raspa" again:

ju - nio,	sie - te de	ju - lio,	San Fer - min.	¡A	Pam-plo-na he-mos de
xu nyo	sye te ðe	xu lyo	san feɾ min	a	pam plo ne mos ðe
June, sev-enth of Ju - ly,		San Fer-min!	To Pam-plo - na		we must

ir	con u - na	me - dia, con u - na	me - dia!	¡A Pam -
iɾ	kon u na	me ðya kon u na	me ðya	a pam
go,	wear-ing a	stock - ing, wear-ing a	stock - ing.	To Pam -

plo-na he-mos de	ir	con u - na	me - dia y un cal - ce - tin!
plo ne mos ðe	iɾ	kon u na	me ðya iun kal se tin
plo - na	we must go,	wear-ing a	stock-ing, one "cal - ci - tin."

211

Take a Chance, Learn a Dance

The A section arm and foot movements for
"La raspa" imitate the motion of filing with a rasp.
A rasp is a file with small cutting teeth on the surface.

Practice these movements for "La raspa."

**Preparation for
A section:**

**Final form
for A section:**

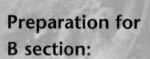

**Preparation for
B section:**

**Final form for
B section:**

Begin the dance with your left foot. Each time you repeat
a 4-beat pattern, start on the opposite foot forward.

Perform the dance with a partner as you listen to "La raspa."

Art Gallery

La Zandunga

Diego Rivera (1866–1957) was known mostly for his murals such as this one. The people in this painting are dancing in a traditional Mexican style.

Something Old and Something New

CONCEPT
RHYTHM
SKILLS
LISTEN, SING, READ
LINKS
CULTURES, DANCE, READING

Dancing is a great way to express yourself! "El nido" is a popular *bailecito* (little dance) in northern Argentina and Bolivia. **Listen** to the song while you tap the beat.

EL NIDO

The Nest

South American Folk Song

CD 9:29

Spanish: En el te - cho de mi ran - cho Ba-jo el

Pronunciation: en el te cho ðe mi ɾan cho βa xoel

English: In the roof - top of my cot - tage live a

a - ler-o en un hue-co Ba-jo el a - ler-o en un

a leɾ oen un xwe ko βa xoel a leɾ oen un

pair_____ of nest-ing lin-nets, live a pair of nest-ing

hue - co. Cuan-do em-pie-za a - ma - ne - cer En mi rar -

xwe ko kwan doem pye ɾa ma ne seɾ en mi ɾaɾ

lin-nets. Lis - ten to the hap-py song. I hope it

los me en_ tre - ten-go Co-mo can - tan y re-

los men tɾe teng go ko mo kan tan i ɾe

lasts the whole day long._ And my heart is filled with

to - zan Con a - le-gres a - le - te-os. Tra la

to san kon a le gɾes a le te os tɾa la

glad - ness to hear their mer - ry roun - de - lay._

Global Voices

Listen to this song about raising little chicks. It is from Azerbaijan, a mountainous country in western Asia. The Caucasus Mountains are located in Azerbaijan.

 LISTENING CD 10:1

MAP

UNITED STATES

AZERBAIJAN

Cip-cip cücələrim

by Gambar Huseynli and Tofig Mutallibov

Refrain

Cip-cip cücələrim,
Cheep-cheep, my chicks,

Cip-cip-cip-cip cücələrim,
Cheep-cheep, cheep-cheep, my chicks,

Mənim qəşəng cücələrim,
My beautiful chicks,

Tükü ipək cücələrim!
Chicks whose feathers are like silk!

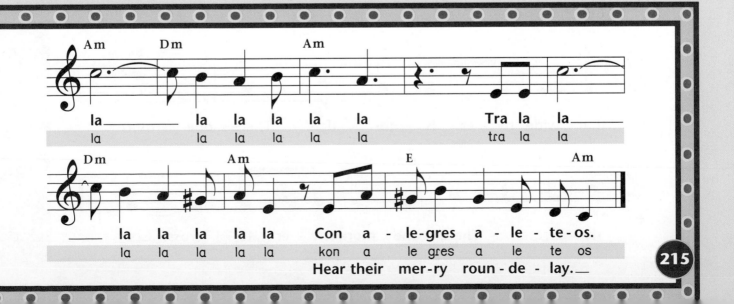

la_____ la la la la la   Tra la la_____
la   la la la la la   tra la la

_____ la la la la la   Con a - le - gres a - le - te - os.
la la la la la   kon a   le gres a   le te os

Hear their mer-ry roun-de-lay.__

Animals Go with Ostinatos

Find familiar rhythms in "One More River." This American folk song tells the story of Noah, who saved his family and many animals from a great flood.

One More River

CD 10:2

Nineteenth Century American Folk Song

Verse

1. Old No-ah, he built him-self an ark;
2. The an-i-mals went in one by one;
3. The an-i-mals went in two by two; } There's one more riv-er to
4. The an-i-mals went in three by three;
5. The an-i-mals went in four by four;

cross.
He built it out of hick'-ry bark;
The el-e-phant chew-ing a car-a-way bun;
The rhi-no-cer-os and the kang-a-roo; } There's
The bear, the bug, and the bum-ble-bee;
The hip-po-po-ta-mus stuck in the door;

Refrain

one more riv-er to cross. There's one more riv-er, And

that wide riv-er is Jor-dan, There's one more

riv-er, There's one more riv-er to cross._____

Clap this ostinato:

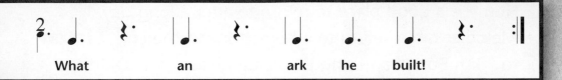

What an ark he built!

Perform this ostinato with pats and snaps:

snap

pat

Riv-er to cross, riv-er to cross, just one riv-er to cross.

Clap the first ostinato while you sing the verse of "One More River." **Perform** the second ostinato while you sing the refrain.

CONCEPT
MELODY
SKILLS
LISTEN, PERFORM,
IDENTIFY
LINKS
CULTURES,
READING

Home is a good place to return to after a long day. Melodies often return to a home tone at the end. **Listen** to "Bim Bom," and sing the first and last tone. Did the melody of "Bim Bom" return to the same pitch on which it started, its home tone?

The words to this song do not have any meaning, but they are fun to sing. **Sing** "Bim Bom."

BIM BOM

CD 10:5

Jewish Folk song

Clap the rhythm of the "Bim Bom" playalong.

Sing the pitch syllables of the playalong as you listen.

Play the pitch syllables on a pitched instrument.

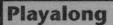
Playalong

la,   la,   mi   la,   la,   mi   la,   la,   la,   mi   la,

re   la,   mi   mi   so,   la,

re   la,   mi   mi   so,   la,

Tagging the Tonal Center

Look at music for "Moon and Me." Are the starting and ending pitches the same?

Sing the melody.

Moon and Me

CD 10:8

Words and Music by Bill Harley

Verse

1. Ev' - ry - bod - y else has closed their eyes,
2. I can see her shin - ing in the sky, through the
3. If there was a wish that I might try, I

it's as qui - et as can be. Ev' - ry - one will sleep un -
branch-es of the wil - low tree. Me here in my bed and
think I know what it would be. One night I'd have wings and

The End (Fine)

til sun - rise, ev' - ry - one but moon and me.
her so high, just us two, the moon and me.
then we'd fly to - geth - er, just the moon and me.

Sing the final tone of "Moon and Me." The tonal center, or home tone, of this melody is *do*.

Refrain

Moon and me,   moon and me,   no one but the moon and me.

Go to the beginning, until the end (D.C. al Fine)

I can see her shin-ing, shin-ing down on me,   just us two, the moon and me.

In "Moon and Me," *do* is the tonal center, and in "Bim Bom," *la* is the tonal center. Discover the tonal center of this mystery tune. Begin by singing the melody using pitch syllables.

What is the name of this mystery tune?

THINK! **Why do you think the tonal center is sometimes called the home tone?**

CONCEPT
TEMPO
SKILLS
IDENTIFY, DESCRIBE, SING
LINKS
READING, VISUAL ARTS, HISTORY

Check Your Speed!

Look around you. Things are moving all around. What moves fast? What moves slow? How fast do you go?

Clap the beat as you say the nursery rhyme "Mary Had a Little Lamb." Change the speed of the words as you say the rhyme. How did the speed of the beat change?

Sometimes the tempo of a song changes. **Pat** the beat while you listen to "Draw a Bucket of Water." Did you hear and feel a tempo change?

Draw a Bucket of Water

CD 10:11

African American Play-Party Song

1.-4. Draw a buck-et of wa-ter For my on-ly daugh-ter.

There's
{ none in the bunch, we're all out the bunch,
one in the bunch, and three out the bunch,
two in the bunch, and two out the bunch,
three in the bunch, and one out the bunch,

(Four times)

You__ go un-der, sis-ter Sal-ly.

Sing the African American song "Draw a Bucket of Water."

THINK! How does the mood of the song change when the tempo changes?

The ♪ sign is an **eighth rest**. It shows when there should be no sound on one eighth of a beat. (Remember that ♪ is an eighth note.) How many eighth rests (♪) are in this song?

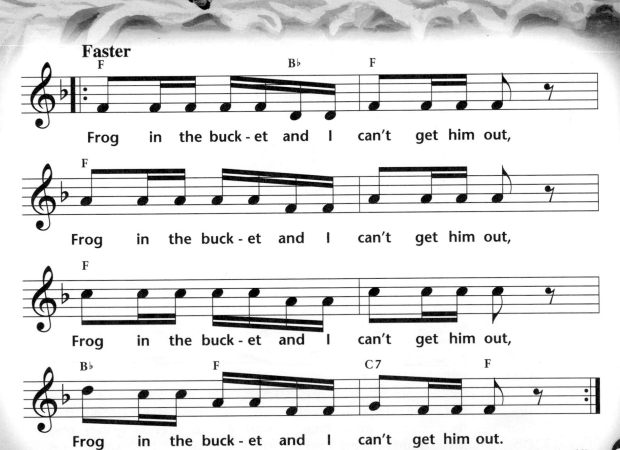

Faster

Frog in the buck-et and I can't get him out,

Frog in the buck-et and I can't get him out,

Frog in the buck-et and I can't get him out,

Frog in the buck-et and I can't get him out.

Unit 6 Express Yourself!

223

Russian to the Beat!

During the refrain of "Kalinka," the tempo gradually accelerates, or gets faster. The Italian musical term for this kind of tempo is **accelerando**.

Sing this Russian folk song.

CD 10:14

Little Snowball Bush

Russian Folk Song
English Words by MMH

Refrain

Russian: Ka лин - ка, ка - лин - ка, ка - лин - ка мо -
Pronunciation: ka lin ka ka lin ka ka lin ka mɔ
English: Ka - lin - ka, ka - lin - ka, ka - lin - ka____

я! В'са - ду я - го - да ма - лин - ка, ма - лин - ка мо -
ya vsa du ya gɔ da ma lin ka ma lin ka mɔ
mine! In the gar - den grows a ber - ry so sweet and____

я! Ка - я. Ах,_____
ya ka ya ax
fine. *Ka* - fine. Oh,_____

Verse

Под__ сос - но - ю, под__ зе - лё - но - ю,
pɔd__ sɔs nɔ yu pɔd__ zɛ lyo nɔ yu
1. Un - der the__ pine tree, un - der the_ green tree,
2. Stur - dy_____ pine tree, shad - y ev - er - green tree,
3. Oh,__ my good_ friend, do not__ for - sake me,

Sergei Prokofiev (1891–1953) was born in Russia. He began composing when he was only five years old. He composed ballets, operas, symphonies, music for films, and pieces for piano.

 LISTENING CD 10:18

Troika by Sergei Prokofiev

Prokofiev wrote "Troika" to describe an exciting ride in a sleigh. A troika is a Russian sleigh pulled by three horses.

Спать	по-ло	-жи	-те___	вы	ме	-ня.	Ах-
spat	pɔ	ʒi	tɛ	vɪ	mɛ	nʸa	a
There	I'll___	lay___	me___	down	to	sleep.	Ah!
Do	not___	wake me	with your	rust-	ling	sound.	Ah!
Pro-	mise that	al-ways	you will	stand	by	me!	Ah!

Ай___	лю-ли,	лю-ли,	ай___	лю	-ли,___	
aɪ	lyu	li	lyu	li	aɪ	lyu	li
Ay,___	liu-li,	liu-li,	ay,___	liu	-li,___	

Go back to 𝄋 and sing to the end
(D.S. al Fine)

Спать	по-ло	-жи	-те___	вы	ме	-ня!	Ка-
spat	pɔ	ʒi	tɛ	vɪ	mɛ	nʸa	ka
There	I'll___	lay___	me___	down	to	sleep.	*Ka-*
Do	not___	wake me	with your	rust-	ling	sound.	Ka-
Pro-	mise that	al-ways	you will	stand	by	me!	Ka-

225

Smooth Move

CONCEPT
EXPRESSION
SKILLS
SING, PERFORM,
IDENTIFY
LINKS
CULTURES,
READING

There are many ways to add expression to music. Music can be smooth and connected. This is called **legato**. Music can also be short and choppy. This is called **staccato**. Performing music legato or staccato makes it more expressive. The song "Shoo Fly Pie and Apple Pan Dowdy" has lots of expression. **Sing** the song.

? THINK! Do you think "Shoo Fly Pie and Apple Pan Dowdy" should be performed legato or staccato? Why?

Shoo Fly Pie and Apple Pan Dowdy

CD 10:19

Music by Guy Wood
Words by Sammy Gallop

Swing Rhythm

1., 3. Shoo fly pie___ and ap-ple pan dow-dy makes your
2. Shoo fly pie___ and ap-ple pan dow-dy makes the

eyes light up,___ your tum-my say, "How-dy."
sun come out___ when heav-ens are cloud-y. }

Shoo fly pie___ and ap-ple pan dow-dy,___ I

End (Fine)

nev-er get e-nough of that won-der-ful stuff.___

Ma-ma, when you bake,_ Ma-ma, I

don't want cake; Ma-ma, for my sake,_

Go back to the beginning and sing to the end (Da Capo al Fine)

go to the ov-en___ and make some ev-er-lov-in'___ sh,

No Strings Attached

Staccato is shown by a dot above or below a note ( ).

Legato is marked by a flowing line over a phrase ( ).

Instruments in the string family are played with a bow. By using the bow, players can produce staccato and legato sounds. Sometimes string instruments are played by plucking the strings with the fingers. This produces a short sound called **pizzicato**.

Listen to "Holiday for Strings" by David Rose.

 LISTENING CD 10:22

Holiday for Strings by David Rose

Holiday for Strings

In this music for strings, there are times when the strings play only pizzicato and other times when they play legato using bows. Work in groups to find a way to move when the strings play pizzicato, and a different way when they play legato sections of the music.

Listening Map for Holiday for Strings

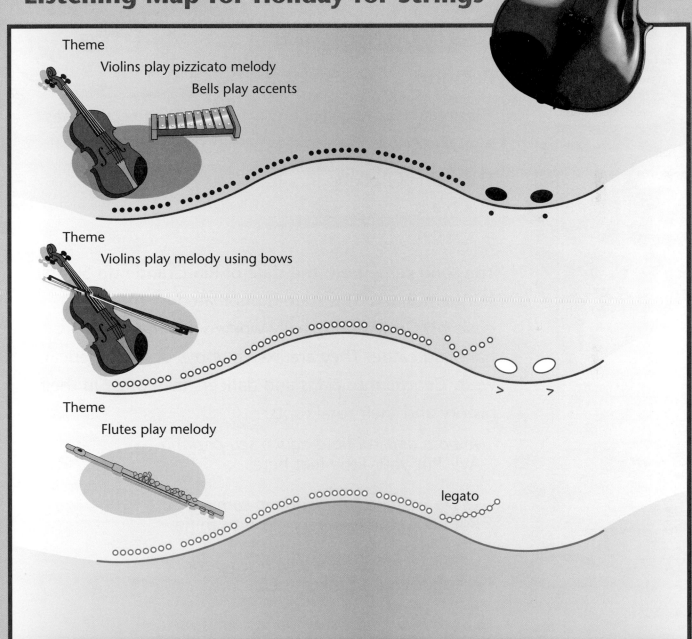

Theme
Violins play pizzicato melody
Bells play accents

Theme
Violins play melody using bows

Theme
Flutes play melody

legato

LESSON 7

CONCEPT
FORM
SKILLS
LISTEN,
PERFORM
LINKS
CULTURE,
SOCIAL STUDIES

Singing Brazilian Style!

LOG ON

Log on to
music.mmhschool.com
to learn more about folk
music from Brazil.

Global Voices

Some music from Brazil has its roots in folk music. Brazil has a rich tradition of folk music. "Pezinho" is a folk song from Brazil. **Listen** to the song.

MAP

UNITED STATES

BRAZIL

💿 **LISTENING** CD 10:23

Pezinho

"Pezinho" has two sections, A and B. Each section has four phrases. Some phrases within the sections repeat.

The form of Pezinho is:

A: a b a b

B: c d c d'

The song came from the state of Rio Grande do Sul in southern Brazil. This state is populated by many *gauchos. Gauchos* originally worked in rural areas, handling cattle. They are like cowboys of the American west. *Gaucho* musicians and dancers take pride in their history and their rural roots.

Ai bota aqui, ai bota aqui o seu pezinho
Ay! Put your little feet here.

O seu pezinho bem juntinho com o meu
Put your little feet very close to mine.

Ai bota aqui, ai bota aqui o seu pezinho
Ay! Put your little feet here.

O seu pezinho bem juntinho com o meu
Put your little feet very close to mine.

E depois nào vá dizer, que você se arrependeu
And after, don't go and say that you have regrets.

Art Gallery

Bambini Giocando
by Cándido Portinari

Cándido Portinari is well loved in Brazil for his versions of the daily lives of ordinary people. He painted this in 1960, and the people of Brazil loved it so much that they used it on a stamp in 1978 for Brazilian National Day.

"Pezinho" is a children's song, or *cantiga*. *Cantigas* are sung in a circle. The children hold hands and do what the lyrics tell them, like stomp their feet, clap their hands, and wave a handkerchief.

Meet the Musician

Kleiton and Kledir are Brazilian brothers who have been playing together under that name since 1980. Kleiton and Kledir are famous for performing Brazilian songs, including Pezinho. Since they are from the southern part of Brazil, their music has very different rhythms than the samba. Their style of music is called Brazilian Gaucho.

Name That Form

"Limbo Rock" is a popular rock and roll song from the early 1960s. There is a dance that you can do with this song. All you need is a limbo stick!

Sing the song.

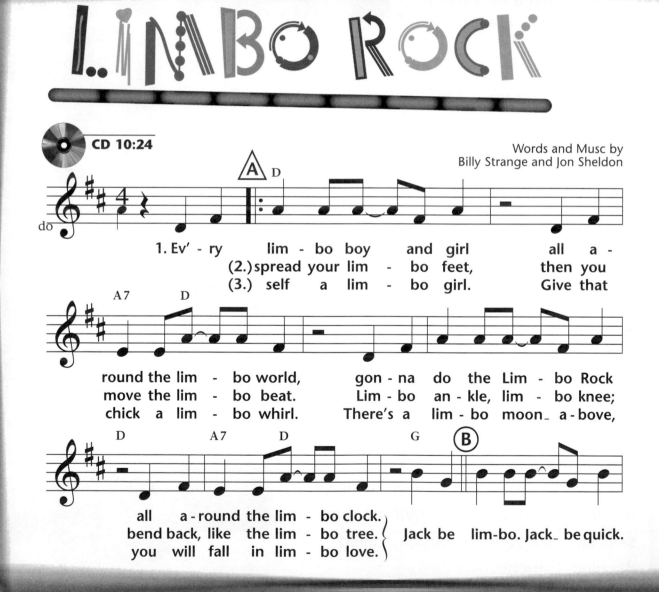

CD 10:24

Words and Musc by
Billy Strange and Jon Sheldon

1. Ev' - ry lim - bo boy and girl all a -
(2.) spread your lim - bo feet, then you
(3.) self a lim - bo girl. Give that

round the lim - bo world, gon - na do the Lim - bo Rock
move the lim - bo beat. Lim - bo an - kle, lim - bo knee;
chick a lim - bo whirl. There's a lim - bo moon_ a - bove,

all a - round the lim - bo clock.
bend back, like the lim - bo tree. Jack be lim-bo. Jack_ be quick.
you will fall in lim - bo love.

In music, sections are often called A and B, or verse and refrain. Inside the sections are smaller parts, called **phrases**. Phrases are sometimes labeled a, b, c, and d.

"Limbo Rock" has two sections, A and B. The A section has four phrases. What is the form of the A section of "Limbo Rock"?

Are any of the phrases in the B section identical or similar? What is the form of the B section of "Limbo Rock"?

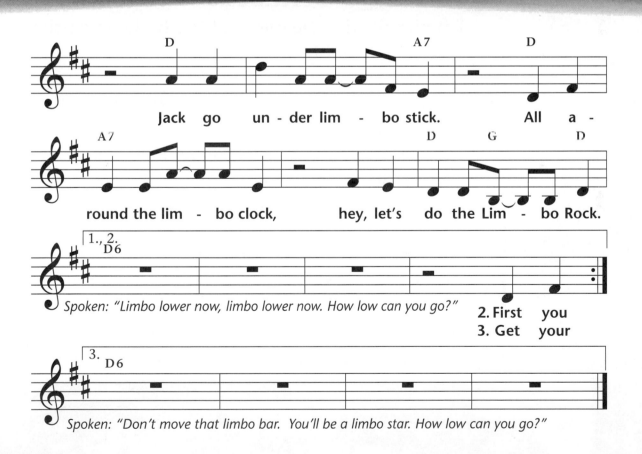

Jack go un - der lim - bo stick. All a - round the lim - bo clock, hey, let's do the Lim - bo Rock.

1., 2.
D6
Spoken: "Limbo lower now, limbo lower now. How low can you go?"
2. First you
3. Get your

3.
D6
Spoken: "Don't move that limbo bar. You'll be a limbo star. How low can you go?"

Cook Up Your Own Rhythms!

CONCEPT
METER
SKILLS
READ, CREATE,
PERFORM
LINKS
READING,
CULTURES,
VISUAL ARTS

A **limerick** is a special kind of poem that describes an event with a funny surprise ending. Limericks have word rhythms in ⅔ meter with three sounds on many of the beats.

I raised a great hullabaloo
When I found a large mouse in my stew.
  Said the waiter, "Don't shout
  And wave it about,
Or the rest will be wanting one too."

THINK!

Describe how the words of the limerick fit with the meter of the body percussion accompaniment below.

As you say the limerick, **perform** this body percussion accompaniment with a partner. There are three motions: pat your legs, clap your hands, and tap. For "tap," you and your partner place your palms together.

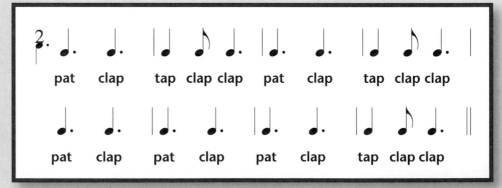

With your partner, choose three of the 2-beat rhythms below and use them to create an 8-beat phrase.

Use at least one pattern that has three sounds on a beat.

End your phrase with a ♩. or a 𝄽. on Beat 8.

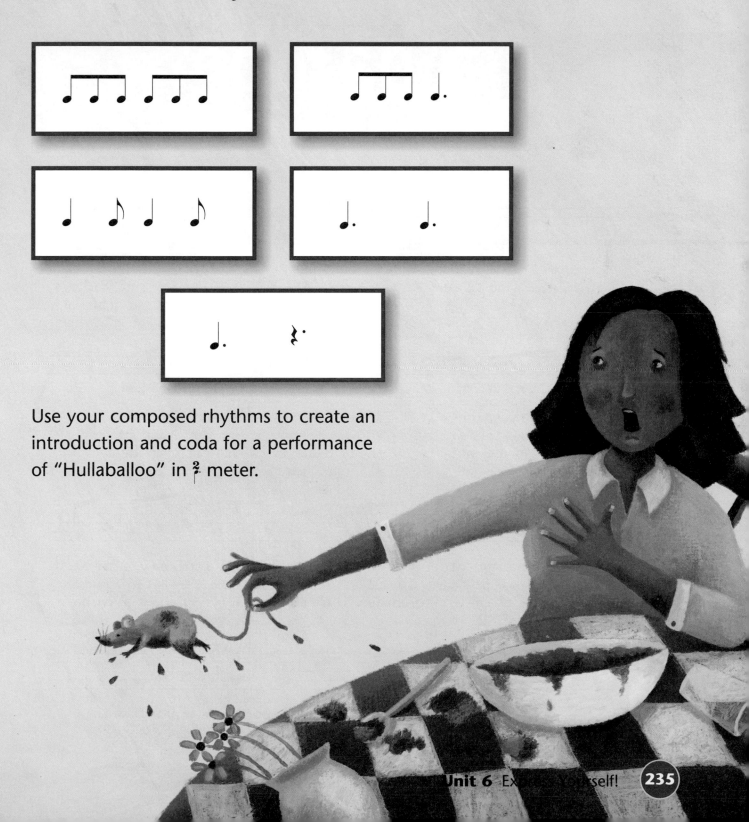

Use your composed rhythms to create an introduction and coda for a performance of "Hullaballoo" in ⅔ meter.

Fun in Mexico

"La bamba" is a fun song to sing in Spanish. It is also a dance. If you go to a Mexican festival, you might sing and dance to "La bamba." **Sing** this song.

CD 10:27

Mexican Folk Song

Spanish: **1. Pa - ra bai - lar la   bam-ba,**   **pa - ra bai - lar la**
Pronunciation: pɑ ɾɑ βai lɑr la   bam ba   pɑ ɾɑ βai lɑr la

(2.) cie - lo,   **pa - ra su - bir al**
sye lo   pɑ ɾɑ su βir al

bam - ba se ne - ce - si - ta̲ u̲ - na   po - ca de   gra - cia,
bam ba se ne se si tau na po ka ðe gɾa sia

cie - lo se ne - ce - si - ta̲ u̲ - na̲ es - ca - le - ra   gran - de,
sye lo se ne se si tau naes ka le ɾa gɾan de

u - na   po - ca de   gra - cia y̲ o - tra co - si - ta y̲ a - rri - ba y̲ a - rri - ba,
u na po ka ðe gɾa sla yo tra ko si ta ya ɾi βa ya ɾi βa

u - na̲ es - ca - le - ra   gran - de y̲ o - tra chi - qui - ta y̲ a - rri - ba y̲ a - rri - ba,
u naes ka le ɾa gɾan de yo tra chi ki ta ya ɾi βa ya ɾi βa

y a - rri - ba y̲ a - rri - ba y̲ a - rri - ba̲ i - ré, por ti se - ré, por ti se - ré,
i a ɾi βa ya ɾi βa ya ɾi βai ɾe por ti se ɾe por ti se ɾe

Spotlight Your Success!

REVIEW

1 Identify the tonal center of each of the melodies below:

a. *do*   **b.** *la*

2

a. *do*   **b.** *la*

3

a. *do*   **b.** *la*

READ AND LISTEN

 **CD 10:31**

1 Which rhythm do you hear?

2 Which rhythm do you hear?

a.

b.

c.

THINK!

1 Explain the meaning of the home tone of a melody.

Describe how you figure out if a song's tonal center is *do* or *la*.

Why do you think composers and performers use sudden and gradual changes in the tempo and dynamics in their music?

Write about how you should change your performance of a song if you see the words *staccato* or *legato* on the score.

CREATE AND PERFORM

Create your own melody and rhythm over 8 beats.

1 Use *so₁ la₁ do re mi so la*

2 Use ⅔ for your meter signature.

3 Use ♩♪, ♫♩, ♩., and 𝄽· to create your rhythm pattern.

4 Decide whether your melody should end on the tonal center of *do* or *la*.

Perform your melody for the class.

Spotlight on Music Reading

Spotlight on Music Reading

Spotlight on Music Reading

CONCEPT
MELODY/RHYTHM
SKILLS
READ, SING

A *Mi-Re-Do* Song

Learn a *mi-re-do* song about the weather.

Find a place in the song that has no sound to a beat
(𝄽), one sound to a beat (♩), or two sounds to a beat
(♫). **Sing** the song with pitch syllables.

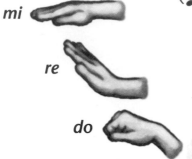

mi

re

do

Rain Is Falling Down

CD 11:1

Traditional English Song

Rain   is   fall - ing   down!   Rain   is   fall - ing   down!

Pit - ter, pat - ter,   pit - ter, pat - ter,   Rain   is   fall - ing   down!

UNIT 1 READING

CONCEPT
MELODY
SKILLS
SING, READ,
PERFORM

Sing Steps and Skips

Melodies can
- move one step at a time.
- skip a step.
- stay on the same step.

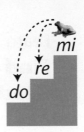

mi
re
do

Sing *mi re do* by steps, by skips, and by repeating.

Sing "Frog in the Meadow" and find where the music moves by steps, by skips, or stays the same.

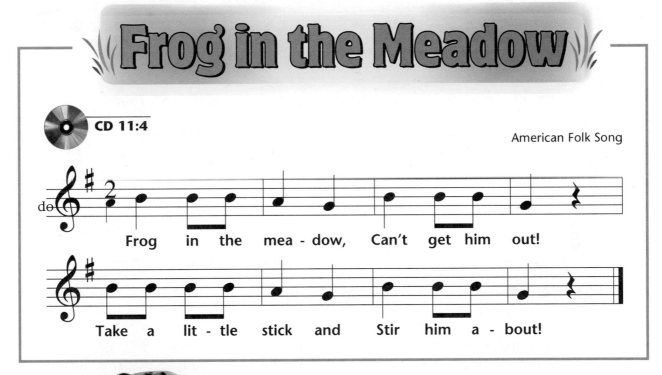

CD 11:4

American Folk Song

do

Frog in the mea-dow, Can't get him out!

Take a lit-tle stick and Stir him a-bout!

What rhythms can you find in this song?

Perform this rhythm with the song.

2

Hide frog! Run a-way!

Play with Rhythms

Learn a Japanese song for jumping rope.
Find ♫ ♩ and 𝄽 in the song.
Read the rhythm of the first line then the whole song.

Kuma San

Honorable Bear

CD 11:7

Japanese Folk Song
English Version by
Marilyn Davidson and Kathy B. Sorensen

Japanese: く ま さん く ま さん ま わ れ み ぎ
Pronunciation: ku ma san ku ma san ma wa ɾe mi gi
English: **Ku - ma san, ku - ma san, turn your-self a - round.**

く ま さん く ま さん りょ う て を つい て
ku ma san ku ma san ɾyo te wo tsui te
Ku - ma san, ku - ma san, hands up - on the ground.

く ま さん く ま さん か た あ し あ げ て
ku ma san ku ma san ka ta a shi a ge te
Ku - ma san, ku - ma san, hop with one foot in the air.

く ま さん く ま さん き よ う な ら
ku ma san ku ma san sa you na ɾa
Ku - ma san, ku - ma san, Sa - yo - na - ra.

Sing the song and hop with the beat.

Practice Reading Pitches

Learn about *do re mi.*

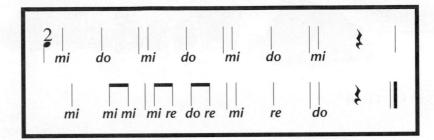

Who's That Yonder?

CD 11:11

African American Spiritual

1. Who's that yon - der dressed in red?

Must be the chil-dren that___ Mo - ses led.

2. Who's that yonder dressed in white?
   Must be the children of the Israelite.

4. Who's that yonder dressed in black?
   Must be the hypocrites a-turnin' back.

3. Who's that yonder dressed in blue?
   Must be the children that are comin' through.

THINK! Both lines of this song
are four measures long. How else are
they alike? How are they different?

A *Do-Re-Mi* Tongue Twister

Find *do re mi* in this song.

CD 11:14

Traditional Tongue Twister
Music by Marilyn Copeland Davidson

Faster each time

do

How much wood would a wood - chuck chuck

if a wood - chuck could chuck wood?

He would chuck, he would, as much as he could,

And chuck as much wood as a wood - chuck would

If a wood - chuck could chuck wood!

Sing another melody, this time with pitch syllables.

do re mi mi mi mi mi mi re re do

re re re do re mi mi mi

March Past of the Kitchen Utensils
from *The Wasps* by Ralph Vaughan Williams

This piece is from an opera called "The Wasps" that is based on a Greek comedy written about 2,500 years ago.

The first theme of this piece begins like the *do-re-mi* melody you just sang.

Listen to "March Past of the Kitchen Utensils" and follow the listening map. Raise a hand each time you hear the *do-re-mi* melody.

Listening Map for March Past of the Kitchen Utensils

CONCEPT
MELODY
SKILLS
READ, SING

Sing with an Added Pitch

You have been singing songs with *do re mi*.
This song has another pitch. What is it?

do do re re mi ?

Let Us Chase the Squirrel

CD 11:18

North Carolina Game Song

do

1. Let us chase the squir - rel, Up the hick'-ry, down the hick'-ry,
2. If you want to catch him, Up the hick'-ry, down the hick'-ry,

Let us chase the squir - rel Up the hick' - ry tree!
If you want to catch him, Learn to climb a tree!

Do, Re, Mi, So, and La

Learn to sing a *pentatonic,* or five-tone, song.
Sing *do re mi so la* then find those
pitches in "Coral."

so la

CD 11:21

American Folk Song

do

1.   O   sail - or   come a - shore. What have you brought for me?
2. Did not take it   from the ground, nor   pick   it   from   a tree;

Red   cor - al, white   cor - al,   cor - al from the   sea.
Lit-tle   in - sects made it   in   the   storm - y, storm - y   sea.

Find the half note ♩ in "Coral." Half notes are held
for two beats.
Practice singing the half note in "Coral."

CONCEPT
MELODY

SKILLS
READ, LISTEN, CREATE

More Pentatonic Melodies

Sing this pentatonic phrase with pitch syllables and letter names.

so so mi   so   la   so mi mi   re   do

G G E   G   A   G E E   D   C

Sing this song about a snowy winter day.

Frosty Weather

CD 11:24

Traditional

do Frost - y   weath - er,   Snow - y   weath - er,

When the wind   blows,   we   all   go   to - geth - er.

Sing this ostinato with "Frosty Weather."

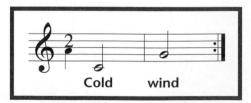

Cold   wind

Imagine it is winter and you are outside at the end of a long, dark night. How would you feel when you saw the sun rise?

 LISTENING CD 11:27

Morning Mood from *Peer Gynt Suite No. 1*, Op. 46
by Edvard Grieg

"Morning Mood" is a piece for orchestra. The composer used a pentatonic melody to set the mood for a daybreak scene. The pitches of the first phrase are the same as those in "Frosty Weather."

Listen to "Morning Mood" and trace the shape of the melody.

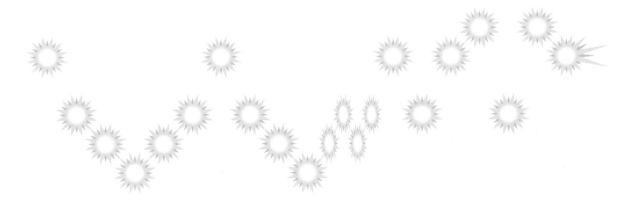

Create your own morning melody by improvising with *do re mi so la*.

Sing a Pentatonic Song

Beep! Beep! Have fun learning a song about a car. There are three yellow patterns in this song. Which yellow melodic pattern in the song has repeated notes? Which pattern moves by steps? Which pattern moves by skips?

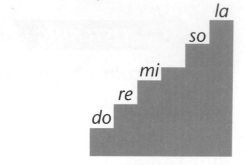

I Have a Car

CD 11:28

American Camp Song

I have a car, it's made of tin.

No - bod - y knows what shape it's in.

It has four wheels and a rum - ble seat.

Hear us chug - ging down the street.

This car from the 1930s has a rumble seat.

Name That Pitch

What is the mystery pitch in the pattern below?

mi mi do ? ? do

Find that pitch in the song.

Old Mister Rabbit

CD 11:31

African American Folk Song

Old Mis-ter Rab-bit you got a might-y hab-it of

Jump-ing in my gar-den and eat-ing all my cab-bage.

Sing Low *La*

Learn another song about a rabbit.
Find the pitches in "See the Rabbit Running" on the pitch stairs.

See the Rabbit Running

CD 11:34

Hungarian Melody
Traditional English Words

See the rab - bit run - ning, from the fox who's cun - ning,

Fox is get - ting thin - ner, chas - ing down his din - ner.

An Added Pitch

Find *do* in this song.   *so*

Identify the new
pitch below *do*.

MAP

UNITED STATES   GUATEMALA

Vamos a la mar

CD 11:37   Let's Go to the Sea

Guatemalan Folk Song
English Version by MMH

Spanish: Va - mos a la mar, tum tum,
English: Let's go to the sea, tum tum,
Pronunciation: ba mos a la maɾ tum tum

a co - mer pes - ca - do, tum tum;
We will eat some fish - es, tum tum;
a ko meɾ pes ka ðo tum tum

bo - ca co - lo - ra - da, tum tum,
Bo - ca co - lo - ra - da, tum tum,
bo ka ko lo ɾa ða tum tum

fri - ti - to y a - sa - do, tum tum.
Fried and hot and spi - cy, tum tum.
fɾi ti to ya sa ðo tum tum

Clap or play this pattern on
shells or wood instruments as
you sing the song again.

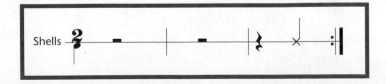

Shells

UNIT 3 READING

CONCEPT
RHYTHM

SKILLS
SING, READ,
CONDUCT

Conduct in Two

Practice measures 6 and 7 of the pattern below.
Read the whole pattern with pitch syllables.

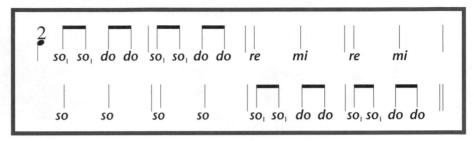

What is the meter of this song?
Conduct in two as you sing it.

1   2

Scotland's Burning

CD 11:41

Traditional Round

Scot - land's burn - ing,   Scot - land's   burn - ing,

Look   out!   Look   out!

Fire!   fire!   fire!   fire!

Pour   on   wa - ter,   Pour   on   wa - ter.

Sing with Low *La* and Low *So*

Move along with the words as you sing "Kreely Kranky." Find the pentatonic pitches in the song.

la
so
mi
re
do
la,
so,

CD 11:44

American Dance Song

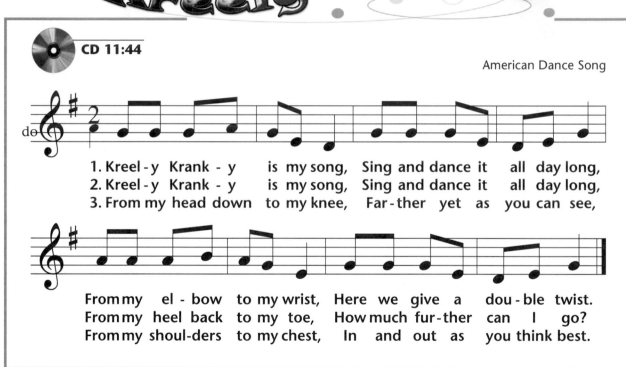

do

1. Kreel - y Krank - y   is my song,   Sing and dance it   all day long,
2. Kreel - y Krank - y   is my song,   Sing and dance it   all day long,
3. From my head down to my knee,   Far - ther yet as you can see,

From my   el - bow to my wrist, Here we give a   dou - ble twist.
From my heel back to my toe,   How much fur - ther can I go?
From my shoul-ders to my chest, In   and out as   you think best.

Sing this pattern and trace the melody.
Identify the pattern in the song.

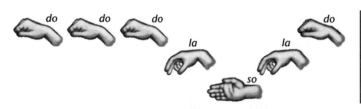

do   do   do
la
la
so
do

do do do la,   so,   la,   do

258

Keep the Beat in Four

Do you have a dog or a cat?
Sing this song.
Pat with the beat as you sing
it again.

Cat and Dog

CD 11:47

South Carolina Folk Song

1. Bought me a dog, bought me a cat.
2. Bought me a coat, bought me a hat.

They both fight but do not mind that.
They don't fit but do not mind that.

Hi ho, my dar - ling.

Find low *la* and low
so in the song.

Music Reading 259

A Pentatonic Song

Long ago, sailors sang songs like this to entertain themselves at sea.

Sing this pattern with pitch syllables.

CD 11:50

Verse

American Folk Song

I've been to Haar - lem, I've been to Do - ver,

I've trav - eled this wide world all o - ver,

O - ver, o - ver, three times o - ver,

Drink what you have to drink and turn the glass - es o - ver.

THINK! Count how many times you find the pattern above, or one like it, in the song.

How are the patterns the same?

How are some of them different?

The form of this song can be shown like this:

A B

What is another name for the form of this song?
Look for clues in the song.

Equal and Unequal

♫ and ♩ get one beat in 4 meter.
In ⅔ meter, each of these rhythms gets one beat:

♩.   𝄽   ♫♫   ♩♪

The last of these rhythms is unequal: long-short.

Read, conduct, and compare these two poems.

Our Washing Machine

Our washing machine
  went whisity whirr
Whisity whisity whisity whirr
One day at noon it went whisity click
Whisity whisity whisity click
Click grr click grr click grr click
Call the repairman
Fix it . . . Quick!

—*Patricia Hubbell*

I woke up in the morning

I woke up in the morning
and I jumped out of bed
put some clothes on my body
and a hat on my head
took a leap to the kitchen
and I ate my toast
listened to the news
from coast to coast
looked out the window
to check the sun
ran out the door
to have some fun

—*Sonja Dunn*

Which of these patterns has equal rhythms and which has unequal?

Click grr, click grr, click grr, click.

I woke up in the morn-ing and I jumped out of bed.

Say the third and fifth lines from "Our Washing Machine." These lines contain this rhythm: ♫♫♩ ♫♫♩

Playful Pizzicato from
Simple Symphony by Benjamin Britten

Simple Symphony is a piece for string orchestra.
In this movement, the string players play a
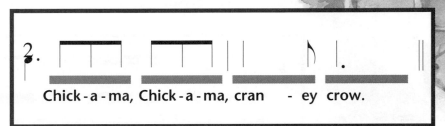 pattern in ⅔ over and over.

Listen to this excerpt from the "Playful Pizzicato"
and softly say *whisity* while the orchestra plays.

Read this rhythm.
Learn a song in ⅔.

2. Chick-a-ma, Chick-a-ma, cran - ey crow.

Chicka-ma, Chicka-ma, Craney Crow

CD 11:54

British Folk Song

Chick - a - ma, chick - a - ma, cra - ney crow,

Went to the well to wash his toe. When he got there his

chick - en was gone. "What time, old fox?"

"One!"
"Two!"
"Three!"
"Four!"

Sixteenth Notes

Four sounds to a beat looks like this.

Pat and say these rhythms from "Golden Ring Around the Susan Girl."

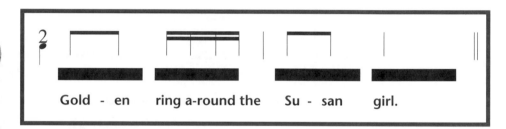

Gold - en   ring a-round the   Su - san   girl.

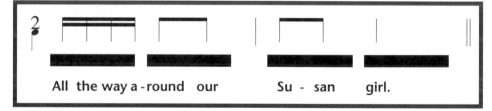

All the way a-round   our   Su - san   girl.

Golden Ring Around the Susan Girl

CD 11:57

American Folk Song

Gold-en ring a-round the Su-san girl, Gold-en ring a-round the Su-san girl,

Gold-en ring a-round the Su-san girl, All the way a-round our Su-san girl.

Play and Sing Sixteenth Notes

Pat this rhythm and then count how many times it is in the song. ♫♫♫

Chicken on the Fence Post

CD 12:1

Play-Party Song

do

F

Chick-en on the fence post, can't dance Jo - sey,

F

Chick - en on the fence post, can't dance Jo - sey,

F

Chick - en on the fence post, can't dance Jo - sey,

F

Hel - lo, Su - san Brown - y - o.

Say and pat the yellow patterns in "Chicken on the Fence Post."

LISTENING CD 11:60

Batuque by Oscar Lorenzo Fernández

Listen to this piece in ABA form from Brazil.
Play the yellow patterns as you listen.

Music Reading 265

Sixteenth Notes and High *Do*

This song is about the rhythm of a clock.
What pitches and rhythms are at the end
of the song?

do¹
la
so
mi
re
do

Clocks

CD 12:4

Traditional

C
Big clocks mark time slow - ly, tick - tock, tick - tock,

C
small clocks mark time fast - er, tick - tock, tick - tock,

C
tick - tock, tick - tock, And the lit - tle watch - es mark time

C
tick - y - tock - y, tick - y - tock - y, tick - y - tock - y, tick - y - tock - y.

266

Sing a playground song with high *do*.

Find the sixteenth notes and high *do* in this game song.

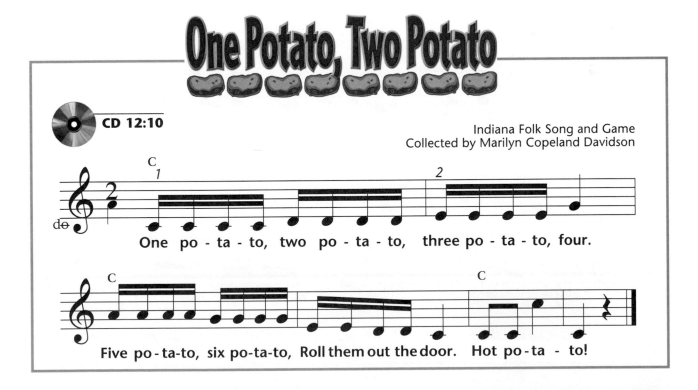

Practice What You Know

Sing and play a game with this pentatonic song.
Sing it first with syllables then with the words.

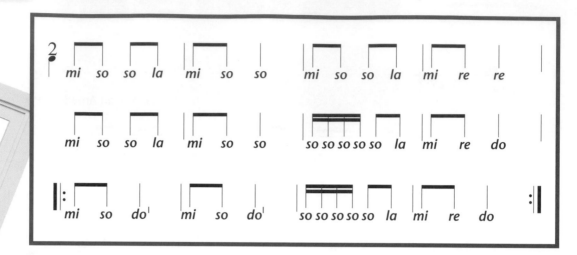

mi	so	so	la	mi	so	so	
mi	so	so	la	mi	re	re	

mi	so	so	la	mi	so	so	
so so so so so	la	mi	re	do			

mi	so	do¹	mi	so	do¹		
so so so so so	la	mi	re	do			

Jingle at the Window

CD 12:13

Ohio Play-Party Song

Pass one win-dow,   ti - de - o,   Pass two win-dows,   ti - de - o,

Pass three win-dows,   ti - de - o,   Jin-gle at the win-dows,   ti - de - o.

Ti - de - o,   ti - de - o,   Jin-gle at the win-dows,   ti-de-o.

Answer That Rhythm

Clap or play these rhythm patterns.

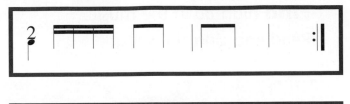

Play them as you sing the song.

Ding Dong Diggy Diggy Dong

CD 12:16

Words and Music by Carl Orff
English Translation by Doreen Hall

Ding dong dig-gy dig-gy dong, Dig-gy dig-gy ding the cat is gone!

Ding dong dig-gy dig-gy dong, Dig-gy dig-gy ding ding dong.

Create an answer rhythm for each pattern above.
Choose an instrument and play your answers.

CONCEPT ◀
MELODY

SKILLS
READ, PLAY, LISTEN

Sing and Listen for High *Do*

Listen to this song. Raise a hand when you hear high *do*.
Find high *do* in the music.
Read and sing the song.

CD 12:19

1845 Singing School Song

Morn-ing bells I love to hear Ring-ing mer-ri-ly loud and clear.

Play instruments with "Morning Bells."

Down and Up: *So Mi Do Mi So Do*[l]

This melody uses the same pitches as "Morning Bells."

Pat the rhythm of this pattern, first slow then fast.
Read the melody with pitch syllables.

Compare the direction of this melody with that of "Morning Bells."

 LISTENING CD 12:22

Galop of Sancho's Donkey from
Don Quixote by Georg Philipp Telemann

This music is part of a collection of pieces about Don Quixote and his adventures with his pal, Sancho Panza. It sounds as if Sancho's donkey takes a few fast steps then a few long steps.

Listen to "The Galop of Sancho's Donkey" and raise a hand each time you hear the "Morning Bells" pitches going down and up.

Don Quixote and his friend, Sancho Panza

Play an Inner Hearing Game

Sing the song as you conduct the beats in two.
This song starts on which beat?

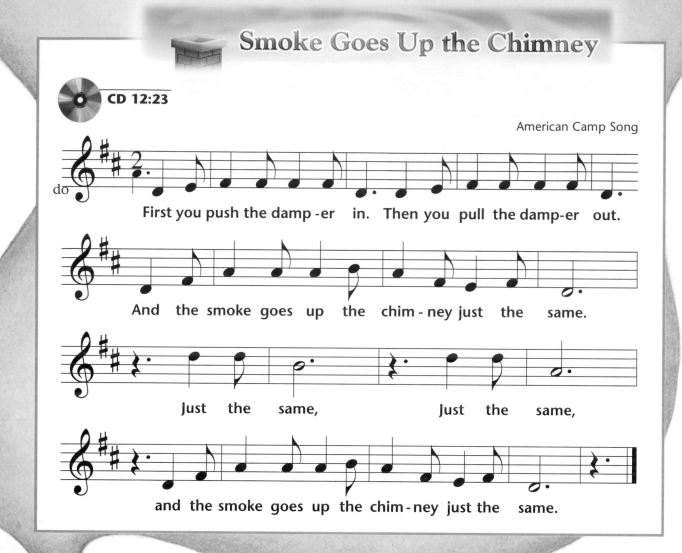

Smoke Goes Up the Chimney

CD 12:23

American Camp Song

do

First you push the damp-er in. Then you pull the damp-er out.

And the smoke goes up the chim-ney just the same.

Just the same, Just the same,

and the smoke goes up the chim-ney just the same.

Sing the song again. This time think the pitches of the yellow section instead of singing them out loud.
Clap or tap this ostinato with the song.

Start on a Pickup Note

The pickup in this song is an eighth note.

Remember that there are two eighth notes to a beat and ♪ ♪ = ♫ An ♪ gets one-half is a beat in ² meter.

Read and sing as you conduct this song in two.

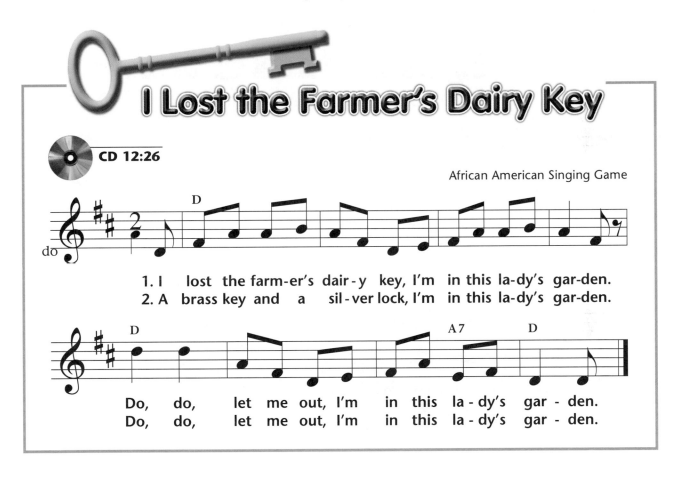

I Lost the Farmer's Dairy Key

CD 12:26

African American Singing Game

1. I lost the farm-er's dair-y key, I'm in this la-dy's gar-den.
2. A brass key and a sil-ver lock, I'm in this la-dy's gar-den.

Do, do, let me out, I'm in this la - dy's gar - den.
Do, do, let me out, I'm in this la - dy's gar - den.

CONCEPT
RHYTHM
SKILLS
READ, SING

Eighth Notes and Eighth Rests

Clap this rhythm from the Mexican song "Que llueva."

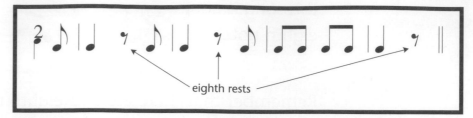

eighth rests

An eighth rest (𝄾) gets one-half beat of silence in ⅖ meter.

Que llueva

It's Raining

CD 12:29

Mexican Children's Game Song

Spanish: **1.–2.** Que   llue - va, que   llue - va, la   ra - na_es-tá_en la
Pronunciation: **1.–2.** ke   ywe   βa   ke   ywe   βa   la   ra   naes   taen   la
English: **1.–2.** It's   rain - ing, it's   rain - ing, the   frog   is   in   the

cue - va; los   pa - ja - ri - tos   can - tan, la   lu - na se   le -
kwe   βa   los   pa   xa   ɾi   tos   kan   tan   la   lu   na   se   le
cave, And the   par - a - keets are   sing - ing, the   sil - ver moon is

van - ta. ¡Que sí,   que no!
βan ta ke si   ke   no
ris - ing. Oh, yes!   Oh, no!

1. Que cai - ga_un cha - pa - rrón.
   ke   kai   gaun cha   pa   r̄on
   The rain   is   fall - ing down.
2. Le can - ta_el la - bra - dor.
   le   kan   tael   la   βɾa   ðor
   The farm - er   sings the song.

Whole Notes

Learn an Appalachian folk song about a robin.
Find the whole note. In ⁴₄ meter, a whole note (𝅝) is a sound that lasts four beats.

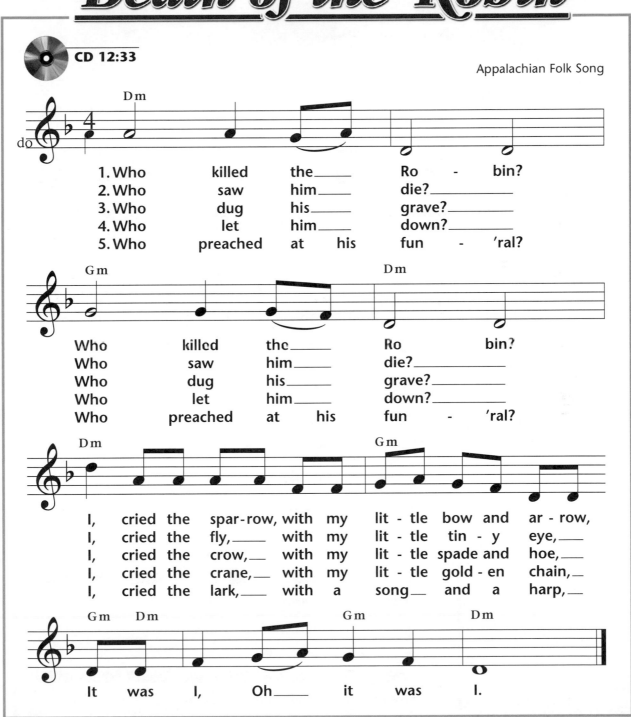

Death of the Robin

CD 12:33

Appalachian Folk Song

Dm

1. Who   killed   the____   Ro - bin?
2. Who   saw   him____   die?_____
3. Who   dug   his____   grave?_____
4. Who   let   him____   down?_____
5. Who   preached   at   his   fun - 'ral?

Gm   **Dm**

Who   killed   the____   Ro   bin?
Who   saw   him____   die?_____
Who   dug   his____   grave?_____
Who   let   him____   down?_____
Who   preached   at   his   fun - 'ral?

Dm   **Gm**

I,   cried the   spar-row, with   my   lit - tle   bow   and   ar - row,
I,   cried the   fly,____ with   my   lit - tle   tin - y   eye,____
I,   cried the   crow,__ with   my   lit - tle spade and   hoe,__
I,   cried the   crane,__ with   my   lit - tle gold - en   chain,__
I,   cried the   lark,____ with   a   song__ and   a   harp,__

Gm   Dm   **Gm**   **Dm**

It   was   I,   Oh____   it   was   I.

Dotted Half Notes and Whole Notes

Find the whole note in this Creole folk song.
There are also dotted half notes. In 𝄴 meter a 𝅗𝅥. is a sound
that lasts three beats.

Read this rhythm from the song.

Sing with Dotted Half Notes

Find the dotted half notes.

Sing "Little Tommy Tinker," first in unison then as a canon.

Traditional

CD 12:39

Little Tom-my Tink - er   sat up - on   a clink - er, And

he be - gan to   cry,   "Ma!   Ma!"___

Poor   lit - tle   in - no - cent   guy.

Rhythms in ⅜ Meter

Read and sing this folk song from Tennessee.

My Horses Ain't Hungry

CD 12:42

Tennessee Folk Song

do

G   C   G

My hors-es ain't hun-gry, They won't eat your hay,

G   C   G

So I'll get on my po-ny, I'm go-ing a-way.

Sing and play this harmony part with the song.

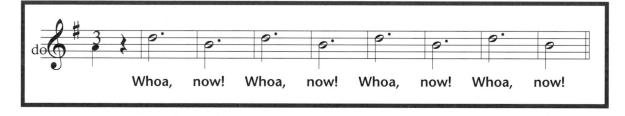

do

Whoa, now! Whoa, now! Whoa, now! Whoa, now!

Rhythms of Celebration

Find the dotted half notes (♩.) in this African song celebrating the harvest.

Find the upbeat in the song.

Play this ostinato on drums or body percussion then play it with the song. Since "Dide" begins on an upbeat, so begin on the first full measure.

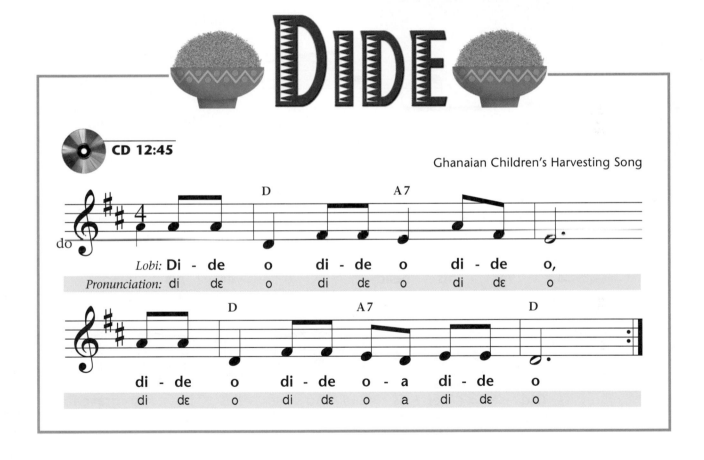

CD 12:45

Ghanaian Children's Harvesting Song

Lobi: **Di - de o di - de o di - de o,**
Pronunciation: di dɛ o di dɛ o di dɛ o

di - de o di - de o - a di - de o
di dɛ o di dɛ o a di dɛ o

UNIT
6
READING
CONCEPT
RHYTHM
SKILLS
READ, SING

A Song in 2.

Pat each of these rhythm patterns a few times.
Count how often each pattern is found in the song.

CD 12:49

British Children's Singing Game

Old Roger

1. Old Ro - ger is dead and he lies in his grave,
2. They plant - ed an ap - ple tree o - ver his head,
3. The ap - ples were ripe___ and read - y to drop,

Lies in his grave, lies in his grave.
o - ver his head, lies in his grave.
read - y to drop, read - y to drop.

Old Ro - ger is dead and he lies in his grave
They plant - ed an ap - ple tree o - ver his head
The ap - ples were ripe___ and read - y to drop

I ah I O I ay!

4. There came an east wind a blowing them off...
5. There came an old woman a pickin' them up...
6. Old Roger jumped up and gave her a knock...
7. Which made the old woman go hippety hop...

Military Music in $\frac{2}{2}$

In $\frac{2}{2}$ meter

$\frac{1}{2}. = \frac{1}{2}.\frac{1}{2}. = $

Find the dotted half notes ($\frac{1}{2}.$) in "Taps."

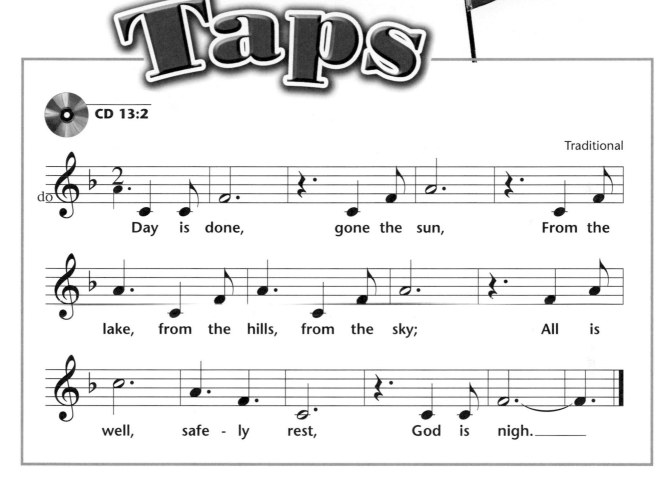

CD 13:2

Traditional

do

Day is done, gone the sun, From the

lake, from the hills, from the sky; All is

well, safe - ly rest, God is nigh._____

LISTENING CD 13:1

Semper Fidelis by John Philip Sousa

John Philip Sousa wrote "Semper Fidelis" for the United States Marine Band.

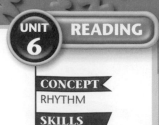

Canons in ⅔ Meter

When you sing in canon, you add texture to a song. **Sing** two canons in ⅔ meter.

CD 13:5

Words by Mary Ann Hoberman
Music by Marilyn Davidson

1. Spi - ders sel - dom see too well.
2. Spi - der bod - ies are two - part.
3. Spi - ders al - ways have eight legs.

Spi - ders have no sense of smell.
Spi - der webs are works of art.
Spi - ders hatch straight out of eggs.

Spi - ders spin out silk - en threads.
Spi - ders don't have an - y wings.
Since all these facts are sure - ly so,

Spi - ders don't have se - pa - rate heads.
Spi - ders live on liv - ing things.
Spi - ders are not in - sects, no!

Find the *fermatas*, or holds, in this song.

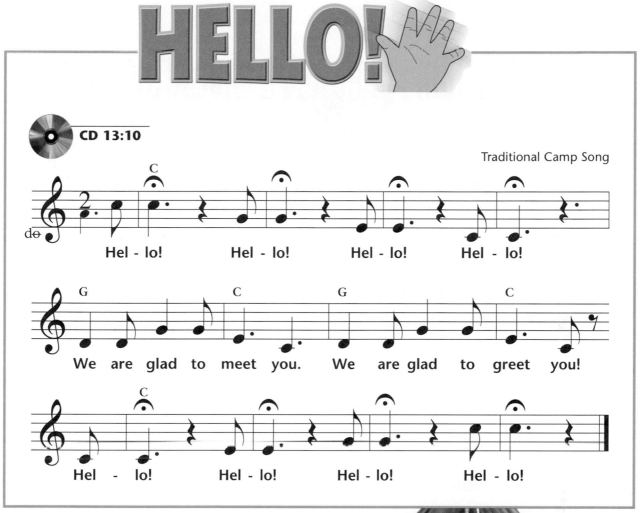

CD 13:10

Traditional Camp Song

Hel - lo! Hel - lo! Hel - lo! Hel - lo!

We are glad to meet you. We are glad to greet you!

Hel - lo! Hel - lo! Hel - lo! Hel - lo!

Tonal Centers

Find the tonal center in this song.

Cornstalk Fiddle and a Shoestring Bow

CD 13:13

Traditional

Verse

1. I made me a fid - dle and I made me a bow,
2. I tuned up my fid - dle and I went to a dance.

and I learned to play the fid - dle like Cot - ton Eye Joe.
__ I tried to make some mu - sic but I did - n't get a chance. }

Refrain

Corn - stalk fid - dle and a shoe - string bow,

It's the ver - y best fid - dle in the coun - ty - o!

3. Cotton Eye Joe lived 'cross the creek.
   He learned to play the fiddle 'bout seven days a week.
   (Refrain)

4. I've made lots of fiddles and I've made lots of bows.
   But I never learned to fiddle like Cotton Eye Joe!
   (Refrain)

Refrain Countermelody

Corn - stalk fid - dle, And if that ain't fid - dl - in' then I don't know.

Follow the Melody, Listen for Form

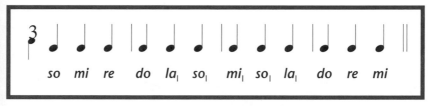

LISTENING CD 13:16

Circus Music from *The Red Pony Suite*

by Aaron Copland

The piece is in three sections—like a 3-ring circus! The first and last sections are the same. What is the form?

Read and sing this pattern.

Le cirque (The Circus), 1890-1891
by Georges Seurat

so mi re do la₁ so₁ mi₁ so₁ la₁ do re mi

Listen for this pattern in "Circus Music."
Follow the sections in the listening map.

Listening Map for Circus Music

UNIT
6 READING

CONCEPT
RHYTHM
SKILLS
READ, SING

Sing with Ties

In $\frac{4}{4}$ a whole note (𝅝) is held for four beats.

Find the whole notes in "Over My Head." How many do you see?
What do you notice about the whole notes?
How long are these sounds?

CD 13:17

African American Spiritual

O-ver my head,_____ I hear mu-sic in the air._____

O-ver my head,_____ I hear mu-sic in the air._____

O-ver my head,_____ I hear mu-sic in the air._____

There must be a God some - where._____

Sing this ostinato or play it on a pitched instrument. Begin the ostinato on the first full measure of the song.

Ties and Slurs

Read the pattern then sing the song.

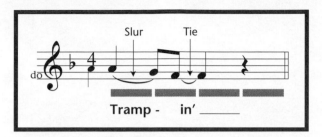

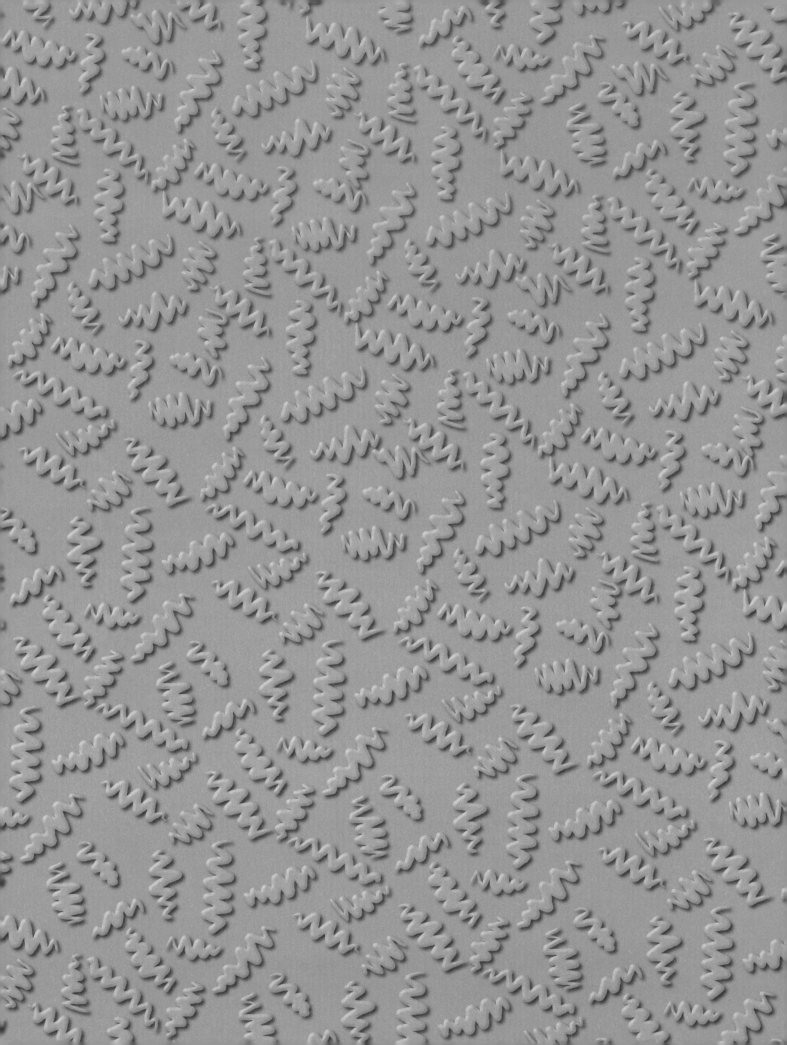

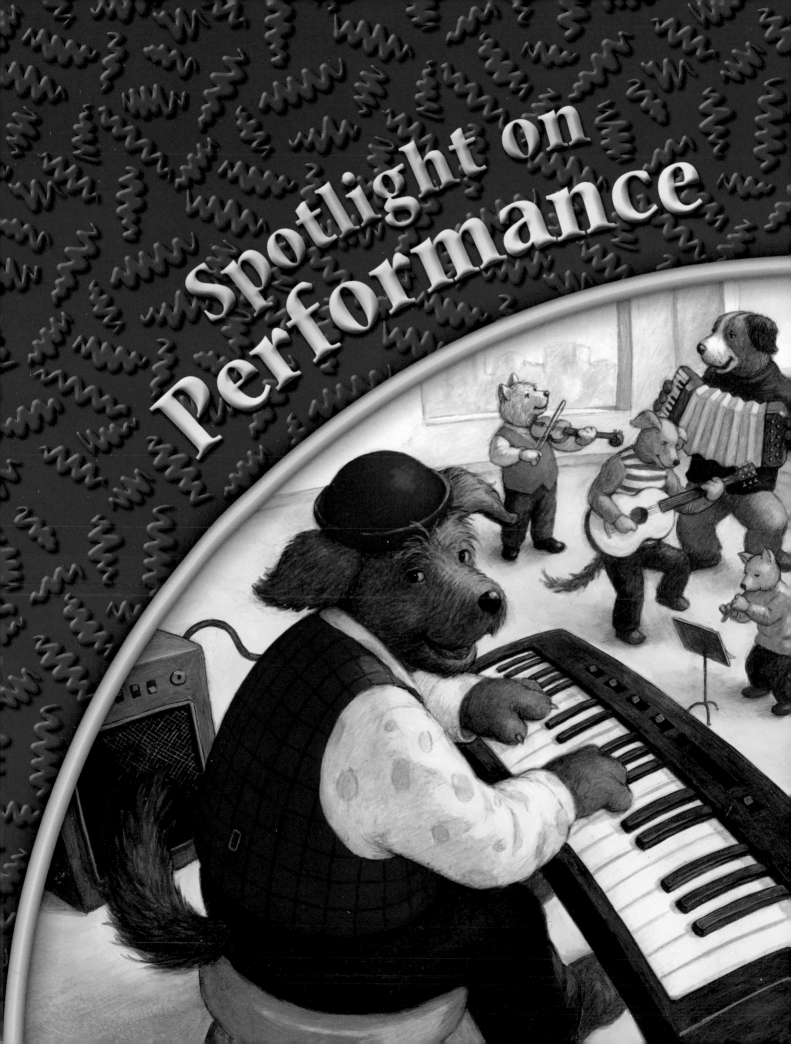

Spotlight on Performance

Spotlight on Performance

Spotlight on Performance

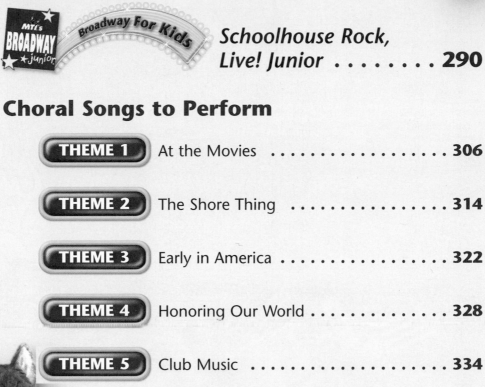

Broadway For Kids

MTI's BROADWAY junior

SCHOOLHOUSE ROCK LIVE! Jr.

Mini musicals specifically designed for classroom study and presentation, featuring scenes and songs from the musical Schoolhouse Rock Live! Junior.

Originally conceived and directed by Scott Ferguson
Book by Scott Ferguson, Kyle Hall, and George Keating
Music and Lyrics by Lynn Ahrens, Bob Dorough, Dave Frishberg, Kathy Mandry, George Newall, Tom Yohe

Musical Numbers

The Preamble

Three Is a Magic Number

Interplanet Janet

Interjections

Schoolhouse Rock Live! Jr.
Harris County Carver Middle School, Hamilton, GA

About Rehearsals

You are about to begin rehearsals for a mini production of *Schoolhouse Rock Live! Jr. Rehearsing* means learning and practicing a show. Below are some words actors use during rehearsals.

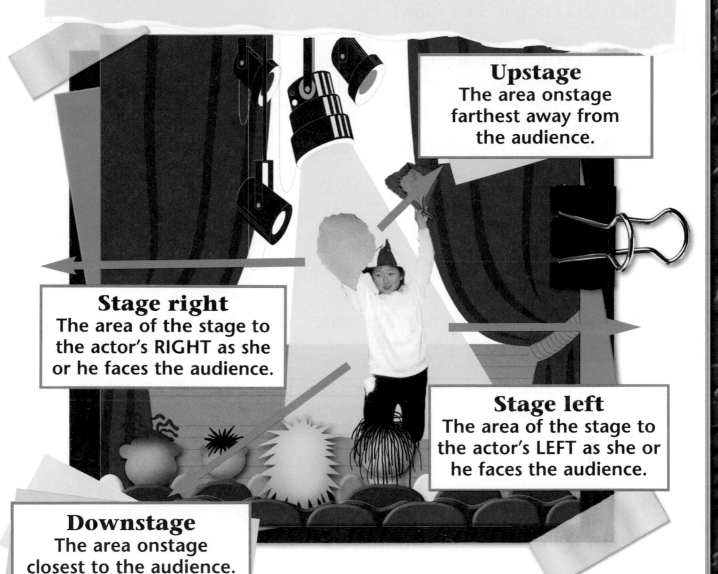

Upstage
The area onstage farthest away from the audience.

Stage right
The area of the stage to the actor's RIGHT as she or he faces the audience.

Stage left
The area of the stage to the actor's LEFT as she or he faces the audience.

Downstage
The area onstage closest to the audience.

About the Script

CHARACTER NAMES are colored **RED**

DIALOGUE is colored **BLUE**

STAGE DIRECTIONS are colored **GREEN**

Scene 1

CHILD 1: Welcome to the theatre!

CHILD 2: Let's put on a show!

CHILD 3: Which one shall we do?

CHILD 4: Let's see, wait. ... *(Pauses, shrugs.)* I don't know.

CHILD 5: We've got lessons to learn!

CHILD 6: We've got time on the clock!

CHILD 7: We're all right here at school. ...

ALL: Why not do SCHOOLHOUSE ROCK!?

(ALL improvise reactions such as "yeah," "that sounds great," etc., as a large scroll is unrolled that reads "SCHOOLHOUSE ROCK LIVE!".)

CHILD 8: Remember those cartoons that you saw on TV about grammar, life, and the great number three?

CHILD 9: Remember "Interplanet Janet"?

CHILD 10: I LOVED that one!

CHILD 11: And singing along with the show was such fun!

CHILD 12: But where should we start?

CHILD 13: We won't keep you guessin'!

ALL: Let's kick things off with a HISTORY lesson!

(Another scroll with "THE PREAMBLE" is unrolled.)

CHILD 14: Presenting the UNITED STATES CONSTITUTION!

The Preamble

CD 13:23

Words and Music by
Lynn Ahrens

All
Hey, do you know a-bout the U. S. A.?

5
Do you know a-bout the gov-ern-ment? Can you tell me 'bout the

8
Con - sti - tu - tion? Hey,

11
learn a-bout the U. S. A.!

Solo
18
In sev-en-teen eight-y-sev-en, I'm told, our found-ing fa-thers

21
did a-gree to write a list of prin-ci-ples for

All
24
keep-in' peo-ple free. The U. S. A. was

27
just start-ing out, a whole brand new coun-try.

30
And so our peo-ple spelled it out, the things that we should

More ➡

293

Scene 2

CHILD 15: That number was great! I learned a lot.

CHILD 16: Speaking of numbers, what else have we got?

CHILD 17: Which song was your favorite?

CHILD 18: My favorite, let's see ... my favorite number's the one about three!

ALL: Yeah, yeah ... let's do it!, I love that one!, (etc.).

(A scroll, reading "THREE IS A MAGIC NUMBER," is unrolled.)

Schoolhouse Rock Live! is one of theater's most creative shows. It is based on the 1970s cartoon series, *Schoolhouse Rock!* The musical uses different styles of music to teach subjects such as grammar, science, math, and American history.

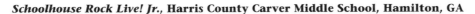

Schoolhouse Rock Live! Jr., Harris County Carver Middle School, Hamilton, GA

Three Is a Magic Number

CD 13:24

Words and Music by
Bob Dorough

One, two, three._____

Trio 1
Three   is a mag - ic num-ber.   Yes, it is,

Trio 2
it's a mag - ic num-ber.   Some-where   in the

veil   of an - cient his - to - ry,___   you get   three

Trio 3
as a mag-ic num-ber.   The past and the pres-ent and the

Trio 4   **Trio 5**
fu - ture,   faith and hope and char - i - ty,   the

heart and the brain and the bo-dy give you three   as a mag-ic

All
num-ber.   A man and a wo - man had_

___ a lit-tle ba - by.   Yes, they did.

Scene 3

CHILD 19: Math is great, now, don't get me wrong ...
But what about science?

CHILD 20: I've got JUST the song ...

(A scroll is unrolled, reading "INTERPLANET JANET" across it.)

CD 13:25

Words and Music by
Lynn Ahrens

They say our so-lar sys-tem is cen-tered a-round the sun.___ Nine plan-ets large and small pa-rad - ing by. But___ some-where out in space there's an-oth-er shin - ing face that you might see some night up in the sky wav - ing "Hi!"___

82 Plu-to, lit-tle Plu-to, is the far-thest plan-et from our sun.___

Coda

86 has - n't seen.___

Scene 4

(The song ends and the CHILDREN begin putting their PROPS away.)

CHILD 21: Is there time for one more?

CHILD 22: If we don't dilly-dally!

CHILD 23: Here's my favorite song, for the big grand finale!

ALL: "INTERJECTIONS!" Yea!

(TWO CHILDREN go to CENTER; one coughing and sneezing, the other playing a doctor.)

Schoolhouse Rock Live! Jr., Gowanda Elementary School, Gowanda, NY

Interjections

Words and Music by Lynn Ahrens

3

All

When Re - gi - nald was home with the flu,_

6 _ uh - huh. The doc - tor knew just what_ to do._ She

9 cured the in - fec - tion with one small in - jec - tion, while

11 Re - gi - nald ut - tered some in - ter - jec - tions.

Solo 1:
Hey! That smarts!

Solo 2:
Ouch! That hurts!

Solo 3:
Yowl! That's not fair, givin' a guy
a shot down there!

4

13

303

Small Group

17 In - ter - jec - tions (Hey!) show ex-cite-ment (Ouch!) or e-mo-tion. (Yow!) They're

19 gen-er-al-ly set a-part from a sen-tence by an ex-cla-ma-tion point,

21 or by a com-ma when the feel-ing's not as strong. So when you're

Small Group

23 hap - py, (Hur-ray!) or sad, (Aw!) or

25 fright-ened, (Eek!) or mad, (Rats!) or ex-

27 ci - ted, (Wow!) or glad, (Hey!) an

29 in - ter - jec - tion starts a sen-tence right!

33 The game was tied at sev-en all,__ uh - huh, when

36 Frank-lin found he had_ the ball._ He made a con-nec - tion in the

39 oth-er di-rec - tion, the crowd start-ed shout-in' out in-ter-jec-tions.

Solo 1:
Aw! You threw
the wrong way!

Solo 2:
Darn! You just
lost the game!

Solo 3:
Hurray! I'm for
the other team!

4

42

Small Group

(Aw!)   (Darn!)   (H'ray!)

46 In - ter - jec - tions show ex - cite - ment or e - mo - tion. They're

48 gen - er - al - ly set a - part from a sen - tence by an ex - cla - ma - tion point,

50 or by a com - ma when the feel - ing's not as strong.

52 In - ter - jec - tions show ex - cite - ment or e - mo - tion. Hal - le -

Solo 1:
Darn! That's the end!

54 lu - jah. Hal - le - lu - jah. Hal - le - lu - jah.___ Yeah!

Take a Bow

At the Movies

Many movies have a special song. Think of a song from your favorite movie. After you saw the movie, what made you remember the song? Here are four great movie songs that you will enjoy singing. You might even know some of them already!

SKILL BUILDER: Eye Contact and Posture

When you are standing on stage at a concert, there are many interesting things to look at. To be a good performer, it is important to keep your eyes on the conductor and stand with good posture.

Follow these steps for good posture when you sing:

- Stand with your feet about shoulder width apart.
- Keep your back straight.
- Place your hands at your sides.

All it takes are the first few notes and the finger snaps. You know right away: It's the creepy tune from *The Addams Family*!

THE ADDAMS FAMILY THEME

from the movie *The Addams Family*

Words and Music by Vic Mizzy

CD 14:1

1. They're creep - y and they're kook - y, mys - te - ri - ous and spook - y, they're
house is a mu - se - um, where peo - ple come to see 'em, they

al - to - geth - er ook - y, the Add - ams Fam - i - ly. 2. Their
real - ly are a scree - um, the Add - ams Fam - i - ly.

Finger snaps
Neat! Sweet! Pe - tite! So

get a witch -'s shawl on, a broom - stick you can crawl on, we're

gon - na pay a call on the Add - ams Fam - i - ly.

The Add - ams Fam - i - ly.

Have you ever been to the circus? There is excitement everywhere you look: scary lions, goofy clowns, flying trapeze artists, and much more. "The Greatest Show on Earth" is a song from a movie that is all about the circus. When you sing this song, you might feel like you are sitting in the audience!

The Greatest Show on Earth

from the movie *The Greatest Show on Earth*

CD 14:4

Music by Victor Young
Words by Ned Washington

1. Come to the cir - cus and laugh your cares a -
men - dous, stu - pen - dous as cir - cus - es should

way. Come to the cir - cus! See the cir - cus!
be! The Ben - gal ti - ger and the li - on,

If we're not ve - ry care - ful life can o - ver - work us.
the tra - peze art - ist does a leap that's death de - fy - ing.

Come see the clowns who play their part, and wear a
A land of mirth, your mon - ey's

smile though they hide a bro - ken heart._____ 2. Tre -

308

CONCEPT
MELODY
SKILLS
SING

The Muppet Movie tells the story of how the Muppets became famous. In the beginning of the movie, Kermit the Frog sings this song about a rainbow. Rainbows mean different things for different people. What do you think of when you see a rainbow in the sky?

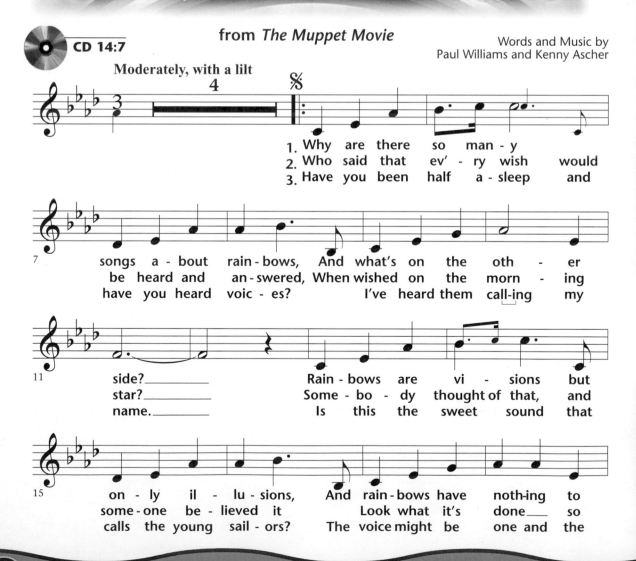

The Rainbow Connection

from *The Muppet Movie*

CD 14:7

Words and Music by
Paul Williams and Kenny Ascher

Moderately, with a lilt

1. Why are there so man - y
2. Who said that ev' - ry wish would
3. Have you been half a - sleep and

songs a - bout rain - bows, And what's on the oth - er
be heard and an - swered, When wished on the morn - ing
have you heard voic - es? I've heard them call - ing my

side?_____ Rain - bows are vi - sions but
star?_____ Some - bo - dy thought of that, and
name._____ Is this the sweet sound that

on - ly il - lu - sions, And rain - bows have noth - ing to
some - one be - lieved it Look what it's done___ so
calls the young sail - ors? The voice might be one and the

CONCEPT
MELODY
SKILLS
SING

Fairy tales have happy endings when the characters believe in themselves and their dreams. In the movie *Shrek*, Shrek doesn't get upset by things other people think about him. His dreams come true because he believes in himself.

I'm a Believer

CD 14:10

from the movie *Shrek*

Words and Music by Neil Diamond

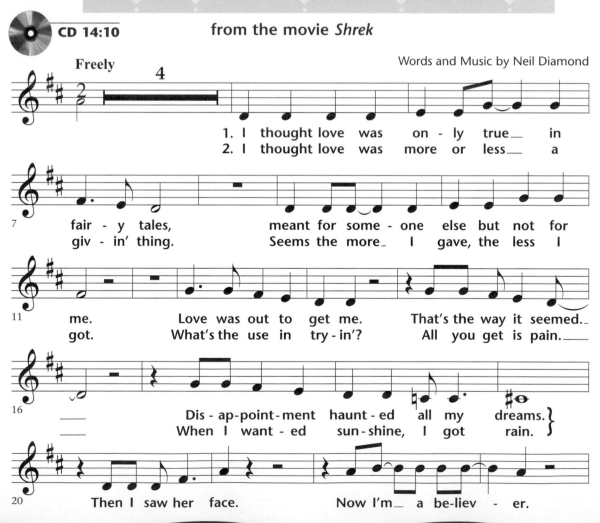

Freely

1. I thought love was on-ly true in fair-y tales, meant for some-one else but not for me. Love was out to get me. That's the way it seemed.___ Dis-ap-point-ment haunt-ed all my dreams. Then I saw her face. Now I'm___ a be-liev-er.

2. I thought love was more or less___ a giv-in' thing. Seems the more___ I gave, the less I got. What's the use in try-in'? All you get is pain.___ When I want-ed sun-shine, I got rain.

Not a trace of doubt in my mind.

I'm in love. I'm a be-liev - er. I could-n't leave

1. her if I tried. 2. tried. Then I saw her

Sing 3 times

face. Now I'm a be-liev - er.

LISTENING CD 14:13

My Favorite Things from *The Sound of Music*

by Richard Rodgers and Oscar Hammerstein II

Listen to "My Favorite Things" from the original production of *The Sound of Music.* The scene below is from the movie starring Julie Andrews. It was made six years after the musical opened on the Broadway stage.

Scene from *The Sound of Music*

The Shore Thing

Ahoy there, matey! Visiting the ocean shore can be exciting. You can ride the waves, relax in the sunshine, or take a boat trip to go fishing. You may discover many amazing sea creatures, too. When you sing the next few songs, imagine you are at the shore. Don't forget your swim suit!

VOICE BUILDER: Breathing

Good singers make sure they control their breathing. You can begin to learn to control your breathing with these exercises:

- Imagine you are holding a milkshake as large as the room. Drink the air through a giant straw.

- As you breathe in, imagine that your ribs grow larger.

Practice your breath control by singing this exercise.

ah____   ah____   ah____

💿 **CD 14:14**

Steadily

American Folk Song

1. When o'er the si-lent seas a-lone, for days and nights we've
sails a-back we near-er come; kind words are said of

8 cheer - less gone, Oh! they who've felt it know how sweet some
friends and home; but soon, too soon we part in pain to

to Coda

11 sun - ny morn__ a sail to meet, some sun - ny morn a sail to meet!
sail the si - lent seas a - gain, to

Refrain

15 Spark - ling on deck is ev' - ry eye: Ship a - hoy! ship a - hoy! our

18 joy - ful cry when an - sw'ring back we faint - ly hear: Ship a -

D.S. al Coda

21 hoy! ship a - hoy! What cheer! what cheer! 2. Now__

Coda

24 sail the si - lent seas a - gain.

CONCEPT
MELODY
SKILLS
SING

This silly song comes from the province of Newfoundland, which is in Canada. A herring is a type of fish that lives in the Atlantic and Pacific Oceans. Many people in Newfoundland like herrings so much, they sing a song about them.

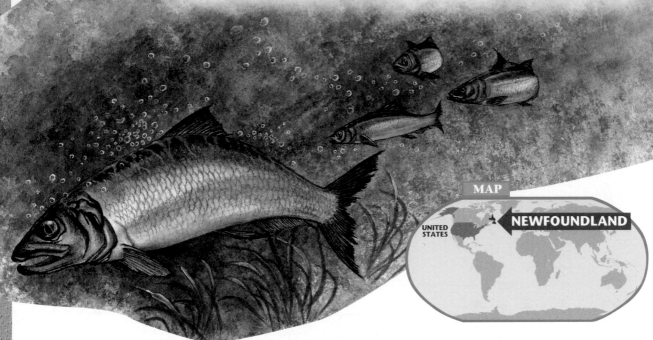

MAP

UNITED STATES   NEWFOUNDLAND

THE HERRING

CD 14:17

Folk Song from Newfoundland, Canada

With gusto

1. O what will we do with the old her-rings' heads? We'll get some loaves and sell them for bread. O
2. O what will we do with the old her-rings' fins? We'll get some nee-dles and sell them for pins. O O
3. O what will we do with the old her-rings' backs? We'll get a boy and we'll call him Jack. O O
4. O what will we do with the old her-ring's scales? We'll get some can-vas and sew it for sails. O O

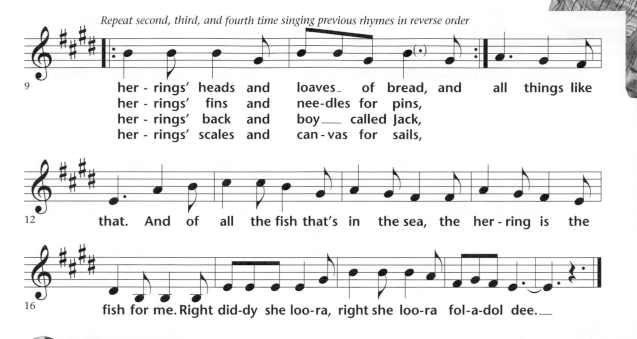

Repeat second, third, and fourth time singing previous rhymes in reverse order

9
her - rings' heads and loaves__ of bread, and all things like
her - rings' fins and nee-dles for pins,
her - rings' back and boy__ called Jack,
her - rings' scales and can - vas for sails,

12
that. And of all the fish that's in the sea, the her - ring is the

16
fish for me. Right did-dy she loo-ra, right she loo-ra fol-a-dol dee.__

LISTENING CD 14:20

Two in a Boat American Folk Song

Children who grow up on the shore often sing songs about the water. "Two in a Boat" is a fun song that children sing in different parts of the United States.

Listen to the Revels Children's Chorus perform this song. They pronounce the words very clearly. This helps the audience understand the meaning of the song.

Revels Children's Chorus members sing and dance at Harvard University, Cambridge, Massachusetts.

CONCEPT
EXPRESSION
SKILLS
SING

All over the world, people love the sound of the sea. "El arroyo que murmura" is a folk song from Cuba. It describes the gentle sound of a brook as it winds its way to the sea. How do the melody and rhythm of the song make you feel?

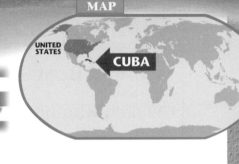

MAP

UNITED STATES → CUBA

El arroyo que murmura

The Murmuring Brook

CD 14:21

Folk Song from Cuba
English Words by Ruth De Cesare

Moderately

Spanish: El a - rro - yo que mur - mu - ra y que la lu - na re -
Pronunciation: el a ɾo yo ke muɾ mu ɾa i ke la lu na ɾe -
English: Mur - mur - ing brook is so love - ly as it's re - flect - ed in

8
tra - ta, cuan - do sus ra - yos de pla - ta a - tra - vie - san la_es - pe -
tra ta kwan do sus ɾa yos ðe pla ta a tra βye san les pe -
moon - beams. Sil - ver rays cross - ing the dark - ness make it ap - pear as a

12
su - ra. El sin - son - te de voz pu - ra
su ɾa el sin son te ðe βos pu ɾa
sweet dream. Soon the mock - ing - bird's sing - song will

17 que_a - le - gra_el mon - te y_el lla - no, la pal - ma de
kea   le   gɾel mon te iel   ya no   la pal ma ðe
fill woods and plain with its sing - ing; and the green palm

20 ver - de gua - no que_el son de vien - to se me - ce
ßeɾ   ðe gwa no kel son de ßyen to se me se
wav - ing; and the wind as it blows oh so soft - ly

D.C. al Fine

23 y que sus pi - rar pa - re - ce, e - se_es el pun - to cu - ba - no
i   ke sus pi ɾaɾ pa   ɾe se e ses el pun to ku ßa no
seems to sigh now as it moves, the soul of Cu - ba in its whis-p'ring.

CONCEPT
FORM
SKILLS
SING

Wouldn't it be great to travel underwater in your very own submarine? You could take your friends to explore underwater caverns and chase gigantic octopuses. The famous pop group the Beatles thought this would be neat, too. They wrote about an imaginary trip in the song "Yellow Submarine."

YELLOW SUBMARINE

CD 14:25

Words and Music by
John Lennon and Paul McCartney

1. In the town____ where I was born lived a man____ who sailed the sea, and he told____ us of his life in the land____ of sub-ma-rines. 2. So we

sailed____ up to the sun till we found____ the sea of green, and we lived____ be-neath the waves in our yel-low____ sub-ma-rine.

Early in America

Life in the early days of the United States was very different from today. In these early times, many different groups of people helped build our country. Native Americans, African Americans, Europeans, and many other groups all shared parts of their culture.

The Minutemen were a group of American soldiers during the Revolutionary War. They named themselves the Minutemen because they said they could be ready for anything in a minute. Here is a song about these soldiers. Guess how long it takes to sing it!

CD 14:28

Music by Mary Lynn Lightfoot
Words by Lee Brandon

Spirited

mf

Min-ute-man! Min-ute-man! Read-y in on-ly a

min-ute! 1. In the time it takes to sing this song, the Min-ute-man so
2. time it takes to sing this song, the Min-ute-man with

brave and strong; put a-side his work or play and came a-run-ning
mus-ket long; took the green at Lex-ing-ton and faced the Red-coats

night or day, in the time it takes to sing this song! 2. In the
in the sun, in the time it takes to sing this

21 song! 3. In the time it takes to sing this song, the

25 Con-cord Min-ute-man so strong; faced the Brit-ish flag un-furled; a

29 shot was heard a-round the world in the time it takes to sing this

grad. accel. to end

33 song! 4. In the time it takes to sing this song, the Min-ute-man so

38 brave and strong; put a-side his work or play and came a-run-ning

f

42 night or day,_____ in the time it takes to sing this song!

VOICE BUILDER: Singing Phrases

To be a good singer, it is important to sing long phrases well. Practice these steps while you sing the exercise below:

- Imagine your mouth is shaped like a tall tree. Keep the corners of your mouth from spreading outward.
- Change smoothly from one note to the next.
- Use good breath control.

ah_____
oh_____

Choral Songs to Perform (323)

African Americans have played an important part in the history of the United States. "Open the Window, Noah" is an African American **spiritual**. This is one style that African Americans created in the 1800s.

Open the Window, Noah

CD 15:1

African American Spiritual

O-pen the win-dow, No - ah, O-pen the win-dow,

No - ah, O - pen the win - dow, No - ah,

1., 2. | Last time

O - pen the win-dow, Let the dove come in. dove come in.

Solo

1. The lit - tle dove flew in the win - dow and mourned,
2. The lit - tle dove brought back the ol - ive leaf,

All

O - pen the win - dow, Let the dove come in.

Solo

The lit - tle dove flew in the win - dow and mourned,
The lit - tle dove brought back the ol - ive leaf,

All

D.S. (last time al Fine)

O - pen the win - dow, Let the dove come in.

CONCEPT
MELODY
SKILLS
SING

In early American times, Native American people lived all over North America. The "Buffalo Dance Entrance Song" is sung by a group of Native Americans called the Hopi who live in Arizona. This song begins a Hopi ceremony. It welcomes dancers to the center of the village.

Buffalo Dance Entrance Song

CD 15:4

Hopi Social Dance Song
As sung by Tsung-ayeh (Wil Numkena)

ya   ya   he   ha - a   we   yo - o   ha   ya

2   ya   ya   we   ha - a   we   yo - o   ha   ya   he

3   ya   he   ha - a   we   ya   e   ya   yo - o_____   we

4   ya   e   ha - a   we   ya - a   he - e   na

*Fourth time end
(Fine)*

5   he - e   yo   ha   he   yo   we   ha__   hi   ye   ne - e   ya

CONCEPT
MELODY
SKILLS
SING

"In Good Old Colony Times" is a silly American folk song about three troublemakers. They lived in the time before the United States became independent. When you sing this song, you will discover the trouble these three get themselves into.

In Good Old Colony Times

CD 15:8

American Folk Song
Words adapted by Phyllis Kaplan

1. In__ good old col-on-y times when__ we__ lived un-der the king, Three__ rogu-ish chaps fell in-to mis-haps, be-cause they could not sing,
2. O the first he was__ a mil-ler and the sec-ond he was__ a wea-ver, And the third he was a tail-or man, Three rogu-ish chaps to-ge-ther.
3. O the mil-ler, he__ stole corn; and the wea-ver, he__ stole yarn, And the tai-lor man ran right__ a-way with the broad-cloth un-der his arm.
4. The__ mil-ler was drowned in the dam, and the wea-ver got hung__ in his yarn, And the tai-lor tripped as he ran__ a-way with the broad-cloth un-der his arm.

Be-cause they could not sing, Be-cause they could not sing, Three__ rogu-ish chaps fell in-to mis-haps, be-cause they could not sing.

Many African Americans settled on islands off the coast of Georgia, called the Georgia Sea Islands. "Uncle Jessie" is a song that children from the Georgia Sea Islands sing.

Uncle Jessie

CD 15:11

Georgia Sea Islands Folk Song

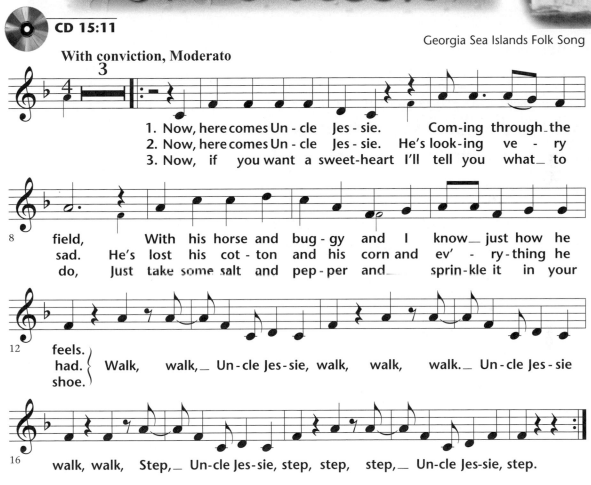

With conviction, Moderato

1. Now, here comes Un - cle Jes - sie. Com-ing through the
2. Now, here comes Un - cle Jes - sie. He's look-ing ve - ry
3. Now, if you want a sweet-heart I'll tell you what to

field, With his horse and bug - gy and I know just how he
sad. He's lost his cot - ton and his corn and ev' - ry - thing he
do, Just take some salt and pep - per and sprin-kle it in your

feels.
had. { Walk, walk, Un - cle Jes - sie, walk, walk, walk. Un - cle Jes - sie
shoe. }

walk, walk, Step, Un-cle Jes-sie, step, step, step, Un-cle Jes-sie, step.

LISTENING CD 15:14

Uncle Jessie African American Folk Song

Listen to Janice Turner sing "Uncle Jessie." She learned this song on the playground when she was young. How would you describe her voice?

Honoring Our World

We share the world with many different people, animals, and plants. If we want our planet to stay healthy, we need to respect all these living things. It is important for us to leave the world healthy for people in the future. Here are some songs that will help us remember to take care of Earth.

SKILL BUILDER: How Did You Do?

When you finish practicing or performing, it is always good to take a minute to think about how you sang a piece. You can think about your own performance. You can also think about your choir's performance. Thinking and talking about your performance helps you find ways you can improve.

Here are some questions you can ask yourself after you sing:
- Was this a good performance? Why or why not?
- How could I sing this song better?
- How could my choir sing this song better?
- What parts of this song are hard for me to sing?
- Did I look at the conductor during the entire song?

CD 15:15

OH MAMA BAKUDALA

Xhosa Folk Song

Xhosa: **Oh   ma-ma ba-ku-da-la   ba-be   than - da-za.**
Pronunciation: o   ma ma ba ku da la   ba be   tan   da za

Ba - be   than - da - za,   ba - be   than - da - za.
ba be   tan   da za   ba be   tan   da za

CONCEPT
RHYTHM
SKILLS
SING

"I Walk in Beauty" was written by a Native American woman named Arlene Nofchissey Williams who is from the Navajo tribe. Many Native Americans now perform versions of her song in their own traditional languages. For the Navajo people, beauty means living in harmony with the world.

I WALK IN BEAUTY

CD15:19

Words and Music by
Arlene Nofchissey Williams

Heh neh - yah - nah, heh yah heh yah - nah, heh neh - yah - nah,

heh yah hee yoh,___ heh yah hee yoh.___ ___ heh yah hee yoh.___ I

yearn for Beau - ty, yes I do, yes I do; I learn of___ Beau - ty,

yes I do, you know I do; I beam with Beau - ty, just for you and on - ly you, heh

yah,___ heh yah hee yoh. Heh neh - yah - nah, heh yah heh yah - nah,

heh neh - yah - nah, heh yah hee yoh,___ heh yah hee yoh.

CONCEPT
FORM
SKILLS
SING

Raffi is a songwriter from Canada. He has written songs for children for many years. Many of his songs have a message that tells people to take good care of our world. After you learn to sing "Evergreen, Everblue," share its message with your friends and family.

Evergreen, Everblue

CD 15:23

Words and Music by Raffi

Ev-er-green, ev - er - blue, As it was in the be-gin-

- ning, we've got to see it through. Ev-er-green,

ev - er - blue, At this point in time, it's up to me,

1., 2., 3.   4.   *Fine*

it's up to you.   3. So come

1. Am - a - zon   is call-ing,   With
2. O - cean's wave   is rumbling,   Help this plan-et Earth!   With
(3.) all   u - nit - ed   na-tions,   With

voic - es from the jun - gle,
voic - es from the sea - way,   Help this plan-et Earth!
Chil-dren of one moth - er,   With

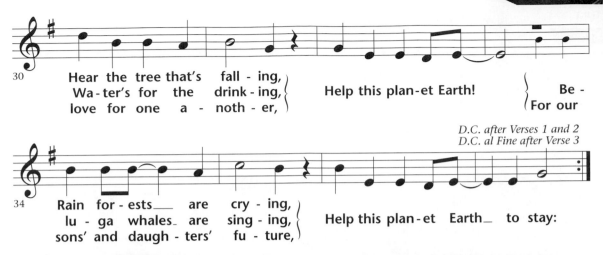

30 Hear the tree that's fall - ing,
    Wa - ter's for the drink - ing,   } Help this plan-et Earth!   { Be -
    love for one a - noth - er,   For our

D.C. after Verses 1 and 2
D.C. al Fine after Verse 3

34 Rain for - ests__ are cry - ing,
    lu - ga whales_ are sing - ing,   } Help this plan-et Earth_ to stay:
    sons' and daugh - ters' fu - ture,

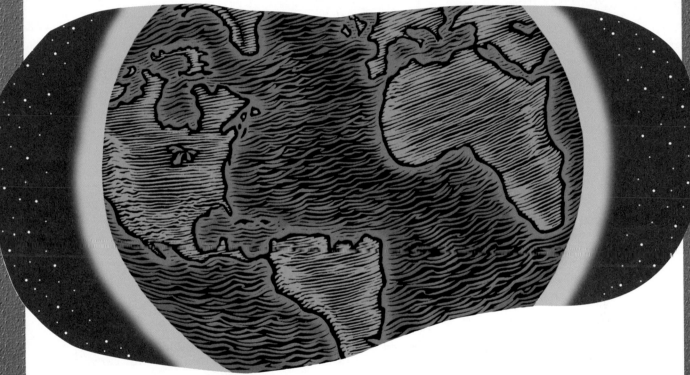

 **LISTENING** CD 15:26

Have to Have a Habitat by Bill Oliver

Listen to Bill Oliver sing "Have to Have a Habitat." Habitats are places where people and animals live, like forests, oceans, or fields. Bill is also known as "Mr. Habitat." Everywhere he goes he sings a message to respect the planet.

Choral Songs to Perform

CONCEPT
RHYTHM
SKILLS
SING

There is one easy way for everyone to help keep our world healthy and clean: Recycle! Glass, newspapers, plastic bottles, and cans are only some of the things we can recycle. "Recycle Rap" will get your head nodding to the beat and make you want to clean up the trash at your feet.

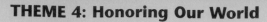

Recycle Rap

CD 15:27

Words and Music by Teresa Jennings

Lis-ten up, friends, you've got to help with our plan. Or we could

all be liv-in' in a gar-bage can. Just save your glass and your tin cans, a-

lu-mi-num, too. Re-cy-cling is the thing to do!

Re-cy-cle, re-cy-cle, re-cy-cle, now! There's noth-in' to it if you

just know how. So tell your bro-ther and your sis-ter and your tea-cher, too:

Club Music

Have you ever wanted to join a club? The four songs in this theme are about a special music club. All the club members love to sing, and everyone is welcome to share their songs. The excitement begins as soon as you open the door to the clubhouse. Sing "Consider Yourself" and join the club!

VOICE BUILDER: Singing Vowels

Vowels are a very important part of singing. When you sing vowels, make your mouth into the shape of an oval. Keep your jaw loose and relaxed, too. Your voice will then mix well with other people's voices.

The five basic vowel sounds are: *oo, oh, ee, eh, ah.* Use these sounds to sing the exercise below:

Repeat at higher pitch levels

oo___   oo___   oo___
oh___   oh___   oh___
ee___   ee___   ee___
eh___   eh___   eh___
ah___   ah___   ah___

 LISTENING CD 15:30

Consider Yourself from *Oliver!* by Lionel Bart

Listen to the cast from the movie *Oliver!* sing "Consider Yourself." The characters in *Oliver!* are from London, England. Do they sing the words differently than you? How are they different?

Consider Yourself

CD 16:1   from the musical *Oliver!*

Words and Music by Lionel Bart

1. Con - sid-er your-self___ at home,   Con-sid-er your-self___
   sid-er your-self___ well in: Con-sid-er your-self___

___ one of the fam - i - ly   We've tak-en to you___ so strong.
___ part of the fur - ni-ture.   There is - n't a   lot___ to spare;

It's clear   we're   go-ing to   get a - long! 2.Con -
Who cares?   What - ev - er we've got we share!

Con - sid - er your-self___ our mate,   We don't want to have___

___ no fuss   For   af - ter some con - sid - er - a - tion,

1.
we can state: Con - sid-er your-self__ one of us.   2. Con -

2.
sid-er your - self_____   one of us.____

Choral Songs to Perform   335

CONCEPT
MELODY
SKILLS
SING

The music club sings many different music styles. They sing along with pop songs on the radio and the golden oldies, too. But one style they all love is dance songs. You will feel the swinging beat as you sing this song. It will make you want to "Flip, Flop and Fly!"

Flip, Flop and Fly

CD 16:4

from the movie *Chicken Run*

Words and Music by
Charles E. Calhoun and Lou Willie Turner

When I get the blues gon-na

get me a rock-in' chair.__ When I get the blues gon-na

get me a rock-in' chair.__ When the

blues o-ver-take me, gon-na rock right a-way from here.__

Flip, flop, fly,__ I'll see you by and by.__

CONCEPT
HARMONY
SKILLS
SING

One day the kids arrive at the clubhouse and something has eaten all the snacks. They discover big paw prints on the ground outside the door. It looks like a bear has broken in! Where did the bear go? Sing this song and imagine you have joined their search.

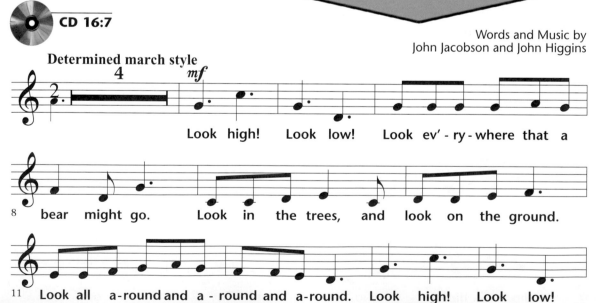

Look High, Look Low

CD 16:7

Words and Music by
John Jacobson and John Higgins

Determined march style

mf

Look high! Look low! Look ev'-ry-where that a
bear might go. Look in the trees, and look on the ground.
Look all a-round and a-round and a-round. Look high! Look low!

Look high! Look low! Look ev' - ry-where that a

37 Look all a - round and a - round and a - round. Look high!

bear might go. Look o - ver there, look to and fro.

40 Look low! Look ev' - ry - where that a bear might go.

ff

Where in the world did she go? Where in the world did she go?

43 Look o - ver there, look to and fro. Where in the world did she go?

CONCEPT
HARMONY
SKILLS
SING

Every year, the kids in the club
take a field trip. Some of the club
members want to visit the big city
and see tall skyscrapers. Other members
think the club should go hiking in the mountains.
There is only one way to settle this argument: Sing!

with "I Love the Mountains"

CD 16:10

1st time: sing Song #1
2nd time: sing Song #2
3rd time: sing both melodies together

Words and Music by
John Jacobson
and Alan Billingsley

Choral Songs to Perform   341

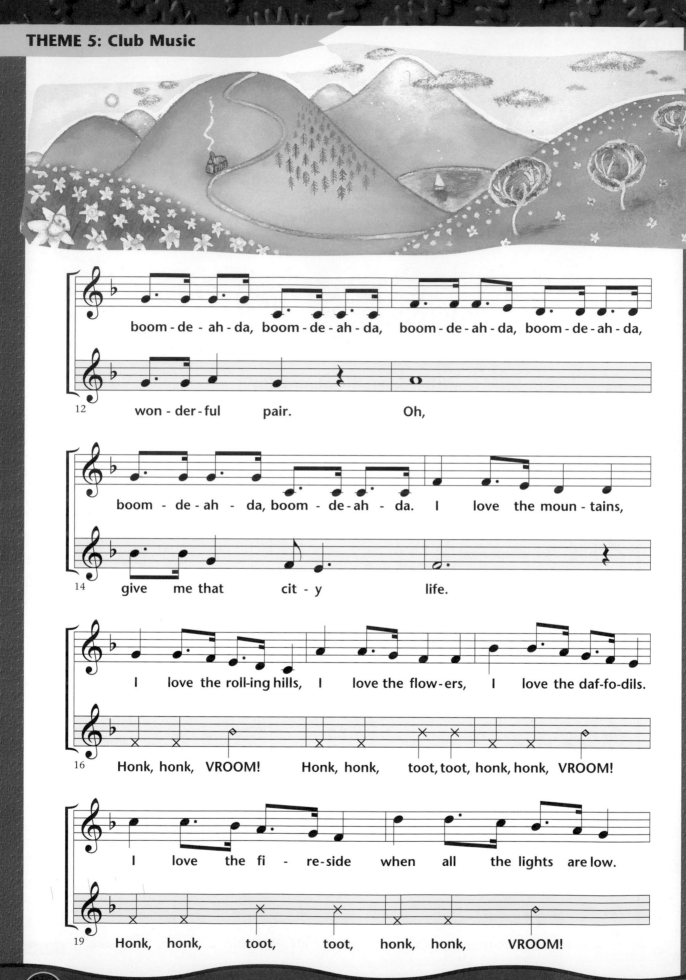

CONCEPT
RHYTHM
SKILLS
PLAY

There Was An Old Lady

—*Dennis Lee*

There was an old lady
    Whose kitchen was bare,
So she woke up the cat
    Saying, "Time for some air!"

She sent him to buy her
    A can of sardines.
But the cat ambled back
    With a bagful of beans.

She sent him to buy her
    A packet of cheese
But the cat reappeared
    With a carton of bees.

She sent him to buy her
    A brisket of beef.
But the cat hurried home
    With a red autumn leaf.

She sent him to buy her
  A dish of ice cream.
But the cat skated in
  With a whole hockey team.

She sent him to buy her
  A plate of spaghetti.
But the cat strutted up
  With a bride and confetti.

She sent him to buy her
  A thermos of tea.
But the cat waddled back
  With a dinosaur's knee.

The fridge was soon bulging,
  And so was the shelf.
So she phoned for a hot dog
  And fetched it herself.

Voice

Da da dum, da da dum, da da dum dum dum!

The Gebeta Board

This folk tale comes from Ethiopia, a country in Africa. Learn these music patterns before you read the story.

Play them when you see their symbol in the story.

Once there was a small boy who tended his family's cattle.  He would watch them all day grazing on the land. He had nothing to do but count them over and over again.

One day his father carved a beautiful gebeta game board for him from the hard, smooth wood of an olive tree. The boy hugged the game in his arms. He now would have games to play while he tended the cattle.

The next day the boy proudly carried the gebeta board with him to the grazing land. He saw four poor men trying to make a fire to cook their food.

"Come, boy," they called to him. "We are hungry and must cook this meat. Where can we find wood?"

"Take this game board to cook your meal. It will be all the wood you need," said the boy. He handed them the game and sadly walked away.

"Wait! Take this shovel in exchange for your kindness," said the four men.  The boy took the shovel and continued to follow the cattle.

He soon saw a man digging a well with his hands.

"Oh, I shall never find water. And my family is so thirsty," cried the man.

"Here, take my shovel," said the boy. "It will help you reach water quickly."

"Wait! Please take this bag of grain in exchange," called the man. The boy thanked him, took the bag of grain, and continued on. After a while he saw a mother and her hungry child.

"Oh, where shall we find food. My child is starving," cried the woman.

"Take my bag of grain. It shall keep your family fed for many days," said the boy.

As he walked away the woman cried to him, "We have nothing to give you but this stick of wood. Please take it."

The boy thanked her and began to lead the cattle back home. When he reached the village an old woman cried, "Please may I have your stick of wood? My old husband feels so cold. I must start a fire for him!"

"Of, course," said the boy. He handed her the wood and began to head home.

"Wait!" said the old woman. "Our eyes have grown bad and we can no longer play games. Take our gebeta board in exchange for your kindness." The boy thanked her, led the cattle home and walked in his front door with the board.

"Anything exciting happen today, son?" asked the father.

"Nothing special," said the boy. He sat down with his father on the floor for a long night of games on his gebeta board.

Isabela and the Troll

This wonderful folk tale comes from Spain. Learn these music patterns before you read the story.

Play them when you see their symbol in the story.

Once upon a time in Spain, there lived an nine-year-old girl with a lovely voice named Isabela.

She lived in a village of white houses. Her favorite thing in the whole world was a coral ring her mother had given her.

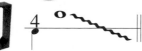

One morning Isabela went to the fountain very early. As she walked, she sang her favorite song. When she got there, she took off her coral ring and placed it on the ground. Suddenly, she heard terrible laughter behind her. *Ha, ha, ha!*

Ha, ha, ha!

She turned around to see what it was. Standing behind her was an ugly, gray troll. He was grinning horribly at her.  She screamed and tried to run, but he threw a brown sack over her and tossed her over his shoulder. Then he picked up the ring and put it in his pocket.

"My fortune is now made!" giggled the troll. The troll took his sack to the main plaza in the village.

"Here I have a singing sack. Magic's in it, too. Place some money in my hat and it will sing for you." Many people gathered and tossed coins in the hat.

The troll shook the sack and whispered to the girl, "Sing, sing, sing or I'll keep your little ring." Isabela was afraid, so she began to sing. The people were amazed and threw more coins into the hat.

That night he carried the sack to a house in the village and knocked on the door. Isabela's mother answered. The troll yelled, "Here I have a singing sack. Magic's in it, too. Place some money in my hat and it will sing for you."

Isabela's mother missed her daughter. She placed some coins in the hat to cheer herself up. Isabela began to sing her song, more sadly than before.

"That is my Isabela's voice," thought her mother. "If I call out he will run away. I must think of something."

At the end of the song, Isabela's mother invited the troll in for dinner. After a huge meal, the troll lay his head down on the kitchen table and fell fast asleep.

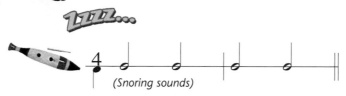
(Snoring sounds)

Isabela's mother quickly untied the sack and Isabela jumped out into her mother's arms. They grabbed their meanest goat and shoved him into the sack. Then Isabela carefully searched the troll's pockets until she found her coral ring.

In the morning, the troll headed to the next house. When he got there, he whispered, "Sing, sing, sing or I'll keep your little ring," but nothing happened. He pinched the sack but all he heard was "maaaa."

"I'll teach you!" the troll screamed at the sack. He tore it open and to his surprise an angry goat jumped out! The goat was so mad he chased the troll out of the village and far away. And the ugly troll was never seen again!

Spotlight on
Celebrations

Spotlight on Celebrations

Songs for Our Country

Singing songs about pride in our country brings Americans together. Katharine Lee Bates wrote "America, the Beautiful" after a trip to Pike's Peak in Colorado.

America, the Beautiful

CD 16:13

Music by Samuel Ward
Words by Katharine Lee Bates

1. O beau-ti-ful for spa-cious skies, For am-ber waves of grain.
2. O beau-ti-ful for he-roes proved In lib-er-at-ing strife,
3. O beau-ti-ful for pa-triot dream That sees be-yond the years,

For pur-ple moun-tain maj-es-ties A-bove the fruit-ed plain.
Who more than self their coun-try loved, And mer-cy more than life.
Thine al-a-bas-ter cit-ies gleam, Un-dim'd by hu-man tears.

A-mer-i-ca! A-mer-i-ca! God shed His grace on thee,

And crown thy good with broth-er-hood, From sea to shin-ing sea.

You're a Grand Old Flag

Words and Music by George M. Cohan

CD 16:16

You're a grand old flag, you're a high - fly - ing flag;

And for - ev - er in peace may you wave;

You're the em - blem of the land I love,

The home of the free and the brave.

Ev' - ry heart beats true un - der red, white, and blue,

Where there's nev - er a boast or brag;

But should auld ac - quaint - ance be for - got,

Keep your eye on the grand old flag.

355

CONCEPT
RHYTHM
SKILLS
SING

Americans like to sing about their country, their people, and their flag.

☆This Is America☆

CD 16:19

Words and Music by Teresa Jennings

This is A - mer - i - ca. A - mer - i - ca.

This is A - mer - i - ca. A - mer - i - ca.

A land of cour - age, faith, and hon - or.

A land of true e - qual - i - ty.

A land of hope and pride. A___ land of u - ni - ty.

(2nd time) D.S. al Fine
Fine

A___ land of lib - er - ty.

Yankee Doodle Boy

CD 16:22

Words and Music by George M. Cohan

I'm a Yan-kee Doo-dle Dan - dy,

A Yan - kee Doo - dle, do or die;

A real live neph-ew of my Un - cle Sam,

Born on the Fourth of Ju - ly.

I've got a Yan-kee Doo-dle sweet - heart,

She's my Yan-kee Doo-dle joy.

Yan-kee Doo-dle came to Lon-don, just to ride the po - nies,

I am a Yan-kee Doo-dle boy.

Hispanic Heritage Month

September 15 to October 15 is Hispanic Heritage Month in the United States. During this time people celebrate the ways Hispanics have worked to help make our country great. People from many backgrounds gather to have fun and learn about Hispanic art, food, culture, and music.

"Pajarillo barranqueño," a song from Mexico, is a favorite at Mexican get-togethers!

Pajarillo barranqueño

Little Bird

CD 16:25

MAP

UNITED STATES

MEXICO

Mexican Folk Song
English Words by Linda Worsley

Spanish: 1. Pa - ja - ri - llo, pa - ja - ri - llo, _____ pa - ja -
Pronunciation: pa xa ɾi yo pa xa ɾi yo pa xa

English: 1. Lit - tle bird, _____ pa - ja - ri - llo, _____ Lit - tle
2. Who is this _____ pa - ja - ri - llo, _____ in the

ri - llo ba - rran - que - ño, _____ ¡qué bo - ni - tos o - jos
ɾi yo βa ɾan ke nyo ke βo ni tos o xos
bird _____ there on the hill - side, _____ Oh, what pret - ty eyes you
tree _____ there sweet - ly sing - ing? _____ Go and tell her not to

tie - nes lás - ti - ma que ten - gan due - ño!
tye nes las ti ma ke ten gan dwe nyo
have, and what a shame you have a mas - ter. _____
sing, be - cause her song has left me weep - ing. _____

Los Lobos live in Los Angeles, California.

Flor de huevo by Los Lobos

The members of Los Lobos have performed together since they were high school friends in Los Angeles, California. They have mixed traditional Mexican music with other styles to come up with their own sound. One member of Los Lobos says that they "like bringing music together to bring people together."

Listen to the first composition of Los Lobos.

Children in Mexico like to say this rhyme to learn to count. Some of the words don't mean anything at all. They are just fun to say!

**Una de dola,
de tela canela,
zumabaca la vaca,
de bire birón.
cuéntalas bien
que las once son:
uno, dos, tres, cuatro,
cinco, seis, siete, ocho,
nueve diez, once.**

Sukkot is a harvest festival that lasts for seven days. Jewish people build a small shelter called a *sukkah* and decorate it with autumn fruits and vegetables.

CHAG ASIF
Harvest Time

CD 17:1

Words and Music by S. Levy Tannai
English Version by L. Koulish

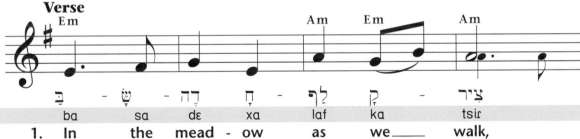

Refrain

Em	Bm	Em	D		Em

Hebrew: חַג אָ - סִיף, חַג אָ - סִיף כֵּן יִר - בֶּה - דֵיר וּ - כֵן יוֹ - סִיף.
Pronunciation: xag a sif xag a sif ken yir be və xen yo sif
English: **Har-vest time, har-vest time. Gath-er in the gold-en wheat.**

Verse

Em		Am	Em	Am

בָּ - שָׂ - דֶה - חָ - לֶף קָ - צִיר
ba sa dε xa laf ka tsir

1. In the mead - ow as we____ walk,
2. Draw the wa - ter from the____ well,
3. Thanks for days that come and____ go, The

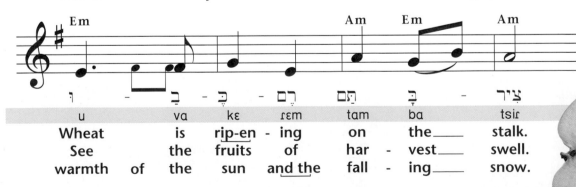

Em		Am	Em	Am

וּ - בַ - כֶּ - רֶם תָּם בַּ - צִיר
u va kε rεm tam ba tsir

Wheat is rip-en - ing on the____ stalk.
See the fruits of har - vest swell.
warmth of the sun and the fall - ing____ snow.

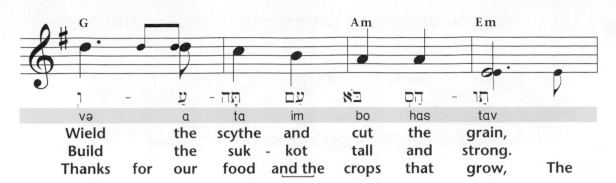
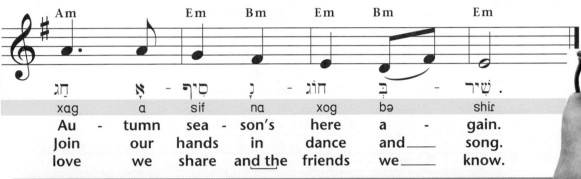

Eating meals in a *sukkah* reminds people of the huts that their ancestors built during harvest time.

Will you be meeting some spooky friends on Halloween night? Watch out, or one of them just might say BOO!

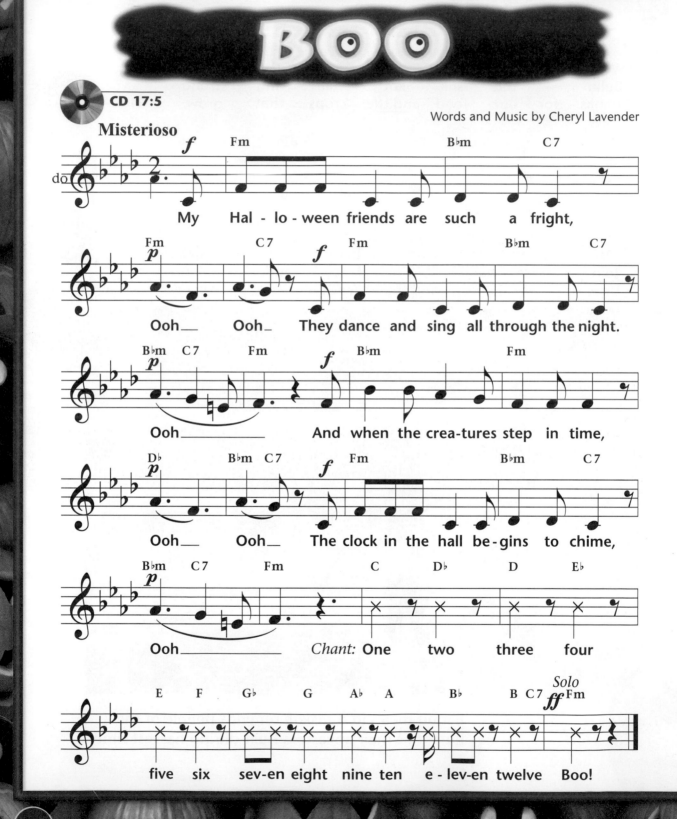

CD 17:5

Words and Music by Cheryl Lavender

Misterioso

My Hal-lo-ween friends are such a fright,

Ooh__ Ooh__ They dance and sing all through the night.

Ooh_____ And when the crea-tures step in time,

Ooh__ Ooh__ The clock in the hall be-gins to chime,

Ooh_____ *Chant:* **One two three four**

five six sev-en eight nine ten e-lev-en twelve Boo!

Danse Macabre by Camille Saint-Saëns

The French composer Camille Saint-Saëns began his
musical career when he was a child. By the time he was
22, he was a famous composer. "Danse Macabre" is one
of his most popular pieces.

Listening Map for Danse Macabre

 CD-ROM

Use *Orchestral Instruments* **CD-ROM**
to learn more about the violin.

Map Key

- violin
- orchestra
- xylophone
- wind

Thanksgiving is a time to be with family and friends. Here is a song about one friend that no Thanksgiving should be without!

My Friend Tom

CD 17:9

Words and Music by
John Jacobson and Alan Billingsley

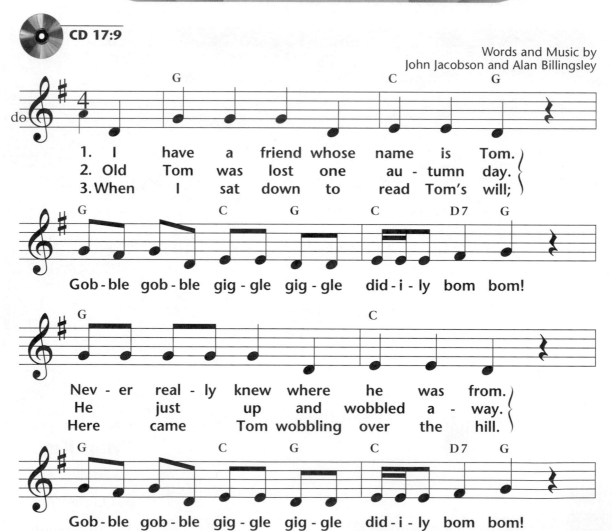

1. I have a friend whose name is Tom.
2. Old Tom was lost one au-tumn day.
3. When I sat down to read Tom's will;

Gob-ble gob-ble gig-gle gig-gle did-i-ly bom bom!

Nev-er real-ly knew where he was from.
He just up and wobbled a-way.
Here came Tom wobbling over the hill.

Gob-ble gob-ble gig-gle gig-gle did-i-ly bom bom!

Find rhyming words in "My Friend Tom" for 'gobble'
and 'giggle.'

Seasonal Songs

Everyone loves this song about a jolly man made of snow.

Frosty, the Snowman

CD 17:12

Swing Rhythm

Words and Music by
Steve Nelson and Jack Rollins

1. Fros-ty, the Snow-man, was a jol-ly, hap-py soul,___ With a
   Fros-ty, the Snow-man, is a fair-y tale, they say,___ He was
   Fros-ty, the Snow-man, was a-live as he could be,___ And the

corn-cob pipe and a but-ton nose_ And two eyes made out of coal.
made of snow, but the chil-dren know_ How he
chil-dren say he could laugh and play_ Just the

came to life one day. There
same as you and me.

Coda

must have been some mag - ic in that old silk hat they found; For

(Go back to the beginning then to the 3rd ending.)

when they placed it on his head, He be - gan to dance a-round. Oh,

2. Frosty, the Snowman, knew the sun was hot that day,
   So he said, "Let's run and we'll have some fun
   Now before I melt away."
   Down to the village, with a broomstick in his hand,
   Running here and there all around the square,
   Sayin' "Catch me if you can."

   He led them down the streets of town right to the traffic cop,
   And he only paused a moment when he heard him holler "Stop!"
   For Frosty, the Snowman, had to hurry on his way,
   But he waved good-bye sayin', "Don't you cry,
   I'll be back again some day."

The story of Hanukkah tells of how a little oil kept the holy lamps in a temple in Jerusalem burning for eight days. The holiday is celebrated by lighting candles. Families gather each evening to watch the candles being lit.

Oy Chanuke

O Hanukkah

CD 17:15

Yiddish Words by M. Rivesman
Jewish Folk Song
English Words by MMH

Yiddish: אַ, נער - שיי אַ טוב - יון אַ ,כה - נו - ח אוי,כה - נו - ח אוי

Pronunciation: o xɑ nu kɑ o xɑn u kɑ ɑ yɔn tɛf ɑ she nəɾ ɑ

English: O Ha-nuk-kah, O Ha-nuk-kah, a beau-ti-ful sea-son, a

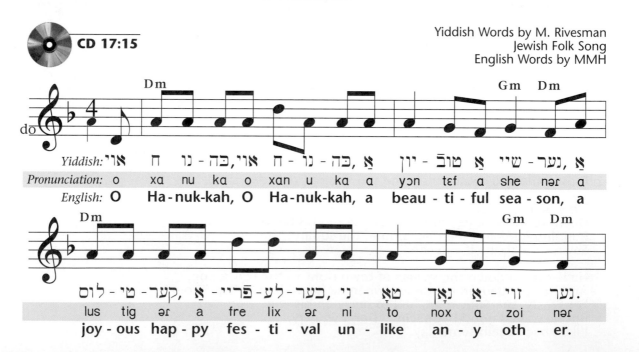

.נער זוי - אַ נאָך אַ - ני טאַ ,קער-לע-פֿרײַ-אַ ,קער-טי - לוס

lus tig əɾ ɑ fre lix əɾ ni to nox ɑ zoi nəɾ

joy - ous hap - py fes - ti - val un - like an - y oth - er.

CONCEPT
FORM
SKILLS
SING

The Eight Days of Hanukkah!

CD 17:19

Words and Music by George David Weiss

Verse

Solo Dm   A7   *Group* A7

"One" is for the tem - ple walls that did-n't fall.____
(Did-n't fall.)

Solo Dm   A7   *Group*

"Two" is for the men who fought, God bless 'em all.____
(Bless 'em all.)

Solo Gm   Gm   Dm

"Three" is for the oil they found, e - nough for just one day.

E   E   A7   Bb7   A7 *Group*

"Four" is for the mir-a-cle that came their way. It burned for eight days.

Solo Dm   A7   *Group* A7

"Five" is for the hope and faith that would-n't die.____
(Would-n't die.)

Solo Dm   Gm   *Group*

"Six" is for the To - rah scrolls that still sur - vive.____
(Still sur-vive.)

CONCEPT
RHYTHM
SKILLS
SING

There are presents to buy, boxes to wrap, and yummy goodies to bake. There is so much to do before Christmas day! Sing this song and find out which jolly fellow also has lots to do before the big day!

It's Time to Get Ready for Christmas

CD 17:22

Words and Music by
Emily Crocker and John Higgins

Refrain

It's time to get read-y for Christ-mas.

San-ta's in a hur-ry to pack his sleigh. Time to get read-y for

Christ-mas, soon it will be Christ-mas Day,

soon it will be Christ-mas Day.

1. I sew the ears on ted-dy bears. I
2. I il-lus-trate the pic-ture books. I

CONCEPT
RHYTHM

SKILLS
SING

Get ready to spread some holiday cheer!
This popular Christmas song from Wales
will put everyone in the holiday spirit!

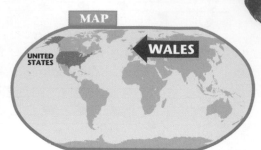

Deck the Hall

CD 17:25

Welsh Carol

1. Deck the hall with boughs of hol - ly,
2. See the blaz-ing yule be-fore us,   Fa la la la la, la   la la la,
3. Fast a - way the old year pass-es,

'Tis the sea - son to be jol - ly,
Strike the harp and join the cho-rus,   Fa la la la la, la   la la la,
Hail the new, ye lads and lass - es,

Don we now our gay ap - par - el,
Fol - low me in mer - ry mea-sure,   Fa la la la la la, la la la,
Sing we joy-ous all to - geth - er,

Troll the an-cient yule - tide car - ol,
While I tell of yule - tide trea-sure,   Fa la la la la, la   la la la.
Heed - less of the wind and weath - er,

This Christmas carol was first sung many years ago in France.

Listen for which instruments play in "Pat-a-Pan."

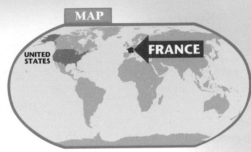

CD 17:28

French Carol Tune
English Version by Merrill Staton

Verse

1. Wil - lie take your lit - tle drum, Rob-in bring your flute and come.
2. When the lit - tle child was born long a - go that Christ - mas morn,
3. Now we cel - e - brate this day on our in - stru - ments we play.

Play a joy - ous tune to-day.
Shep-herds came from fields a - far, } Tu - re - lu - re - lu, pat-a-pat-a-pan,
Let our voi - ces loud-ly ring, }

Play a joy - ous tune to - day on this joy - ous hol - i - day.
Shep-herds came from fields a - far guid-ed by the shin - ing star.
Let our voi - ces loud-ly ring, as our song and gifts we bring.

CONCEPT
TEXTURE
SKILLS
SING, PLAY

CD 18:1

African American Spiritual

Play this accompaniment as the group sings "Amen."

Left Right

This African American spiritual is another holiday favorite.

CD 18:4

African American Spiritual

Swing Rhythm

Go,   tell   it   on   the   moun - tain,

O - ver___ the hills and   ev - 'ry - where.

Go,   tell   it   on   the   moun - tain,

That   Je - sus   Christ___ is   born.

When the short parade of the Christmas *posadas* is over, the party begins. Food and drinks like sweet bread and hot chocolate are served. Children may also break a *piñata*!

¡Dale, dale, dale!

CD 18:7

Mexican Folk Song
English Version by MMH

Spanish: En las no - ches de po - sa - das,
Pronunciation: en las no ches de po sa ðas
English: On the nights of Las Po - sa - das,

la pi - ña - ta es lo me - jor,
la pi nya ta es lo me xor
chil - dren strike the bright pi - ña - ta.

Y los ni - ños más a - le - gres
i los ni nyos mas a le gres
See the hap - py, hap - py chil - dren

le pe - gan con gran fer - vor.
le pe gang kong gran fer βor
as they swing and swing all night.

Refrain

Da - le, da - le, da - le, no pier - das el ti - no,
ða le ða le ða le no pyer ðas el ti no
Da - le, da - le, da - le, do not lose your bal - ance.

Mi - de la dis - tan - cia, que hay en el ca - mi - no.
mi ðe la ðis tan syn keal en el ka mi no
Turn and turn and turn and you will find your tar - get.

Que si no le das de un pa - lo te pi - llo,
ke si no le ðas ðeun pa lo te pi yo
For if you should miss it with a cra - zy wild swing,

Por - que tie - nes ca - ra, de pu - ro zo - rri - llo.___
poɾ ke tye nes ka ɾa ðe pu ɾo so ɾi yo___
You will feel so fool - ish that__ you'll run and hide.__

CONCEPT
RHYTHM
SKILLS
SING, LISTEN

Kwanzaa is an African American celebration of the family, community, and culture. It uses words from Swahili, an African language. Kwanzaa lasts seven days. One day celebrates *Ujamaa*. Its message is that people are stronger when everyone works together to help each other.

 **CD 18:11**

Words and Music by Stan Spottswood

1. U - ja - maa means we should cre - ate our own
2. Don't on - ly buy, start to pro - duce. In the

stores and shops and bus-'ness - es.
end, my friend, you'll

have suc - cess.

Kuumba is another principle of Kwanzaa. Its message is that when people in a community are creative, the community stays strong. Art and music are ways to express feelings, ideas, and thoughts.

Use *World Instruments* CD-ROM to learn more about African instruments.

 LISTENING CD 18:14

Chants du Burgam by Doudou N'Diaye Rose

Doudou N'Diaye Rose is from Senegal. He is one of the most famous African drummers in the world.

 Art Gallery

Beaded Hair

Music is an important part of what makes a group of people who they are. This painting was created by Amos Ferguson (born in 1920). He was born in the Bahamas. He worked with his father on their farm until he decided to be a painter.

BEEDED hAIR PAINT By MR. AMOS FERGUSON 1984

CONCEPT
RHYTHM
SKILLS
LISTEN, SING

Dr. Martin Luther King, Jr., believed that all people should have the same chance in life. He taught that differences in people should bring them together, not separate them.

 LISTENING CD 18:15

Down by the Riverside African American Spiritual

People sing songs like this African American spiritual to remember the spirit of Dr. King's message of peace and freedom.

This spiritual tells about the journey to freedom.

I'm on My Way

CD 18:16

Swing Rhythm

African American Spiritual

1. I'm on my way (I'm on my way) to the free-dom land.

_____ (to the free-dom land) I'm on my way (I'm on my

way) to the free-dom land. _____ (to the free-dom land)

"Integration is an opportunity to participate in the beauty of diversity."

— Dr. Martin Luther King, Jr.

_____ I'm on my way (I'm on my way) to the free-dom land.

land, (to the free-dom land)_____ I'm on my way, Great

God, I'm on my way._____

2. I'll ask my brother to come and go with me, *(3 times)*
   I'm on my way, Great God, I'm on my way.

3. I'll ask my sister to come and go with me, *(3 times)*
   I'm on my way, Great God, I'm on my way.

4. I'm on my way, and I won't turn back, *(3 times)*
   I'm on my way, Great God, I'm on my way.

5. I'm on my way to the freedom land, *(3 times)*
   I'm on my way, Great God, I'm on my way.

CONCEPT
MELODY
SKILLS
SING, LISTEN

The Chinese New Year is a time to be with family and friends. It is a time to give thanks. Family members, living and dead, are remembered during this family celebration.

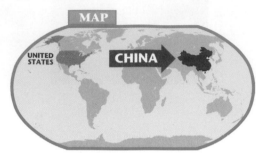

Chinese New Year Song

CD 18:19

Traditional Chinese Song
Arranged by Chooi-Theng Lew
English Version by John Higgins

Mandarin: 每 條 大 街 小 巷 每 個 人 的 嘴 隶
Pronunciation: mei tiao da ji shiao shiang mei gʌ ɾʌn di tsuei li
English: **Up and down the streets to-day, There's a joy-ful sound you'll hear.**

見 面 第 一 句 話 都 是 恭 禧 恭 禧
jiɛn miɛn di i chü hwa do shι gung shi gung shi
Fam - i - ly and friends all say: Bless-ings for the New Year!

恭 禧 恭 禧 恭 禧 你 呀 恭 禧 恭 禧 恭 禧 你
gung shi gung shi gung shi ni ya gung shi gung shi gung shi ni
Hap-py, hap-py, hap-py New Year! Gong xi, gong xi, gong xi ni!

Use *World Instruments* **CD-ROM** to learn more about Asian instruments.

The Year-Naming Race Chinese Folk Tale

Each year of the Chinese calendar is named for an animal. Listen to a story that tells how the years got their names.

Name the animals of the Chinese calendar.

Rat   Ox   Tiger

Rabbit   Dragon   Snake

Horse   Goat   Monkey

Rooster   Dog   Pig

Valentine's Day is a day to remember the ones you love. Show your friends you care. Sing this song with a special friend!

This a Way and That a Way

CD 18:24

Words and Music by
John Jacobson and Alan Billingsley

Refrain

This a way and that a way and that a way and this a way. All that I have to say is, "I like you!" A one way or an-o-ther way, an-oth-er way or a one way. All I'm a-bout to say is, "I hope you like me too."_____

Verse

When we are sing - ing to - geth -

er, we have a beau - ti - ful

tone._____ I hope we'll

stay friends for - ev - er, 'cause

Go back to the beginning and sing to the End.
(Da Capo al Fine)

I don't like sing - ing a - lone! Oh!

LISTENING CD 18:27

Born to Be with You

Bluegrass Song

Good friends are lucky to find each
other. This song was popular in the
1950s. Here it is again in bluegrass style.

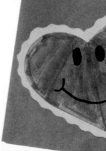

CONCEPT
RHYTHM
SKILLS
SING

Abraham Lincoln was born in 1809 in Kentucky, but spent much of his life in Illinois. Because of his courage and strength, he is now known as one of the greatest American presidents.

Out from the Wilderness

CD 18:28

Music Attributed to J. Warner
Words by Robert Quackenbush

1. Ol' Abe Lincoln came___ out from the wilderness,
2. Ol' Abe Lincoln always spoke for our liberty,
3. Ol' Abe Lincoln believed in our freedom rights, be-

Out from the wilderness, out from the wilderness,
Spoke for our liberty, spoke for our liberty,
lieved in our freedom rights, believed in our freedom rights,

Ol' Abe Lincoln came___ out from the wilderness,
Ol' Abe Lincoln always spoke for our liberty,
Ol' Abe Lincoln believed in our freedom rights,

Down in Illinois.
Down in Illinois.
Down in Illinois.

Lincoln

Lincoln
stares
from our classroom wall.
History says
he was lanky tall.

History says
that he borrowed books
and some people laughed
at his rumpled looks.

Born in a cabin,
he would be
the President
who set slaves free.

He gave the Gettysburg Address.
Except for George Washington
Lincoln was best
of all presidents,
and wise.

I can sort of see that
when I stare at his eyes.

—*Myra Cohn Livingston*

Abraham Lincoln,
the 16th President
of the United States,
guided the country
through difficult times.

Sing this song about a funny stew.

WELCOME

Mrs. Murphy's Chowder

CD 18:31

Words and Music by Oscar Brand

Verse

G

Won't you   bring   back,   won't you   bring   back

G   D

Mis - sus Mur - phy's   chow - der?   It   was   tune - ful,   ev - 'ry

D   G

spoon-ful   made   you yo - del   loud - er.   Af - ter din - ner,

D   G   D

Un - cle   Ben   used   to   fill   his   foun - tain   pen

D   G   D   G

From   a   plate   of   Mis - sus   Mur - phy's   chow   -   der.

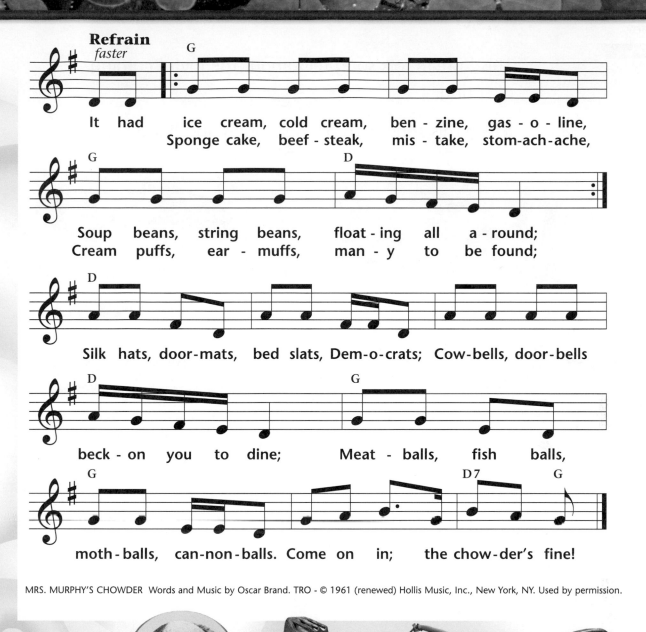

Refrain
faster

It had ice cream, cold cream, ben - zine, gas - o - line,
Sponge cake, beef - steak, mis - take, stom-ach-ache,

Soup beans, string beans, float - ing all a - round;
Cream puffs, ear - muffs, man - y to be found;

Silk hats, door-mats, bed slats, Dem-o-crats; Cow-bells, door-bells

beck - on you to dine; Meat - balls, fish balls,

moth - balls, can-non-balls. Come on in; the chow-der's fine!

MRS. MURPHY'S CHOWDER Words and Music by Oscar Brand. TRO - © 1961 (renewed) Hollis Music, Inc., New York, NY. Used by permission.

LISTENING CD 19:1

Brafferton Village/Walsh's Hornpipe

Irish Folk Music

Listen for the dance steps in this performance by The Chieftains and Kathryn Tickell.

Seasonal Songs

This Korean folk song tells about the joyful coming of spring.

Sing this song with pitch syllables and hand signs.

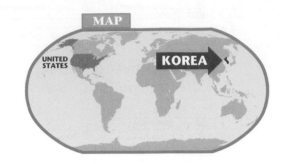

MAP

UNITED STATES   KOREA

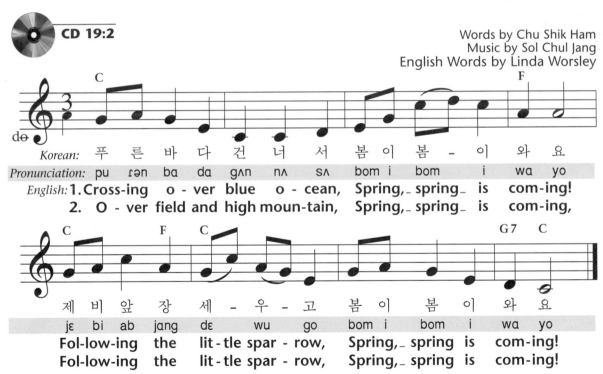

Bohm

Spring Has Come!

CD 19:2

Words by Chu Shik Ham
Music by Sol Chul Jang
English Words by Linda Worsley

Korean: 푸 른 바 다 건 너 서 봄이 봄 - 이 와 요
Pronunciation: pu ɾən ba da gʌn nʌ sʌ bom i bom i wa yo
English: 1. Cross-ing o - ver blue o - cean, Spring, spring is com-ing!
2. O - ver field and high moun-tain, Spring, spring is com-ing,

제 비 앞 장 세 - 우 - 고 봄이 봄 이 와 요
jɛ bi ab jaŋ dɛ wu go bom i bom i wa yo
Fol-low-ing the lit-tle spar - row, Spring, spring is com-ing!
Fol-low-ing the lit-tle spar - row, Spring, spring is com-ing!

CD-ROM

Use *World Instruments* CD-ROM
to learn more about Asian instruments.

May Day was first celebrated in Europe. It was a day of games and feasting that celebrated the end of winter and the return of the sun.

Find five notes moving up stepwise in "May Day Carol."

May Day Carol

CD 19:6

English Folk Song

1. I have been wan-d'ring all this___ night and
2. My song is done and I must be gone, no

some time of this day. And now re-turn-ing
long-er can I stay. So bless you all, both

home a-gain, I've brought you a branch of May.
great and small, and send you a joy-ful May.

CONCEPT
METER
SKILLS
SING

Earth Day is a day to remind people to look at the planet and decide what needs to be done to protect its beauty. This song is a reminder that the beauty of the earth is for everyone to enjoy.

Just Like the Sun

CD 19:9

Words and Music by Raffi

1. Just like the birds that keep on fly - ing, Just like the
2. Just as the flow - ers keep on bloom-ing, Just like the

wind that keeps on blow-ing, I see a wave of o-ceans roll-ing
leaves that keep on turn - ing I feel the change of sea-sons flow-ing

on and on, Just like the sun, these gifts are here for ev-ery-one.
on and on, Just like the sun, these gifts are here for ev-ery-one.

Just like the trees that keep on giv-ing,   Just like the
Just like the moon that keeps on shin-ing,   Just like the

grass that keeps on grow-ing,   I hear the sound of chil-dren sing-ing
stars that keep on twink-ling,   I know a world of won-ders play-ing

on and on,   Just like the   sun, these gifts are here for
on and on,   Just like the

Go back to the beginning and sing to the end
(D.C. al Fine)

ev-ery-one.   sun, these gifts are here for ev-ery-one.

Move with the beat as you sing the song.

CONCEPT
RHYTHM
SKILLS
SING, LISTEN

Cinco de Mayo celebrates the victory of a small Mexican army over a large French army. Today people celebrate with dancing, music, and good things to eat. This song is about a sweet, warm drink made with corn.

El atole

The Atole

CD 19:12

Mexican Folk Song
Adapted by José-Luis Orozco
English Words by Linda Worsley

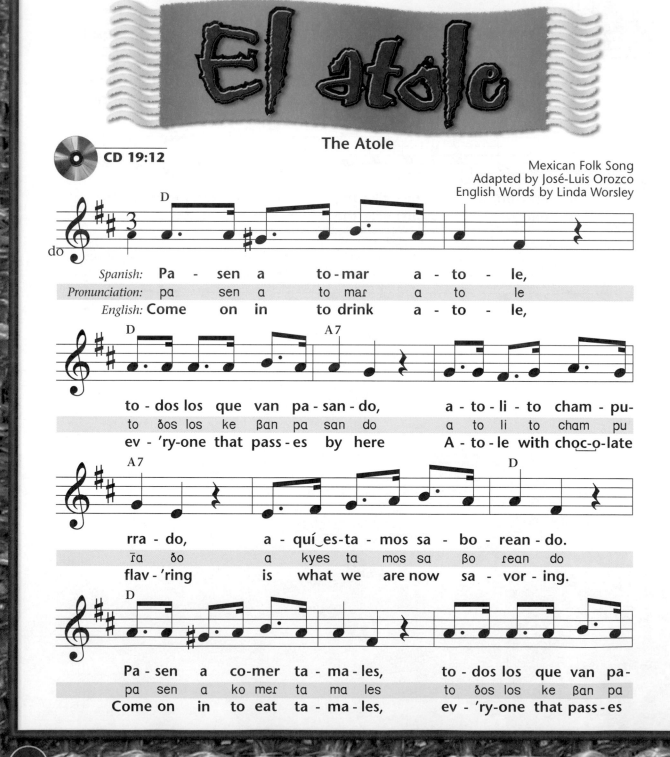

Spanish: **Pa - sen a to - mar a - to - le,**
Pronunciation: pa sen a to maɾ a to le
English: **Come on in to drink a - to - le,**

to - dos los que van pa - san - do, a - to - li - to cham - pu-
to ðos los ke βan pa san do a to li to cham pu
ev - 'ry-one that pass - es by here A - to - le with choc-o-late

rra - do, a - quí es-ta - mos sa - bo - rean - do.
ɾa ðo a kyes ta mos sa βo ɾean do
flav - 'ring is what we are now sa - vor - ing.

Pa - sen a co - mer ta - ma - les, to - dos los que van pa-
pa sen a ko meɾ ta ma les to ðos los ke βan pa
Come on in to eat ta - ma - les, ev - 'ry-one that pass - es

396

san - do, ta - ma - li - tos ca - lien - ti - tos,
san do ta ma li tos ka lyen ti tos
by here. Hot and spi - cy fresh ta - ma - les,

a - quí es - ta - mos dis - fru - tan - do.
a kyes ta mos dis fɾu tan do
We just love to eat ta - ma - les.

 LISTENING CD 19:16

 CD-ROM

Use *World Instruments* **CD-ROM** to learn more about Mexican instruments.

Los mariachis Mexican Folk Song

Mariachi music began in Mexico in the 1800s. The instruments in mariachi groups are usually violins, guitars, vihuelas, guitarrons, and trumpets.

Playing the Recorder

C

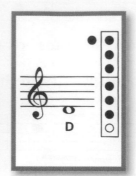

D

E

F

F#

G

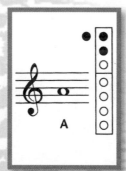

A

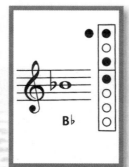

B♭

B

C'

D'

Glossary of Instruments

A

accordion a hand-held keyboard instrument that is played by pressing keys or buttons while air is forced through the instrument. It is often played while standing and held by straps over the shoulders, **CD 21:10**

B

bagpipe a member of the woodwind family that is played by blowing air through a tube into the bag and then pressing the bag so that the air is forced out through the pipes, **88 CD 21:11**

banjo a member of the string family that is played by plucking or strumming the strings, **31 CD 21:20**

bass drum a large member of the percussion family that gives a deep sound when hit, **CD 20:32**

bassoon a member of the woodwind family that is played by blowing into the reed while covering holes along the body with fingers, **CD 20:15**

cello the second-largest member of the string family in an orchestra, which is held between the knees and played by bowing or plucking the strings, **178 CD 20:6**

clarinet a member of the woodwind family that is played by blowing into the mouthpiece while covering holes along the body with fingers, **31 CD 20:12**

conga a percussion instrument used in Latin America that has a low-pitched sound when struck, **CD 21:30**

cymbal A dish-shaped percussion instrument that is often played by hitting one against another to make a clashing sound, **CD 20:37**

djembe a West African percussion instrument that is a drum made from pottery or wood and played with the hands, **CD 21:2**

double bass the largest instrument of the string family in an orchestra, which is held upright and played by bowing or plucking the strings, **CD 20:7**

flute a member of the woodwind family that is played by blowing across a hole at one end while covering holes along the body with fingers, **CD 20:10**

French horn a member of the brass family that is played by buzzing the lips into the mouthpiece while pressing keys with fingers, **CD 20:20**

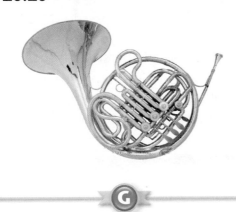

güiro a Latin American percussion instrument that is made from a gourd and has a bumpy surface that is scraped with a stick to make a sound, **CD 21:33**

guitar a popular string instrument that is played by plucking or strumming the strings, **14** **CD 21:13**

harp one of the oldest instruments in the string family, played by plucking or strumming the strings with fingers, **CD 20:8**

koto a long, flat, Japanese string instrument that is played by plucking its 13 strings, **CD 21:53**

Glossary of Instruments 401

mandolin a member of the string family that is similar to a guitar, but it has a different body shape and 8 metal strings, **CD 21:16**

maracas Latin American percussion instruments played in pairs by shaking when held at the handles, **CD 21:35**

oboe a double-reed woodwind instrument that is played by blowing into the reed while covering holes along the body with fingers, **CD 20:13**

piano a percussion instrument that is played by pressing the keys on the keyboard, **155 CD 20:41**

piccolo one of the smaller members of the woodwind family that is a small flute that plays high pitches, **CD 20:11**

saxophone a member of the woodwind family that is played by blowing into the mouthpiece while pushing the keys along the body with fingers, **CD 20:16**

shekere an African percussion instrument that is a hollow gourd covered with a net of beads or seeds and is played by shaking, **CD 21:8**

slit drum a percussion instrument used in Africa, Asia, and the South Pacific that is formed by hollowing a tree trunk through a slit on one side and played by hitting with sticks, **CD 21:9**

snare drum a member of the percussion family that is played by hitting the top of the drum with drumsticks to vibrate wires along the bottom, **31 CD 20:35**

spoons a common object used as a percussion instrument by holding two together and hitting them against the body. Musicians often use special spoons fastened together with a wooden handle, **15 CD 21:23**

taiko drum a barrel-shaped Japanese percussion instrument that is played with sticks, or *bachi*, **CD 21:51**

tambourine a small, hand-held percussion instrument that has metal disks attached loosely around the rim and is played by shaking or hitting it with the hand, **31 CD 20:36**

timpani percussion instruments that are a set of large kettle-shaped drums, played with mallets and tuned to different pitches, **CD 20:26**

trombone a large, low-pitched member of the brass family, which is played by buzzing the lips into the mouthpiece while moving the slide in and out, **CD 20:21**

trumpet the smallest, highest-pitched member of the brass family, which is played by buzzing the lips into the mouthpiece while pressing keys with fingers, **CD 20:18**

tuba the largest, lowest-pitched member of the brass family, which is played by buzzing the lips into the mouthpiece while pressing keys with fingers, **CD 20:22**

viola a member of the string family slightly larger than the violin, which is held under the chin and played by bowing or plucking the strings, **CD 20:5**

violin the smallest member of the string family in an orchestra, which is held under the chin and played by bowing or plucking the strings, **31 CD 20:4**

xylophone a percussion instrument that is played by hitting the wooden bars with small wooden hammers, or mallets, **CD 20:30**

Glossary of Terms

A

accelerando gradually getting faster, **224**

accompaniment a musical background to a melody, **191**

allegro fast tempo, **67**

B

bar line (‖) a line that marks the end of a measure, **15**

beat the pulse felt in most music, **8**

C

canon a song form with two or more voices in which the melody is introduced and imitated one or more times; similar to a round, **141**

chord three or more pitches sounded together, **191**

choreographer a person who creates a pattern of dance movements to go with music, **112**

choreography a pattern of dance movements to go with specific music, **112**

coda a short section added to the end of a piece of music, **155**

conductor a person who leads performers using special patterns of arm movements, **106**

contrast combining one musical idea with a different one, **74**

countermelody a contrasting melody written to go with a song, **60**

D

dotted half note (𝅗𝅥.) a note equal to one half note plus one quarter note, **177**

downbeat the first beat of each measure, **170**

downstage the space on the stage closest to the audience, **291**

dynamics the loudness or softness of music, **63**

E

eighth notes (♫) musical notes that show two sounds to a beat, **15**

eighth rest (𝄾) a rest that lasts on half of a beat, **223**

F
---

first ending (⌐1.) a sign that tells you to go back to the beginning of the song and sing to the second ending, **100**

form the order of phrases or sections, or the plan, of a piece of music, **46**

forte (*f*) loud, **63**

H
---

half note (𝅗𝅥) a note that shows a sound that is two beats long, **58**

harmony two or more pitches sung or played at the same time, **192**

high *do* the pitch one octave higher than the *do* that begins the scale, **139**

I
---

identical exactly the same, **128**

interlude a short musical connection between sections or verses of a song, **152**

L
---

largo slow tempo, **67**

leap one way a melody moves; to move higher or lower by jumping over two or more pitches, **148**

legato smooth and connected, **226**

limerick a funny, five-line rhyming poem, **234**

low *la* the pitch *la* that lies below *do*, **98**

low *so* the pitch *so* that lies below *do*, **98**

M
---

measure a unit used to group notes and rests, **15**

melody a pattern of pitches that moves upward, downward, or stays the same; a tune, **12**

meter the pattern of beats grouped in a measure of music, **106**

meter signature the symbol that tells how many beats are grouped in each measure and what kind of note equals one beat, **15**

O

ostinato a musical pattern that repeats over and over, **131**

P

pentatonic a scale having only five pitches, **140**

phrase a short section of music that is one musical thought, **91**

piano (*p*) soft, **63**

pitch how high or low a sound is, **12**

pizzicato played by plucking a stringed instrument, **228**

Q

quarter note (♩) the symbol for one sound to a beat, **15**

quarter rest (𝄽) a symbol for silence the length of one quarter note, **15**

R

refrain a section of a song that is repeated after each verse, **91**

repeat sign (:‖) a symbol that tells you to repeat part of a piece of music, **96**

repetition using the same musical idea more than once, **74**

rhythm combinations of longer and shorter sounds and silences, **9**

rondo a piece of music in which the A section always returns, with different sections in between, such as ABACA, **155**

round a type of canon; a short song for three or more voices in which each voice begins at a different time, **141**

S

scale a group of pitches in order from lowest to highest, **140**

second ending (⌐2.⎺⎺⎺) the ending after the first ending of a song, **100**

similar having many but not all qualities the same, **128**

sixteenth note (♪) four notes that equal one beat, **136**

skip one way a melody moves; to move higher or lower by jumping over a pitch, **148**

spiritual an African American folk song, many of which began as religious songs, **324**

staccato short and choppy, **226**

staff the five lines and four spaces on which musical notes are written, **20**

stage left the space to the left of the actor when facing the audience, **291**

stage right the space to the right of the actor when facing the audience, **291**

step one way a melody moves; to move higher or lower to the next pitch, **148**

tempo the speed of the beat, **66**

tie (⌢ or ⌣) a curved line that connects two notes of the same pitch and means that the sound should be held for the length of both notes, **70**

tonal center the home tone or pitch around which a melody seems to center; often the last pitch, **206**

tone color the special sound of each instrument or voice, **26**

treble clef or **G clef** (𝄞) tells that the notes on the second line of a staff are called G, **187**

unison all instruments or voices playing or singing the same notes at the same time, **141**

upbeat the last beat of each measure, **170**

upstage the space on the stage farthest away from the audience, **291**

verse a section of a song that is repeated using the same melody but different words, **91**

whole note (𝅝) a note to show a sound that lasts four beats, **180**

whole rest (▬) a rest to show a silence that lasts four beats, **180**

Z

zamba an Argentinean dance that has its own special movements, **111**

CREDITS

Illustration: Barry Ablett: 342-343. Ann Barrow:128, 129. Rose Mary Berlin: 63. Kristin Barr: v, Spotlight on Reading (2). Delana Bettoli: 216-217. Blair Bostick: 138, 139. Ka Botzis: 28-29. Vicki Bradley: 8 –9. S.G. Brooks: 365. Priscilla Burris: 204-205. Carlos Caban: 87. Gina Capaldi: 132, 133. Carly Castillon: 186-187. Antonio Castro: 305. Emilie Chollat: 104, 105. Peter Church: iv, 312, Spotlight on Concepts (2). Jack Crane: 116. Carolyn Croll: 272. Renee Daily: 48-49, 60-61 Billy Davis: 1, Spotlight on Celebrations (2). Nancy Davis: 136, 136-137. Viviana M. Diaz: 318-319. Sarah Dillard: 225. Robert Dombrowski: 310-311. Bob Doucet: 306-307. Leslie Evans: 152-153. Peter Fasolino: 346, 347, 348. Jeff Fillbach: 244. Ruth Flanigan: 366-367. Andrea Gabriel: 56-57. J.D. Gentry: 264. Justin Gerard: 94. Mariano Gil: 78,79. Renee Graef: vi, Spotlight on Performance (2). Diane Greenseid: 320-321. Gershom Griffith: 148-149. Mizue Ono Hamilton: 103. Yu-Mei Han: 222-223. Judy Hand: 112-113. Amanda Harvey: 332-333, 336-337, 338, 340. Linda Howard Bittner: 344, 345. Tim Jones: 326. Fiona King: 176-177, 330, 331. Diana Kizlauskas: 58-59. Loretta Krupinski: 226. Fran Lee: 12-13. Laura Logan: 96-97, 100-101. Katherine Lucas: 234-235. Loretta Lustig: 170-171. Stephen Marchesi: 47. Erin Mauterer: 106-107. Deborah Maze: 393. Sue Mell: 359. Elise Mills: 220-221. Carol Newsom: 206-207, 263. Tim Nihoff: 74, 76-77. Cheryl Kirk Noll: 146-147. Laurie O'Keefe: 53. Ed Olson: 64. Rik Olson: 260-261. Kathleen O'Malley: 90, 273. David Opie: 6-7. Frank Ordaz: 249. John Perlock: 192-193. Tamara Petrosino: 385. Gary R. Phillips: 140-141. Ilene Richard: 243. Cecile Schoberle: 24, 24-25. Stacey Schuett: 248-249. Wendy Smith-Griswold: 316. Dick Smolinski: 208-209, 245. Craig Spearing: 72-73. Bridget Starr Taylor: 68-69. Judy Stead: 258. Thomas Stefflbauer: 349, 350, 351. Lydia Taranovic: 246, 246-247. Mary Teichman: 66-67. Jeremy Tugeau: 250. Neecy Twinem: 76-77. Lin Wang: 324. Laura Watson: 308-309. Paula Wendland: 322, 323. Elizabeth Wolf: 154-155. Jason Wolff: 11, 254-255. Nicole E. Wong: 314-315.

Photography Credits: all photographs are by Macmillan/McGraw-Hill (MMH) except as noted below.

Allan Landau/MMH: iv-vii: (tcr tr). A-H: (bcl tl br). 2-6. 11. 15: (tr br). 19. 35: (l r cl cr). 37: (bl bc br). 38. 54: (b). 55: (1-5). 70. 71: (bc). 91. 93: (bl). 162-163. 202-203. 204. 212: (1-4). 306. 403: (tcl bl). 404: (tl).

Cover i: Jade Albert/MMH. iv-vii: (t tc tcl tl b bcl bl) C Squared Studios/Getty Images; (tr r cr br) Royalty-Free/Corbis. A-H: (bl) PhotoDisc/Getty Images; (tl cl) Rubberball; (b) Comstock; (tcr) Barbara Penoyar/Getty Images; (tr) Royalty-Free/Corbis. A: (tr) PhotoDisc. C: (cr) Hulton-Deutsch Collection/Corbis; (cl) PhotoDisc. E: (c) Comstock. G: (inset r) PhotoDisc. G-H: (bkgd) Corbis. H: (t) PhotoDisc. 6-9: (t) MetaCreations/Kai Power Photos. 10-11: (bkgd) MetaCreations/Kai Power Photos. 12: (tr c) PhotoDisc Green/Getty Images. 13: (bkgd) MetaCreations/Kai Power Photos. 14: (br) Bettmann/Corbis. 14-15: (t) Corel. 15: (tr) PhotoDisc. 16-17: (bkgd) PhotoDisc Green/Getty Images; (t) Corel. 18-19: (bkgd) Corbis. 20: (b) R.W. Jones/Corbis. 20-21 22 23: (bkgd) Corel. 21: (tr) Tony Freeman/PhotoEdit. 24: (br) Artville LLC. 25: (tr br cr) Artville LLC; (c) Fine Arts in Hungary/Hungarian National Gallery. 26: (cr) Popperfoto/Getty Images. 26-27 28-29: (t) Corel. 30: (tr) Nik Wheeler/Corbis; (b) argenphoto/Stock Sudamérica; (cl) Jacques Jangoux/Alamy. 30-31: (bkgd) Francesco Venturi/Corbis. 31: (br) MarKamusic; (tc c) Corbis; (cl cr) PhotoDisc. 32: (b) Craig Lovell/Corbis. 32-33: (bkgd) Francesco Venturi/Corbis. 33: (tr) Suzanne Murphy-Larronde Photography; (bcl) Haydee Mendizabal/Images of Eyes Gallery; (cr) MarKamusic. 34-35: (bkgd t) Charles O'Rear/Corbis. 35: (bl) Lynn Goldsmith/Corbis. 36: (cl) Louise Gubb/The Image Works; (cr) Carol Beckwith & Angela Fisher/HAGA/The Image Works. 36-37: (bkgd t) Charles O'Rear/Corbis. 37: (tr) PhotoDisc. 40: (t) Corbis. 41: (br) PhotoDisc. 42-43: (tc) Steve Satushek/Image Bank/Getty Images; (b) Jamie Marcial/SuperStock. 43: (tr) Roy Ooms/Masterfile; (cr) Giel/Taxi/Getty Images. 44: (tl) Chuck Keeler, Jr./Corbis; (bl) James Urbach/Superstock. 45: (tr) Jeffry W. Myers/Corbis; (b) Ariel Skelley/Corbis. 46-47: (bkgd) PhotoDisc; (t) Wetzel and Company. 50: (b) The Granger Collection, NY; (l) Carnegie Museum of Natural History; (r) Mike Greenlar/The Image Works. 50-51: (t) Rufus Grider/Newberry Library, Chicago/ SuperStock. 51: (b) Carnegie Museum of Natural History; (bl) Getty Images; (tr br) Marilyn "Angel" Wynn/Nativestock. 52: (tr) Michael Okoniewski-New York State Fair/HO/AP Images; (bl) Stuart Ramson/AP Images; (cr) Marilyn "Angel" Wynn/Nativestock. 52-53: (t) Rufus Grider/Newberry Library, Chicago/SuperStock. 54: (l) PhotoDisc. 54-55: (bkgd) Corel. 55: (tr br) PhotoDisc. 62-63: NASA. 64: (br) Scala/Art Resource, NY. 64-65: (bkgd) Corbis. 66-67 68-69: (t) Fukuhara/Corbis. 67: (l) PhotoDisc. 70-71: (bkgd) Sandro Vannini/Corbis. 71: (tr) Ted Spiegel/Corbis. 72-73: Digital Vision/PunchStock. 78 80: (r) PhotoDisc. 81: (r) Fox Model 500 English horn, Courtesy Fox Products Corporation, South Whitley, IN. 82-83: (c) Bruce Forster/Stone/Getty Images. 84: (l) Lindsay Hebberd/Corbis. 85: (t bc bl br) Shane Morgan/MMH; (tr) Annie Griffiths Belt/Corbis. 86: (b) Melville B. Grosvenor/National Geographic/Getty Images; (c cl) Hideo Haga/HAGA/The Image Works; (cr) David Grossman/The Image Works. 88: Topham Picture Point/The Image Works. 89: (l) Shane Morgan/MMH; (r) Yann Layma/Stone/Getty Images. 90-91: (t) Corel. 92: (b) The Thomson Collection/Art Gallery of Ontario; (tr) Nik Wheeler/Corbis. 92-93: (t) Corel. 93: (r) Artville LLC. 94-95: (t) Image Farm Graphics. 96: (tr) Lebrecht Music & Arts Photo Library; (t) Image Farm Graphics. 96-97: (bkgd) Corel; (t) Image Farm Graphics. 98: (br) The Granger Collection, NY. 98-99 100-101: (bkgd t) MetaCreations/Kai Power Photos. 102: (b l) Ariadne Van Zandbergen/Lonely Planet Images; (tl) James Marshall/The Image Works. 102-103: Christine Osborne/Corbis. 103: (t) Penny Tweedie/Corbis. 104: (b) Ariadne Van Zandbergen/Lonely Planet Images. 104-105: (bkgd) Christine Osborne/Corbis. 106: (bkgd) PhotoDisc; (l) G. Anderhub/Lebrecht Music & Arts Photo Library. 108: (b) Jon Lusk/Redferns/Getty Images. 108-109: (bkgd) PhotoDisc; (c) altrendo images/Getty Images. 109: (tr) E.Comesana/Lebrecht Music & Arts Photo Library. 110-111: (bkgd) Macduff Everton/The Image Works; (t) Corel. 111: (b cr) MetaCreations/Kai Power Photos. 112-113: (bkgd t) Corel. 113: (br) Mark Richards/Photo Edit. 114-115: (bkgd) Andre Jenny/Alamy; (t) MetaCreations/Kai Power Photos. 115: (cr) Royalty-Free/Corbis. 116-117: (t) MetaCreations/Kai Power Photos. 119: (r) Image Club Graphics. 121: (r) Lebrecht Music & Arts Photo Library. 122-123: (c) Corbis; (l) Diane Meyer. 123: (r) David Young-Wolff/PhotoEdit. 124 125: PhotoDisc. 126: (b) Stephanie Maze/Corbis. 126-127: (bkgd t) Corel; (tc) PhotoDisc. 128-129: (bkgd t) Corel. 130: (c) Grandma Moses Properties Co./Edward Owen/Art Resource, NY. 130-131: (bkgd) Corbis. 132-133: PhotoDisc. 134: (bkgd) James A. Sugar/National Geographic Stock; (c) Erich Lessing/Art Resource, NY. 134-135: (t) Corel. 135: (bkgd) James A. Sugar/National Geographic Stock. 136-137 138-139: Corel. 142: (cl) Werner Forman/Art Resource, NY. 142-143: (bkgd t) Richard T. Nowitz/Corbis; (b) Arnulf Husmo/Stone/Getty Images. 143: (bc) Bob Rowan, Progressive Image/Corbis; (c) Sogne Fjord, Norway, Normann, Adelsteen (1848-1918)/Bonhams, London, UK/Bridgeman Art Library. 144: (tr) Masakatsu Yamazaki/HAGA/The Image Works. 144-145: (bkgd t c) Richard T. Nowitz/Corbis. 145: (cr) The Granger Collection, NY. 146: (b) Lebrecht Music & Arts Photo Library; (br) David Allen Brandt/Stone/Getty Images. 147: (t) Courtesy Sonor Instruments a Division of Hohner, HSS. 150: (b) Corel; (c) Kevin Fleming/Corbis; (cr) PhotoDisc. 150-151: (bkgd t) Corel. 151: (br) Hampton University's Archival and Museum Collection, Hampton University, Hampton, VA. 152-153: Corel. 155: (tr) The State Hermitage Museum, St. Petersburg, Russia/Corbis; (br) Bettmann/Corbis. 156-157: Danny Lehman/Corbis. 159 161 164: PhotoDisc Green/Getty Images. 165: (cr) PhotoDisc; (t) Corbis. 166-167: (bkgd) Philip Coblentz/Brand X Pictures/PunchStock; (t) NASA. 168: (r) National Gallery Collection; By kind permission of the Trustees of the National Gallery, London/Corbis. 168-169: (bkgd) Corbis; (t) NASA. 172-173: (bkgd) John and Lisa Merrill/Corbis. 173: (tr) Hans Georg Roth/Corbis; (br) Hubert Stadler/Corbis. 175: (tr) Blaine Harrington; (bl) Bill Ross/Corbis; (cr) Werner Forman/Art Resource, NY; (r) Jenny & Tony Enderby/Lonely Planet Images/Getty Images. 177: (t) Corbis; (b c) Courtesy Sonor Instruments a Division of Hohner, HSS. 178: (b) Shane Morgan/MMH; (cr) Bettmann/Corbis. 178-179: (bkgd) Bruce Forster/Stone/Getty Images; (t) Corel. 180-181: (bkgd) Corbis; (t) Corel. 182-183: (bkgd) PhotoDisc; (t) Wetzel and Company; (tr) MetaCreations/Kai Power Photos. 183: (tr cr) Rube Goldberg, Inc.; (t) MetaCreations/Kai Power Photos. 184-185: (bkgd) Denis Waugh/Stone/Getty Images; (t) Wetzel and Company. 185: (tr) PhotoDisc; (bc br) David Ball/Index Stock Imagery/Photolibrary; (bl) British Museum, London, UK/Bridgeman Art Library. 186-187: (t) Corel. 188: (c) Robert Landau/Corbis. 188-189: (bkgd) Macduff Everton/Image Bank/Getty Images; (t) Corel. 189: (tr) Peter Turnley/Corbis; (b) PhotoDisc Blue/Getty Images. 190-191: (bkgd) PhotoDisc. 191: (tr) Snark/Art Resource, NY; (cr) Keren Su/Corbis. 194: (inset) Scott Bauer/USDA-ARS. 194-195: (bkgd) K. Pomper/Kentucky State University. 196-197: (bkgd) Ben Mangor/SuperStock. 198: (br) PhotoDisc. 200: (r) PhotoDisc. 206-207 208-209: (t) MetaCreations/Kai Power Photos. 210-211: (b) Morton Beebe/Corbis; (bkgd) Gianni Dagli Orti/Corbis. 211: (r) Gianni Dagli Orti/Corbis. 212: (tr) Bob Krist/Corbis. 212-213: (bkgd) Macduff Everton/Corbis. 213: (c) Schalkwijk/Art Resource, NY/Banco de México Diego Rivera & Frida Kahlo Museums Trust. Av. Cinco de Mayo No. 2, Col. Centro, Del. Cuauhtémoc 06059, México, D.F. 214-215: (t) Corbis. 215: (tr) Dean Conger/Corbis; (c) Jeremy Horner/Corbis; (l) PhotoDisc. 216-217: Corbis. 218-219: (bkgd) MetaCreations/Kai Power Photos. 219: (b) Herbert Knosowski/AP Images. 224: (tr) Image Club Graphics. 225: (tr) Lebrecht Music & Arts Photo Library. 226-227: (t) MetaTools. 228: (tr) Corbis; (bl) David Young-Wolff/PhotoEdit. 228-229: (t) MetaTools. 229: (tr) Corbis. 230-231: (bkgd) Peter Adams/Alamy. 231: (t) Art Resource, NY; (b) Richard Romero/Tyba/BrazilPhotos. 233: (t) Stockbyte/PunchStock; (tr) Michael J. Doolittle/The Image Works. 234-235: PhotoDisc. 236: (tr) Russell Gordon/Aurora Photos. 236-237: (bkgd) Steve Vidler/SuperStock; (t) PhotoDisc. 237: (tr) Steve Vidler/SuperStock. 242 243 247 248: PhotoDisc. 250: (bl) Comstock. 251: (tr) Fine Art Photographic Library, London/Art Resource, NY. 252: (l) MetaCreations/Kai Power Photos. 252-253: (t) Bettmann/Corbis. 254: (tr) Corbis. 257: (l) Comstock. 259: PhotoDisc. 262: Comstock. 264: Artville LLC. 265: PhotoDisc. 268: Comstock. 269: Artville LLC. 270: PhotoDisc. 271: Musee des Beaux-Arts, Pau, France, Giraudon/Bridgeman Art Library. 274: Corbis. 278: (tr) PhotoDisc; (b) Corbis. 280 281: PhotoDisc. 282: (tr bl) MetaCreations/Kai Power Photos. 283: (b) PhotoDisc. 285: (l) Erich Lessing/Art Resource, NY. 290: (b) Music Theatre International (MTI); (bl) Corel. 291: (c) MTI; (cr) Artville LLC. 292: (r) Artville LLC. 293: Image Club Graphics. 295: (tr) PhotoDisc; (b c) MTI. 296 300: PhotoDisc. 302: (b) MTI. 303 307 309 311: PhotoDisc/Getty Images. 313: (b) 20th Century Fox/The Kobal Collection. 313 315 317 319 321 323 325 327 329 313 333: (tr) PhotoDisc. 317: (b r) Roger Ide Photography. 325: (cr) Craig Aurness/Corbis. 327: (cr) SuperStock. 328: (tl) NASA. 331: (br) Harold Wood. 334: (r) Romulus/Warwick/Kobal Collection. 335 337 339 341 343: (tr) Comstock. 344: (bcl bl) Courtesy Sonor Instruments a Division of Hohner, HSS. 345 346: Courtesy Sonor Instruments a Division of Hohner, HSS. 354-355: PhotoLink/Getty Images. 356-357: (1 2) Image Club; (3 5) Steve Cole/Getty Images; (4) C Squared Studios/Getty Images. 359: (t) Paul Natkin/Photo Reserve. 360: (tl) PhotoDisc. 360-361: (tc bc) PhotoDisc; (bkgd) MetaCreations/Kai Power Photos. 361: (b) David H. Wells/Corbis; (cr) PhotoDisc. 362-363: PhotoDisc. 366 367: (bkgd) Corbis. 368: (tr c) PhotoDisc; (tl) MetaCreations/Kai Power Photos. 368-369: (bkgd) Quarasan. 370-371: (1 3) PhotoDisc; (2) Image Club Graphics. 372-373 374-375: PhotoDisc. 376-377: (bkgd) Siede Preis/Getty Images; (t bl l) Steve Cole/Getty Images.378: (tl) Shane Morgan/MMH. 378: (tr) Shane Morgan/MMH. 379: (tl) Travis Morisse/The Hutchinson News/AP Images (tcr) David Young-Wolff/PhotoEdit; (tcl tr) Shane Morgan/MMH. 380: (tr b) PhotoDisc; (bl) Patrick Olear/PhotoEdit; (br) Amos Ferguson/Wadsworth Atheneum Museum of Art; (bcr) Richard Lord/PhotoEdit. 383: (tl) Flip Schulke/Corbis. 384-385: MetaCreations/Kai Power Photos. 386: (tl) Image Club Graphics; (tr) PhotoDisc. 386-387: MetaCreations/Kai Power Photos. 387: (br) Shane Morgan/MMH. 388: (tl) Library of Congress, LC-USZ62-13016. 388-389: (1 2) Image Club; (3 5) Steve Cole/Getty Images; (4) C Squared Studios/Getty Images. 389: (t) Wildside Press; (b) Corbis. 390: (t) MetaCreations/Kai Power Photos; (tl tr) PhotoDisc. 390-391: (bkgd) Corbis; (tc c bc) PhotoDisc. 391: (bcl) MetaCreations/Kai Power Photos; (bl br bcr) PhotoDisc. 392-393: Corbis. 394: (tl bl) PhotoDisc; (br) Corbis. 394-395: (bkgd) PhotoDisc; (tc bc) Corel. 395: (br) Corbis. 397: (b) Joe Sohm/The Image Works. 398: (br r) Bettmann/Corbis. 399: (tl bl br) PhotoDisc/Getty Images. 400: (cl cr) PhotoDisc; (br) Jules Frazier/PhotoDisc Green/Getty Images. 401: (tl br) PhotoDisc. 402: (tl) PhotoDisc. 403: (tl tr) PhotoDisc. 404: (cl br) PhotoDisc.

All attempts have been made to provide complete and correct credits by the time of publication.

Classified Index

Alphabetical Index

My Favorite Things from *The Sound of Music* by R. Rodgers and O. Hammerstein II, **313**

Nigun Atik (Israeli folk dance), **47**

Norwegian Dance, Op. 35, No. 2 by E. Grieg, **145**

William Tell (Overture) (excerpt) by G. Rossini, **64**

Overture from *La forza del destino* (excerpt) by G. Verdi, **201**

Pata Pata by M. Makeba and J. Ragovoy, **35**

Pezinho (Brazilian folk song), **230**

Playful Pizzicato from *Simple Symphony* by B. Britten, **263**

Polovtsian Dances from *Prince Igor* (excerpt) by A. Borodin, **81**

Semper Fidelis by J. P. Sousa, **281**

Sensemayá (excerpt) by S. Revueltas, **161**

Sigh of the Soul for Alyscamp (Fourth Movement) from *Tableaux de Provence* by P. Maurice, **80**

Sonatine for Brass Quintet, First Movement (excerpt) by E. Bozza, **121**

Spinning Song by A. Ellmenreich, **128**

String of Pearls, A, by G. Miller, **12**

Gigue from Suite No. 1 for Cello by J. S. Bach, **178**

Symphony No. 9 ("From the New World"), Largo (excerpt) by A. Dvorák, **81**

Tehahontanekenhnêha' (Rabbit Dance Song), **51**

Tehahontanekenhnêha' (Rabbit Dance story), **50**

Trio for Piano, Violin and Cello No. 39, Finale ("Gypsy Rondo") by F. J. Haydn, **155**

Troika from *Lieutenant Kijé Suite* (excerpt) by S. Prokofiev, **225**

Two in a Boat (American folk song), **316**

Uncle Jessie (African American folk song), **327**

Volta from *Dances from Terpsichore* by M. Praetorius, **121**

Year-Naming Race, The (Chinese folk tale), **385**

Global Voices

Afrakakraba (Akan folk song from Ghana), **102**

Cip-cip cücələrim by G. Huseynli and T. Mutallibov, **215**

Her kommer vennen min (Norwegian folk song), **142**

Pezinho (Brazilian folk song), **230**

Interviews

Brown, Randall (From the Top), **80**

Conway, Eoghan (From the Top), **160**

Gorton, Heidi (From the Top), **200**

McDonald, Jerry Thundercloud, **52**

Park, Ariana and Rexton (From the Top), **40**

Vante, Barbara (From the Top), **120**

INDEX OF SONGS AND SPEECH PIECES

Addams Family Theme, The, **307**

Amen, **376**

America, the Beautiful, **354**

As I Roll My Ball (En roulant ma boule), **100**

Atole, The (El atole), **396**

Ballad of the Bedbugs and the Beetles, The, **206**

Bella bimba (Pretty Girl), **172**

Billy, **7**

Bim Bom, **218**

Blow, Ye Winds, Blow, **192**

Bohm (Spring Has Come!), **392**

Boll Weevil, **171**

Boo!, **362**

Buffalo Dance Entrance Song, **325**

Butterfly, Come Play with Me, **112**

Cat and Dog, **259**

Chan mali chan, **10**

Charlie, **208**

Chicka-ma, Chicka-ma, Craney Crow, **263**

Chicken on the Fence Post, **265**

Chinese Fishing Song (Wang Ü Ger), **190**

Chinese New Year Song (Gong xi fa cai), **384**

Cielito lindo, **166**

Circle 'Round the Zero, **267**

City Life (with "I Love the Mountains"), **341**

Clock, The (La cloche), **67**

Clocks, **266**

Colors of the Wind, **84**

Consider Yourself, **335**

Coral, **249**

Pronunciation Key

Simplified International Phonetic Alphabet

VOWELS

ɑ	father	o	obey	æ	cat	ɔ	paw
e	chaotic	u	moon	ɛ	pet	ʊ	put
i	bee	ʌ	up	ɪ	it	ə	ago

SPECIAL SOUNDS

β	say *b* without touching lips together; *Spanish* nueve, haba
ç	hue; *German* ich
ð	the; *Spanish* todo
ṇ	sound n as individual syllable
ö	form [o] with lips and say [e]; *French* adieu, *German* schön
œ	form [ɔ] with lips and say [ɛ] *French* coeur, *German* plötzlich
ɾ	flipped r; butter
r̄	rolled r; *Spanish* perro
ʇ	click tongue on the ridge behind teeth; *Zulu* ngcwele
ü	form [u] with lips and say [i]; *French* tu, *German* grün
ü̇	form [ʊ] with lips and say [ɪ]
x	blow strong current of air with back of tongue up; *German* Bach, *Hebrew* Hanukkah, *Spanish* bajo
ʒ	pleasure
´	glottal stop, as in the exclamation "uh, oh!" [´ʌ ´o]
~	nasalized vowel, such as *French* bon [bõ]
˥	end consonants *k*, *p*, and *t* without puff of air, such as sky (no puff of air after *k*), as opposed to *kite* (puff of air after *k*)

OTHER CONSONANTS PRONOUNCED SIMILAR TO ENGLISH

ch	cheese	ny	onion; *Spanish* niño
g	go	sh	shine
ng	sing	ts	boats

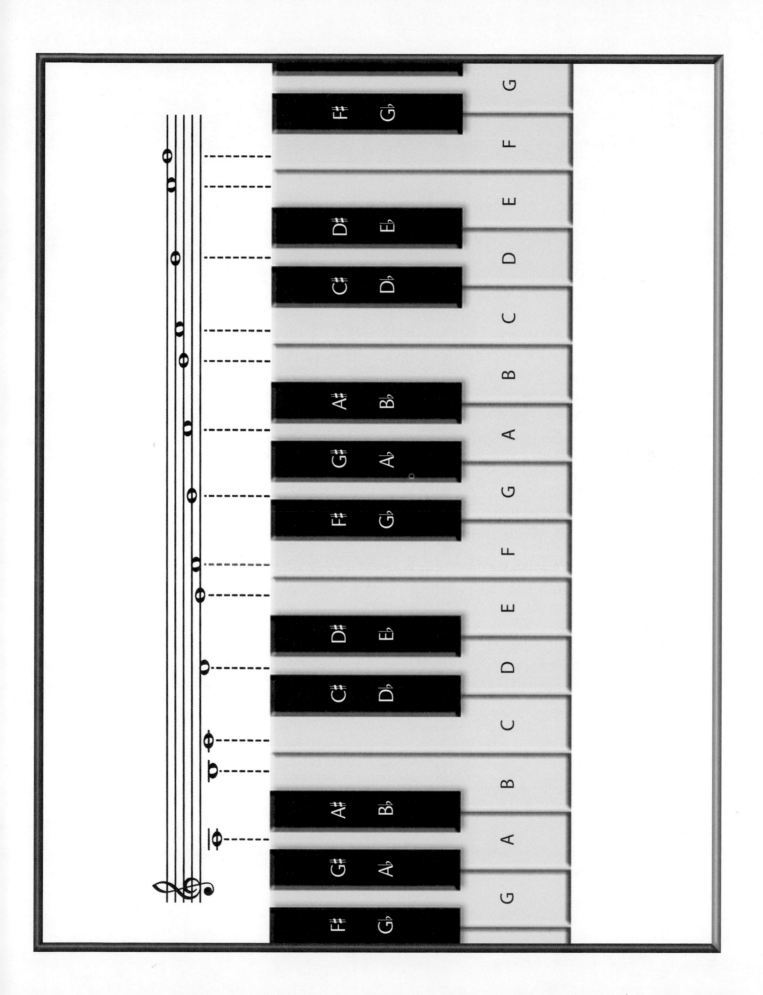